Mary B. Ford

J. F. College

Earl of Southhampton
Shakespear's patron.

Marriage 1598
1592 Earl of Essex
Married.

1594 Wet season, all
fruit killed, memorable
season

A PLAY AT THE BLACKFRIARS.

SHAKESPEARE'S

COMEDY OF

A MIDSUMMER-NIGHT'S DREAM.

EDITED, WITH NOTES,

BY

WILLIAM J. ROLFE, Litt. D.,

FORMERLY HEAD MASTER OF THE HIGH SCHOOL, CAMBRIDGE, MASS.

WITH ENGRAVINGS.

NEW YORK:

HARPER & BROTHERS, PUBLISHERS,

FRANKLIN SQUARE.

1897.

ENGLISH CLASSICS.

EDITED BY WM. J. ROLFE, LITT. D.

Illustrated. 16mo, Cloth, 56 cents per volume; Paper, 40 cents per volume.

SHAKESPEARE'S WORKS.

The Merchant of Venice.
Othello.
Julius Cæsar.
A Midsummer-Night's Dream.
Macbeth.
Hamlet.
Much Ado about Nothing.
Romeo and Juliet.
As You Like It.
The Tempest.
Twelfth Night.
The Winter's Tale.
King John.
Richard II.
Henry IV. Part I.
Henry IV. Part II.
Henry V.
Henry VI. Part I.
Henry VI. Part II.
Henry VI. Part III.

Richard III.
Henry VIII.
King Lear.
The Taming of the Shrew.
All 's Well that Ends Well.
Coriolanus.
The Comedy of Errors.
Cymbeline.
Antony and Cleopatra.
Measure for Measure.
Merry Wives of Windsor.
Love's Labour 's Lost.
Two Gentlemen of Verona.
Timon of Athens.
Troilus and Cressida.
Pericles, Prince of Tyre.
The Two Noble Kinsmen.
Venus and Adonis, Lucrece, etc.
Sonnets.
Titus Andronicus.

GOLDSMITH'S SELECT POEMS.
GRAY'S SELECT POEMS.
MINOR POEMS OF JOHN MILTON.
BROWNING'S SELECT POEMS.
BROWNING'S SELECT DRAMAS.
MACAULAY'S LAYS OF ANCIENT ROME
WORDSWORTH'S SELECT POEMS.

PUBLISHED BY HARPER & BROTHERS, NEW YORK.

☞ *The above works are for sale by all booksellers, or they will be sent by* HARPER & BROTHERS *to any address on receipt of price as quoted. If ordered sent by mail, 10 per cent. should be added to the price to cover cost of postage.*

CONTENTS.

ATHENS RESTORED, FROM THE PNYX.

THE THESEUM RESTORED.

INTRODUCTION
TO
A MIDSUMMER-NIGHT'S DREAM.

I. THE HISTORY OF THE PLAY.

The earliest known reference to *A Midsummer-Night's Dream* is in the *Palladis Tamia* of Francis Meres, published in 1598.* It is the opinion of the best critics that it was

* The passage is as follows: "As Plautus and Seneca are accounted the best for comedy and tragedy among the Latines, so Shakespeare among the English is the most excellent in both kinds for the stage: for comedy, witnes his *Gentlemen of Verona*, his *Errors*, his *Love Labors Lost*, his *Love Labours Wonne*, his *Midsummers Night Dreame*, and his *Merchant of Venice;* for tragedy, his *Richard the 2., Richard the 3., Henry the 4., King John, Titus Andronicus*, and his *Romeo and Juliet.*"

written some years before that date, perhaps as early as 1594. Probably in ii. 1. 88–117 there is an allusion to the unseasonable weather of that summer, which is thus described in the MS. Diary of Dr. Simon Forman :*

" Ther was moch sicknes but lyttle death, moch fruit and many plombs of all sorts this yeare and small nuts, but fewe walnuts : this monethes of June and July wer very wet and wonderfull cold like winter, that the 10. dae of Julii many did syt by the fyer, yt was so cold ; and soe was yt in Maye and June ; and scant too faire dais together all that tyme, but yt rayned every day more or lesse : yf yt did not raine, then was yt cold and cloudye : there were many gret fludes this sommer, and about Michelmas, thorowe the abundaunce of raine that fell sodeinly, the brige of Ware was broken downe, and at Stratford Bowe, the water was never sine so byg as yt was ; and in the lattere end of October, the waters burste downe the bridg at Cambridge, and in Barkshire wer many gret waters, wherwith was moch harm done sodenly."†

* See our *Richard II.* p. 13. We give the passage as it appears in Halliwell's folio ed. of Shakespeare.

† Stowe, in his *Chronicle* (quoted by Halliwell), says of the same year :

"This year, in the month of May, fell many great showers of rain, but in the months of June and July much more ; for it commonly rained every day or night till St. James' day, and two days after together most extremely ; all which notwithstanding, in the month of August, there followed a fair harvest, but in the month of September fell great rains, which raised high waters, such as stayed the carriages, and broke down bridges at Cambridge, Ware, and elsewhere in many places."

Churchyard, in his *Charitie*, published in 1595, refers to the preceding year as follows :

" A colder time in world was never seene:
    The skies do lowre, the sun and moone wax dim ;
    Sommer scarce knowne, but that the leaves are greene.
    The winter's waste drives water ore the brim ;
    Upon the land great flotes of wood may swim.
    Nature thinks scorne to do hir dutie right,
    Because we have displeasde the Lord of Light."

Another passage which has been supposed to have a temporary allusion is v. 1. 52 :

> " The thrice three Muses mourning for the death
> Of Learning, late deceas'd in beggary."

Some make this refer to Spenser's *Teares of the Muses*, 1591 ; others to Spenser's death (in which case, as that event did not occur until January, 1598–99, the lines must have been an addition to the original text) ; and others to the death of Robert Greene, in 1592. It is doubtful, however, whether the passage is anything more than an allusion to the general neglect of learning in that day.

A Midsummer-Night's Dream was first printed in 1600. The following entry appears on the Register of the Stationers' Company :

> "8 Oct. 1600 Tho. Fysher] A booke called a Mydsomer
> nights Dreame."

Fisher then brought it out in quarto form, with the following title-page :

> " A | Midsommer nights | dreame. | As it hath beene
> sundry times pub|*lickely acted, by the Right honoura*|ble, the
> Lord Chamberlaine his | *seruants.* | *Written by William
> Shakespeare.* | Imprinted at London, for *Thomas Fisher*,
> and are to | be soulde at his shoppe, at the Signe of the
> White Hart, | in *Fleetestreete.* 1600."

In the same year another quarto edition appeared with this title :

> " A | Midsommer nights | dreame. | As it hath beene
> sundry times pub|*likely acted, by the Right Honoura*|ble, the
> Lord Chamberlaine his | *seruants.* | *VVritten by VVilliam
> Shakespeare.* | *Printed by Iames Roberts,* 1600."

This edition appears, from internal evidence, to be a re-

It is curious that Churchyard, in the preface to his volume, remarks : " A great nobleman told me this last wet sommer, the weather was too colde for poets." Shakespeare did not find it so, if he wrote this play at that time.

print of the other, perhaps for the use of the players. It was the edition followed when the play was reprinted in the folio of 1623, some of its obvious misprints being copied there. The folio, however, contains some new readings, and White believes that "it was printed from a copy which had been corrected in Shakespeare's own theatre, and probably under his own eye, if not by his own hand." This view is hardly sustained by a careful comparison of the folio readings with those of Fisher's quarto, the latter (as we have pointed out in the notes) being often preferred to the former by most of the modern editors. Fortunately the variations are for the most part unimportant, and there are only one or two passages which furnish any real difficulty.

In the folio of 1623 the play occupies pages 145–162 in the division of "Comedies," and is divided into acts, but not into scenes.

There are few early notices of the representation of this play.* According to a manuscript at Lambeth Palace, it was performed at the Bishop of Lincoln's house on Sunday night, September 27th, 1631 ; but the *name* of the play is a forgery in a later hand. Archbishop Laud exerted his influence to punish this profanation of the Sabbath ; and the following order is taken from a decree made at the time by a self-constituted court among the Puritans :

"Likewise wee doe order, that Mr. Wilson, because hee was a speciall plotter and contriver of this business, and did in such a brutishe manner acte the same with an asses head, and therefore hee shall, uppon Tuisday next, from six of the clocke in the morning till six of the clocke at night, sitt in

---

* There is, however, reason to believe that the play was popular. In 1622, the year before it was reprinted in the 1st folio, Taylor, the Water-Poet, thus refers to it in his *Sir Gregory Nonsense*, v. 1 : "I say, as it is applausfully written, and commended to posterity, in the Midsummer-Night's Dream :—if we offend, it is with our good will : we came with no intent but to offend, and show our simple skill."

the Porter's Lodge at my Lords Bishopps House, with his feete in the stocks, and attyred with his asse head, and a bottle of hay sett before him, and this subscription on his breast :

> Good people I have played the beast,
> And brought ill things to passe :
> I was a man, but thus have made
> Myselfe a silly asse."

Bottom seems then to have been considered the chief character in the play ; and "The merry conceited humors of Bottom the Weaver" were made into a farce or droll,* which was frequently played in private after the suppression of the theatres. "When the publique theatres were shut up," says Kirkman,† "and the actors forbidden to present us with any of their tragedies, because we had enough of that in ernest ; and comedies, because the vices of the age were too lively and smartly represented ; then all that we could divert ourselves with were these humours and pieces of plays, which passing under the name of a merry conceited fellow called Bottom the Weaver, Simpleton the Smith, John Swabber, or some such title, were only allowed us, and that but by stealth too, and under the pretence of rope dancing and the like."

Pepys saw the play performed, September 29th, 1662, and thus records the fact in his *Diary:* "To the King's Theatre, where we saw 'Midsummer's Night's dream,' which I had never seen before, nor shall ever again, for it is the most insipid ridiculous play that ever I saw in my life."

In 1692 the play was changed into an opera under the title of *The Fairy Queen,* and performed in London on a very

---

* "The merry conceited humors of Bottom the Weaver, as it hath been often publikely acted by some of his Majesties comedians, and lately privately presented by several apprentices for their harmless recreation, with great applause." 4to. London, 1661.

† *The Wits,* 4to, London, 1673 (quoted by Halliwell).

splendid scale. In 1716 Richard Leveridge adapted from the play *A Comick Masque of Pyramus and Thisbe*, which was performed at the theatre in Lincoln's Inn Fields, and was printed in London the same year. In 1755 Garrick produced, at Drury Lane, an opera taken from *A Midsummer-Night's Dream*, and entitled *The Fairies*, the parts of the clowns being entirely omitted. In 1763 he brought out the original play, with the interlude restored, but it was coldly received, and was performed only once. It was then cut down to an afterpiece by Colman, under the title of *A Fairy Tale*, the supernatural characters being alone retained. In that form it was somewhat more successful, and was again produced at the Haymarket Theatre in 1777, with the addition of some songs from Garrick's version.

During the present century the play has seldom been put upon the stage, and it is not likely that the experiment will be often repeated. As Hazlitt has said, " the *Midsummer-Night's Dream*, when acted, is converted from a delightful fiction into a dull pantomime. . . . Fancy cannot be embodied any more than a simile can be painted ; and it is as idle to attempt it as to personate *Wall* or *Moonshine*. Fairies are not incredible, but fairies six feet high are so. Monsters are not shocking, if they are seen at a proper distance. When ghosts appear at midday, when apparitions stalk along Cheapside, then may the *Midsummer-Night's Dream* be represented without injury at Covent Garden or at Drury Lane. The boards of a theatre and the regions of fancy are not the same thing."

II. THE SOURCES OF THE PLOT.

" It is probable," says Steevens, " that the hint for this play was received from Chaucer's *Knight's Tale ;*" but there is little resemblance between the tale and the play, except that Theseus and Hippolyta are characters in both, and that Philostrate is the assumed name of Arcite in the tale, while it is the name of the Master of the Revels in the play. The poet was evidently acquainted with the Life of Theseus in North's *Plutarch*, and drew some little material from that source, as the extracts given in our notes will show. For the interlude of Pyramus and Thisbe he was doubtless indebted to Golding's translation of Ovid and Chaucer's *Legende of Goode Women.* Oberon, Titania, and Robin Goodfellow were familiar personages in the popular fairy mythology of the time, but Shakespeare has made them peculiarly his own. The fairy literature of that day has almost entirely perished, and the few fragments that remain afford no evidence that the poet was under any special obligation to it for the incidents of his plot. There is a curious black-letter tract, published in London in 1628 under the title of " Robin Goodfellow; his mad prankes, and merry Jests, full of honest mirth, and is a fit medicine for melancholy " (reprinted by the Percy Society in 1841, and again by the Shakespeare Society in 1845), which, as Collier and Halliwell believe, may have originally appeared much earlier than 1628, and have been seen by Shakespeare. White, on the other hand, in his Introduction to the Play, argues from internal evidence that the " Mad Pranks " was not only written after the *Midsummer-Night's Dream,* but that it was in a measure founded upon this very play ; and we think he makes out his case. The ballad in *Percy's Reliques* entitled " The Merry Pranks of Robin Goodfellow, once attributed to Ben Jonson, was also, as Halliwell admits, probably written after the appearance of the play. The popularity of the comedy doubtless led to the working-up of the old stories concerning Robin Goodfellow in a variety of ways. Collier mentions that in Henslowe's Diary are inserted two entries of money paid to Henry Chettle for a play he was writing in Sept., 1602, under the title of " Robin Goodfellow." Here, as in other instances, Shakespeare had his imitators and plagiarists, but there is no evidence that he imitated or plagiarized from anybody.

As White remarks, " the plot of *A Midsummer-Night's Dream* has no prototype in ancient or modern story."

III. CRITICAL COMMENTS ON THE PLAY.

[*From Drake's "Shakespeare and his Times."* *]

The *Midsummer-Night's Dream* is the first play which exhibits the imagination of Shakespeare in all its fervid and creative power ; for though, as mentioned in Meres's catalogue, as having numerous scenes of continued rhyme, as being barren in fable and defective in strength of character, it may be pronounced the offspring of youth and inexperience, it will ever in point of fancy be considered as equal to any subsequent drama of the poet.

There is, however, a light in which the best plays of Shakespeare should be viewed, which will, in fact, convert the supposed defects of this exquisite sally of sportive invention into positive excellence. A *unity of feeling* most remarkably pervades and regulates their entire structure, and the *Midsummer-Night's Dream*, a title in itself declaratory of the poet's object and aim, partakes of this bond, or principle of coalescence, in a very peculiar degree. It is, indeed, a fabric of the most buoyant and aërial texture, floating as it were between earth and heaven, and tinted with all the magic colouring of the rainbow.

> " The earth hath bubbles as the water has,
> And this is of them."

In a piece thus constituted, where the imagery of the most wild and fantastic dream is actually embodied before our eyes—where the principal agency is carried on by beings lighter than the gossamer and smaller than the cowslip's bell, whose elements are the moonbeams and the odoriferous atmosphere of flowers, whose sport it is " to dance in ringlets to the whistling winds," it was necessary, in order to give a

* *Shakespeare and his Times,* by Nathan Drake, M.D. (London, 1817), vol. ii. p. 299.

Mickle solace would they make him,
And at midnight often wake him,
And convey him from his roome
To a fielde of yellow broome,
Or into the meadowes where
Mints perfume the gentle aire,
And where Flora spreads her treasure,
There they would beginn their measure.
If it chanc'd night's sable shrowds
Muffled Cynthia up in clowds,
Safely home they then would see him,
And from brakes and quagmires free him.
There are few such swaines as he
Now a days for harmonie." *

[*From Hunter's " New Illustrations of Shakespeare."* †]

A Midsummer-Night's Dream ! At the sight of such a
title we naturally ask—Who is the dreamer ? The poet, any
of the characters of the drama, or the spectators ? The
answer seems to be that there is much in this beautiful sport
of imagination which was fit only to be regarded as a dream
by the persons whom the fairies illuded ; and that, as a
whole, it comes before the spectators under the notion of
a dream.

" If we shadows have offended,
    Think but this (and all is mended)
    That you have but slumber'd here,
    While these visions did appear ;
    And this weak and idle theme,
    No more yielding but a dream,
    Gentles, do not reprehend."

Shakespeare was then but a young poet, rising into notice ;
and it was a bold and hazardous undertaking to bring together classical story and the fairy mythology, made still
more hazardous by the introduction of the rude attempts in

---

* See *Shepherd's Pipe, Eglogue I.*
† *New Illustrations of the Life, Studies, and Writings of Shakespeare,*
by Joseph Hunter (London, 1845), vol. i. p. 282.

the dramatic art of the hard-handed men of Athens. By calling it a dream he obviated the objection to its incongruities, since it is of the nature of a dream that things heterogeneous are brought together in fantastical confusion. Yet to a person who by repeated perusals has become familiar with this play, it will not appear so incongruous a composition that it requires such an apology as we find in the epilogue and title. It cannot, however, have been popular, any more than *Comus* is popular, when brought upon the stage. Its great and surpassing beauties would be in themselves a hindrance to its obtaining a vulgar popularity.

There is no apparent reason why it should be called a dream of Midsummer-night in particular. Midsummer-night was of old in England a time of bonfires and rejoicings, and, in London, of processions and pageantries. But there is no allusion to anything of this kind in the play. Midsummer-night cannot be the time of the action, which is very distinctly fixed to May morning and a few days before. May morning, even more than Midsummer-night, was a time of delight in those times which, when looked back upon from these days of incessant toil, seem to have been gay, innocent, and paradisaical. See in what sweet language, and in what a religious spirit, the old topographer of London, Stowe, speaks of the universal custom of the people of the city on May-day morning, " to walk into the sweet meadows and green woods, there to rejoice their spirits with the beauty and savour of sweet flowers, and with the harmony of birds praising God in their kinds." We have abundant materials for a distinct and complete account of the May-day sports in the happy times of old England; but they would be misplaced in illustration of this play; for, though Shakespeare has made the time of his story the time when people went forth " to do observance to the morn of May," and has laid the scene of the principal event in one of those half-sylvan, half-pastoral spots which we may conceive to have been the

most favourite haunts of the Mayers, he does not introduce
any of the May-day sports, or show us anything of the May-
day customs of the time.

[*From Schlegel's " Lectures on Dramatic Literature."* *]

The fairy world here described resembles those elegant
pieces of arabesque, where little genii with butterfly wings
rise, half-embodied, above the flower-cups.   Twilight, moonshine, dew, and spring perfumes are the elements of these
tender spirits; they assist Nature in embroidering her car-
pet with green leaves, many-coloured flowers, and glittering
insects; in the human world they do but make sport child-
ishly and waywardly, with their beneficent or noxious influ-
ences.   Their most violent rage dissolves in good-natured
raillery ; their passions, stripped of all earthly matter, are
merely an ideal dream.   To correspond with this, the loves
of mortals are painted as a poetical enchantment, which, by
a contrary enchantment, may be immediately suspended and
then renewed again.   The different parts of the plot—the
wedding of Theseus and Hippolyta, Oberon and Titania's
quarrel, the flight of the two pair of lovers, and the theatrical manœuvres of the mechanics—are so lightly and happily
interwoven that they seem necessary to each other for the
formation of a whole.   Oberon is desirous of relieving the
lovers from their perplexities, but greatly adds to them
through the mistakes of his minister, till he at last comes
really to the aid of their fruitless amorous pain, their incon-
stancy and jealousy, and restores fidelity to its own rights.
The extremes of fanciful and vulgar are united, when the
enchanted Titania awakes and falls in love with a coarse
mechanic with an ass's head, who represents, or rather dis-
figures, the part of a tragical lover.   The droll wonder of
Bottom's transformation is merely the translation of a met-
aphor in its literal sense ; but in his behaviour during the

* Black's translation, revised ed. (London, 1846), p. 393.

tender homage of the Fairy Queen, we have an amusing proof how much the consciousness of such a head-dress heightens the effect of his usual folly. Theseus and Hippolyta are, as it were, a splendid frame for the picture; they take no part in the action, but surround it with a stately pomp. The discourse of the hero and his Amazon, as they course through the forest with their noisy hunting-train, works upon the imagination like the fresh breath of morning, before which the shades of night disappear.

Pyramus and Thisbe is not unmeaningly chosen as the grotesque play within the play: it is exactly, like the pathetic part of the piece, a secret meeting of two lovers in the forest, and their separation by an unfortunate accident, and closes the whole with the most amusing parody.

[*From Hazlitt's "Characters of Shakespeare's Plays."* *]

Puck, or Robin Goodfellow, is the leader of the fairy band. He is the Ariel of the *Midsummer-Night's Dream;* and yet as unlike as can be to the Ariel in *The Tempest.* No other poet could have made two such different characters out of the same fanciful materials and situations. Ariel is a minister of retribution, who is touched with the sense of pity at the woes he inflicts. Puck is a madcap sprite, full of wantonness and mischief, who laughs at those he misleads— "Lord, what fools these mortals be!" Ariel cleaves the air, and executes his mission with the zeal of a winged messenger; Puck is borne along on his fairy errand like the light and glittering gossamer before the breeze. He is indeed a most epicurean little gentleman, dealing in quaint devices, and faring in dainty delights. Prospero and his world of spirits are a set of moralists; but with Oberon and his fairies we are launched at once into the empire of the butterflies. How beautifully is this race of beings contrasted with the

* *Characters of Shakespear's Plays,* by William Hazlitt (London, 1817), p. 105 fol.

men and women actors in the scene, by a single epithet which Titania gives to the latter—"the human mortals!" It is astonishing that Shakespeare should be considered, not only by foreigners, but by many of our own critics, as a gloomy and heavy writer, who painted nothing but "gorgons and hydras, and chimæras dire." His subtlety exceeds that of all other dramatic writers, insomuch that a celebrated person of the present day said that he regarded him rather as a metaphysician than a poet. In the *Midsummer-Night's Dream* alone, we should imagine, there is more sweetness and beauty of description than in the whole range of French poetry put together. What we mean is this, that we will produce out of that single play ten passages to which we do not think any ten passages in the works of the French poets can be opposed displaying equal fancy and imagery. Shall we mention the remonstrance of Helena to Hermia, or Titania's description of her fairy train, or her disputes with Oberon about the Indian boy, or Puck's account of himself and his employments, or the Fairy Queen's exhortation to the elves to pay due attendance upon her favourite, Bottom ; or Hippolyta's description of a chase, or Theseus' answer? The two last are as heroical and spirited as the others are full of luscious tenderness. The reading of the play is like wandering in a grove by moonlight ; the descriptions breathe a sweetness like odours thrown from beds of flowers.

[*From Verplanck's Introduction to the Play.**]

This is, in several respects, the most remarkable composition of its author, and has probably contributed more to his general fame, as it has given a more peculiar evidence of the variety and brilliancy of his genius, than any other of his dramas. Not that it is in itself the noblest of his works,

* *The Illustrated Shakespeare*, edited by G. C. Verplanck (New York, 1847), vol. ii. p. 5 of *M. N. D.*

or even one of the highest order among them ; but it is not
only exquisite in its kind—it is also original and peculiar in
its whole character, and of a class by itself.   For, although
it be far from rivalling *As You Like It* or the *Merchant of
Venice* in the varied exhibition of human character, or the
gravity or the sweetness of ethical poetry—though it stand
in no rank of comparison with *Othello* or *Lear* in the mani-
festation of lofty intellect or the energy of passion, or in un-
resisted sway over the reader's deeper emotions—yet *Lear*
or *Othello*, or any one of Shakespeare's most perfect comedies, might have been lost by the carelessness of early editors,
or the accidents of time, without any essential diminution of
the general estimate of their author's genius.   Possessing
Hamlet, Romeo and Juliet, Macbeth, and the Roman tragedies, we could place no assignable limit to the genius which
produced them, if exerted on any similar themes of fierce
passion or tragic dignity.   So, again, *As You Like It* is but
another and most admirable exhibition of the same prolific
comic invention which revels as joyously in Falstaff and
Mercutio—of the same meditative poetic spirit, in turns fanciful, passionate, philosophical, which pours forth its austerer
teachings in *Measure for Measure,* or more sweetly comes
upon the ear, " with a dying fall," in the intervals of the loud
jollity of the *Twelfth Night.*   But the *Midsummer-Night's
Dream* stands by itself, without any parallel ; for the *Tempest,*
which it resembles in its preternatural personages and ma-
chinery of the plot, is in other respects wholly dissimilar,
is of quite another mood in feeling and thought, and with,
perhaps, higher attributes of genius, wants its peculiar fas-
cination.   Thus it is that the loss of this singularly beautiful production would, more than that of any other of his
works, have abridged the measure of its author's fame, as it
would have left us without the means of forming any estimate
of the brilliant lightness of his " forgetive" fancy, in its most
sportive and luxuriant vein.   The Poet and his contempora-

ries seem to have regarded this piece, as they well might, as in some sort a nondescript in dramatic literature ; for it happens that, while the other plays published during their author's life are regularly denominated, in their title-page, as "the pleasant comedy," "the true dramatic history," or "the lamentable tragedy," this has no designation of the kind beyond its mere title, in either of the original editions. It has, in common with all his comedies, a perpetual intermixture of the essentially poetical with the purely laughable, yet is distinguished from all the rest by being (as Coleridge has happily defined its character) "one continued specimen of the dramatized lyrical." Its transitions are as rapid, and the images and scenes it presents to the imagination as unexpected and as remote from each other, as those of the boldest lyric ; while it has also that highest perfection of the lyric art, the pervading unity of the poetic spirit—that continued glow of excited thought—which blends the whole rich and strange variety in one common effect of gay and dazzling brilliancy.

There is the heroic magnificence of the princely loves of Theseus and his Amazon bride, dazzling with the strangely gorgeous mixture of classical allusion and fable with the taste, feelings, and manners of chivalry ; and all embodied in a calm and lofty poetry, fitted alike to express the grand simplicity of primeval heroism, and "the high thoughts in a heart of courtesy," which belong to the best parts of the chivalrous character. This is intertwined with the ingeniously perplexed fancies and errors of the Athenian lovers, wrought up with a luxuriant profusion of quaint conceits and artificial turns of thought, such as the age delighted in. The Fairy King and Queen, equally essential to the plot, are invested with a certain mythological dignity, suited to the solemn yet free music of the verse, and the elevation and grave elegance of all their thoughts and images. Their fairy subjects, again, are the gayest and most fantastic of

Fancy's children. All these are relieved and contrasted by the grotesque absurdity of the mock play, and still more by the laughable truth and nature of the amateur "mechanicals" who present it. The critics have, indeed, been disposed to limit the praise of truth and nature, in this part of the play, to the portraiture of green-room jealousies or vanity, such as the Poet might have observed in his own professional life. But in truth he has here contrasted to the finer idealities of heroic and of playful fancy a vivid delineation of vulgar human nature—not confined to any one occupation or class in life, but such as often displays itself in the graver employments of real life, and the higher as well as the lower castes of society. Bottom, for instance, may be frequently found in high official or representative stations, among the legislative and municipal bodies of the world ; and so near (according to Napoleon's well-known adage) is the sublime to the ridiculous, that it depends entirely upon external circumstances, with a little more or a little less sense in himself and his hearers, whether the *Bottom* of the day is doomed to wear the ass's head for life, or becomes the admiration of his companions, and roars "like a nightingale," in his own conceit, from the high stations of the law or the state.

This clustering of the sweetest flowers of fanciful and of heroic poetry around the grotesque yet substantial reality of Bottom and his associates gives to the whole play that mixed effect of the grotesquely ludicrous with the irregularly beautiful which the Poet himself has painted in his picture of Titania "rounding the hairy temples" of the self-satisfied fool—

> With coronet of fresh and fragrant flowers.

All this profusion of pure poetry and droll reality is worked up with the dramatic skill of a practised artist, in embodying these apparently discordant plots and personages into one perfectly connected and harmonious whole, out of which nothing could well be removed without injury to the rest.

[*From Thomas Campbell's Remarks on the Play.**]

Addison says, "When I look at the tombs of departed greatness, every emotion of envy dies within me." I have never been so sacrilegious as to envy Shakespeare, in the bad sense of the word, but if there can be such an emotion as *sinless envy*, I feel it towards him; and if I thought that the sight of his tombstone would kill so pleasant a feeling, I should keep out of the way of it. Of all his works, the *Mid-summer-Night's Dream* leaves the strongest impression on my mind, that this miserable world must have, for once at least, contained a happy man. This play is so purely de-licious, so little intermixed with the painful passions from which poetry distils her sterner sweets, so fragrant with hilarity, so bland and yet so bold, that I cannot imagine Shakespeare's mind to have been in any other frame than that of healthful ecstasy when the sparks of inspiration thrilled through his brain in composing it. I have heard, however, an old critic object that Shakespeare might have foreseen it would never be a good acting play; for where could you get actors tiny enough to couch in flower-blossoms? Well! I believe no manager was ever so fortunate as to get recruits from Fairy-land; and yet I am told that *A Midsum-mer-Night's Dream* was some twenty years ago revived at Covent Garden, though altered, of course not much for the better, by Reynolds, and that it had a run of eighteen nights —a tolerably good reception. But supposing that it never could have been acted, I should only thank Shakespeare the more that he wrote here as a poet and not as a playwright. And as a birth of his imagination, whether it was to suit the stage or not, can we suppose the Poet himself to have been insensible of its worth? Is a mother blind to the beauty of her own child? No! nor could Shakespeare be unconscious that posterity would doat on this, one of his loveliest children.

* Quoted by Verplanck, vol. ii. p. 49 of *M. N. D.*

How he must have chuckled and laughed in the act of placing the ass's head on Bottom's shoulders! He must have foretasted the mirth of generations unborn at Titania's doating on the metamorphosed weaver, and on his calling for a repast of sweet peas. His animal spirits must have bounded with the hunter's joy, while he wrote Theseus's description of his well-tuned dogs and of the glory of the chase. He must have been happy as Puck himself while he was describing the merry Fairy, and all this time he must have been self-assured that his genius was " to put a girdle round the earth ;" and that souls, not yet in being, were to enjoy the revelry of his fancy.

[From Gervinus's " Shakespeare Commentaries."*]*

That which Shakespeare received in the rough form of fragmentary popular belief he developed in his playful creation into a beautiful and regulated world. He here in a measure deserves the merit which Herodotus ascribes to Homer ; as the Greek poet has created the great abode of the gods and its Olympic inhabitants, so Shakespeare has given form and place to the fairy kingdom, and with the natural creative power of genius he has breathed a soul into his merry little citizens, thus imparting a living centre to their nature and their office, their behaviour and their doings. He has given embodied form to the invisible, and life to the dead, and has thus striven for the poet's greatest glory ; and it seems as if it was not without consciousness of this his work that he wrote in a strain of self-reliance that passage in this very play :

> " The poet's eye, in a fine frenzy rolling,
> Doth glance from heaven to earth, from earth to heaven ;
> And as imagination bodies forth
> The forms of things unknown, the poet's pen
> Turns them to shapes and gives to airy nothing

* *Shakespeare Commentaries*, by Dr. G. G. Gervinus, translated by F. E. Bunnett : revised ed. (London, 1875), p. 195 fol. (by permission).

A local habitation and a name.
Such tricks hath strong imagination,
That, if it would but apprehend some joy,
It comprehends some bringer of that joy."

This he has here effected: he has clothed in bodily form those intangible phantoms, the bringers of dreams of provoking jugglery, of sweet soothing, and of tormenting raillery; and the task he has thus accomplished we shall only rightly estimate when we have taken into account the severe design and inner congruity of this little world.

If it were Shakespeare's object expressly to remove from the fairies that dark ghostlike character (iii. 2. 381 fol.) in which they appeared in Scandinavian and Scottish fable; if it were his desire to portray them as kindly beings in a merry and harmless relation to mortals; if he wished, in their essential office as bringers of dreams, to fashion them in their nature as personified dreams, he carried out this object in wonderful harmony both as regards their actions and their condition. The kingdom of the fairy beings is placed in the aromatic flower-scented Indies, in the land where mortals live in a half-dreamy state. From hence they come, "following darkness," as Puck says, "like a dream." Airy and swift, like the moon, they circle the earth; they avoid the sunlight without fearing it, and seek the darkness; they love the moon, and dance in her beams; and above all they delight in the dusk and twilight, the very season for dreams, whether waking or asleep. They send and bring dreams to mortals; and we need only recall to mind the description of the fairies' midwife, Queen Mab, in *Romeo and Juliet*, a piece nearly of the same date as the *Midsummer-Night's Dream*, to discover that this is the charge essentially assigned to them, and the very means by which they influence mortals.

The manner in which Shakespeare has fashioned their inner character in harmony with this outward function is full of profound thought. He depicts them as beings without delicate feeling and without morality, just as in dreams we meet with no check to our tender sensations, and are without moral impulse and responsibility. Careless and unscrupulous, they tempt mortals to infidelity; the effects of the mistakes which they have contrived make no impression on their minds; they feel no sympathy for the deep affliction of the lovers, but only delight and marvel over their mistakes and their foolish demeanour. The poet farther depicts his fairies as beings of no high intellectual development. Whoever attentively reads their parts will find that nowhere is reflection imparted to them. Only in one exception does Puck make a sententious remark upon the infidelity of man, and whoever has penetrated into the nature of these beings will immediately feel that it is out of harmony. They can make no direct inward impression upon mortals; their influence over the mind is not spiritual, but throughout material; it is effected by means of vision, metamorphosis, and imitation. Titania has no spiritual association with her friend, but mere delight in her beauty, her "swimming gait," and her powers of imitation. When she awakes from her vision there is no reflection. "Methought I was enamoured of an ass," she says,—"O, how mine eyes do loathe his visage now!" She is only affected by the idea of the actual and the visible. There is no scene of reconciliation with her husband; her resentment consists in separation, her reconciliation in a dance; there is no trace of reflection, no indication of feeling. Thus, to remind Puck of a past event no abstract date sufficed, but an accompanying indication, perceptible to the senses, was required. They are represented, these little gods, as natural souls, without the higher human capacities of mind, lords of a kingdom, not of reason and morality, but of imagination and ideas conveyed by the senses; and thus they are uniformly the vehicle of the fancy which produces the delusions of love and dreams. Their will, therefore, only extends to the corporeal. They lead a luxurious, merry life, given up to the pleasures of the senses; the secrets of nature and the powers of flowers and herbs are confided to them. To sleep in flowers, lulled with dances and songs, with the wings of painted butterflies to fan the moonbeams from their eyes, this is their pleasure; the gorgeous apparel of flowers and dewdrops is their joy. When Titania wishes to allure her beloved, she offers him honey, apricots, purple grapes, and dancing.

This life of sense and nature is seasoned by the power of fancy, and by desire after all that is most choice, most beautiful, and agreeable. They harmonize with nightingales and butterflies; they wage war with all ugly creatures, with hedgehogs, spiders, and bats; dancing, play, and song are their greatest pleasures; they steal lovely children, and substitute changelings; they torment decrepit old age, toothless gossips, and the awkward company of the players of Pyramus and Thisbe, but they love and recompense all that is pure and pretty. Thus was it of old in the popular traditions; their characteristic trait of favouring honesty among mortals and persecuting crime was certainly borrowed by Shakespeare from these traditions in the *Merry Wives of Windsor*, though not in this play. The sense of the beautiful is the one thing which elevates the fairies not only above the beasts, but also above the ordinary mortal, when he is devoid of all fancy and uninfluenced by beauty. Thus, in the spirit of the fairies, in which this sense of the beautiful is so refined, it is intensely ludicrous that the elegant Titania should fall in love with an ass's head. The only pain which agitates these beings is jealousy, the desire of possessing the beautiful sooner than others; they shun the distorting quarrel; their steadfast aim and longing is for undisturbed enjoyment.

But in this sweet jugglery they neither appear constant to mortals, nor do they carry on intercourse among themselves in monotonous harmony. They are full also of wanton tricks and railleries, playing upon themselves and upon mortals pranks which never hurt, but which often torment. This is especially the property of Puck, who "jests to Oberon," who is the "lob" at this court, a coarser goblin, represented with broom or threshing-flail, in a leathern dress, and with a dark countenance—a roguish but awkward fellow, skilful at all transformations, practised in wilful tricks, but also clumsy enough to make mistakes and blunders contrary to his intention. . . .

We can now readily perceive why, in this work, the "rude mechanicals" and clowns, and the company of actors with their burlesque comedy, are placed in such rude contrast to the tender and delicate play of the fairies. Prominence is given to both by the contrast afforded between the material and the aërial, between the awkward and the beautiful, between the utterly unimaginative and that which, itself fancy, is entirely woven out of fancy. The play acted by the clowns is, as it were, the reverse of the poet's own work, which demands all the spectator's reflective and imitative fancy to open to him this aërial world, whilst in the other nothing is left to the imagination of the spectator. The homely mechanics, who compose and act merely for gain, and for the sake of so many pence a day, the ignorant players, with hard hands and thick heads, whose unskilful art consists in learning their parts by heart, these men believe themselves obliged to represent Moon and Moonshine by name in order to render them evident; they supply the lack of side-scenes by persons, and all that should take place behind the scenes they explain by digressions. These rude doings are disturbed by the fairy chiefs with their utmost raillery, and the fantastical company of lovers mock at the performance. Theseus, however, draws quiet and thoughtful contemplation from these contrasts. He shrinks incredulously from the too-strange fables of love and its witchcraft; he enjoins that imagination should amend the play of the clowns, devoid as it is of all fancy. The real, that in this work of art has be-

come "nothing," and the "airy nothing," which in the poet's
hand has assumed this graceful form, are contrasted in the
two extremes; in the centre is the intellectual man, who
participates in both, who regards the one, namely, the stories
of the lovers, the poets by nature, as art and poetry, and who
receives the other, presented as art, only as a thankworthy
readiness to serve and as a simple offering.

[From Dowden's " Shakspere." *]

In the *Comedy of Errors* (ii. 2. 189–201) occurs the following dialogue:

> "*Luciana.* Dromio, go bid the servants spread for dinner.
>   *Dromio of S.* O, for my beads! I cross me for a sinner.
> This is the fairy land: O spite of spites!
> We talk with goblins, owls, and sprites;
> If we obey them not, this will ensue,—
> They 'll suck our breath, or pinch us black and blue.
>   *Luciana.* Why prat'st thou to thyself and answer'st not?
> Dromio, thou drone, thou snail, thou slug, thou sot!
>   *Dromio of S.* I am transformed, master, am I not?
>   *Antipholus of S.* I think thou art in mind, and so am I.
>   *Dromio of S.* Nay, master, both in mind and in my shape.
>   *Antipholus of S.* Thou hast thine own form.
>   *Dromio of S.*   No, I am an ape.
>   *Luciana.* If thou art chang'd to aught, 't is to an ass."

When Shakspere wrote thus of fairy-land, of the pranks of
Robin Goodfellow, and of the transformation of a man to an
ass, can it be doubted that he had in his thoughts *A Midsummer-Night's Dream?* The play was perhaps so named
because it is a dream-play, the fantastic adventures of a
night, and because it was first represented in midsummer—
the midsummer, perhaps, of 1594. The imagined season of
the action of the play is the beginning of May, for according
to the magnificent piece of mediæval-classical mythology
embodied here, and in the *Knightes Tale* of Chaucer, and

* *Shakspere: a Critical Study of his Mind and Art*, by Edward Dowden (2d ed. London, 1876), p. 66 fol. (by permission).

C

again in *The Two Noble Kinsmen* of Shakspere and Fletcher, this was the month of Theseus' marriage with his Amazonian bride.* . . . *A Midsummer-Night's Dream* was written on the occasion of the marriage of some noble couple—possibly for the marriage of the poet's patron Southampton with Elizabeth Vernon, as Mr. Gerald Massey supposes; possibly at an earlier date to do honour to the marriage of the Earl of Essex with Lady Sidney.†

The central figure of the play is that of Theseus. There is no figure in the early drama of Shakspere so magnificent. His are the large hands that have helped to shape the world. His utterance is the rich-toned speech of one who is master of events—who has never known a shrill or eager feeling. His nuptial day is at hand; and while the other lovers are agitated, bewildered, incensed, Theseus, who does not think of himself as a lover but rather as a beneficent conqueror, remains in calm possession of his joy. Theseus, a grand ideal figure, is to be studied as Shakspere's conception of the heroic man of action in his hour of enjoyment and of leisure. With a splendid capacity for enjoyment, gracious to all, ennobled by the glory, implied rather than explicit, of great foregone achievement, he stands as centre of the poem, giving their true proportions to the fairy tribe upon the one hand, and upon the other to the "human mor-

---

* Titania says to Oberon (ii. 1. 82),

> "And never, since the middle summer's spring,
> Met we on hill, in dale, forest or mead," etc.

Perhaps a night in early May might be considered a night in the spring of midsummer.

† Mr. Massey is obliged to entertain the supposition that the play was written some time before the marriage actually took place (1598), "at a period when it may have been thought the queen's consent could be obtained. . . . I have ventured the date of 1595." Professor Karl Elze's theory, maintained in a highly ingenious paper in *Shakspeare Jahrbuch*, vol. iii., that the play was written for the marriage of the young Earl of Essex, would throw back the date to 1590. There is much to be said in favour of this opinion.

tals." The heroic men of action—Theseus, Henry V., Hector—are supremely admired by Shakspere. Yet it is observable that as the total Shakspere is superior to Romeo, the man given over to passion, and to Hamlet, the man given over to thought, so the Hamlet and the Romeo within him give Shakspere an infinite advantage over even the most heroic men of action. He admires these men of action supremely, but he admires them from an outside point of view. "These fellows of infinite tongue," says Henry, wooing the French princess, "that can rhyme themselves into ladies' favours, they do always reason themselves out again. What! a speaker is but a prater, a rhyme is but a ballad." It is into Theseus' mouth that Shakspere puts the words which class together "the lunatic, the lover, and the poet" as of imagination all compact. That is the touch which shows how Shakspere stood off from Theseus, did not identify himself with this grand ideal (which he admired so truly), and admitted to himself a secret superiority of his own soul over that of this noble master of the world.

Comments by Shakspere upon his own art are not so numerous that we can afford to overlook them. It must here be noted that Shakspere makes the "palpable gross" interlude of the Athenian mechanicals serve as an indirect apology for his own necessarily imperfect attempt to represent fairy-land and the majestic world of heroic life. Maginn (*Shakspeare Papers*, p. 119) writes: "When Hippolyta speaks scornfully of the tragedy in which Bottom holds so conspicuous a part, Theseus answers that the best of this kind [scenic performances] are but shadows, and the worst no worse if imagination amend them. She answers [for Hippolyta has none of Theseus' indulgence towards inefficiency, but rather a woman's intolerance of the absurd] that it must be *your* imagination then, not *theirs*. He retorts with a joke on the vanity of actors, and the conversation is immediately changed. The meaning of the Duke is that, however we may laugh at the silliness of Bottom and his companions in their ridiculous play, the author labours under no more than the common calamity of dramatists. They are all but dealers in shadowy representations of life, and if the worst among them can set the mind of the spectator at work, he is equal to the best."

Maginn has missed the more important significance of the passage. Its dramatic appropriateness is the essential point to observe. To Theseus, the great man of action, the worst and the best of those shadowy representations are all one. He graciously lends himself to be amused, and will not give unmannerly rebuff to the painstaking craftsmen who have so laboriously done their best to please him. But Shakspere's mind by no means goes along with the utterance of Theseus in this instance any more than when he places in a single group the lover, the lunatic, and the poet. With one principle enounced by the duke, however, Shakspere evidently does agree, namely, that it is the business of the dramatist to set the spectator's imagination to work, that the dramatist must rather appeal to the mind's eye than to the eye of sense, and that the co-operation of the spectator with the poet is necessary. For the method of Bottom and his company is precisely the reverse, as Gervinus has observed, of Shakspere's own method. They are determined to leave nothing to be supplied by the imagination. Wall must be plaistered; Moonshine must carry lanthorn and bush. And when Hippolyta, again becoming impatient of absurdity, exclaims, "I am aweary of this moon! would he would change!" Shakspere further insists on his piece of dramatic criticism by urging, through the duke's mouth, the absolute necessity of the man in the moon being *within* his lanthorn. Shakspere as much as says, "If you do not approve of my dramatic method of presenting fairy-land and the heroic world, here is a specimen of the rival method. You think my fairy-world might be amended. Well, amend it with your own imagination. I can do no more unless I adopt the artistic ideas of these Athenian handicraftsmen."

It is a delightful example of Shakspere's impartiality that he can represent Theseus with so much genuine enthusiasm. Mr. Matthew Arnold has named our aristocrats, with their hardy, efficient manners, their addiction to field sports, and their hatred of ideas, "the Barbarians." Theseus is a splendid and gracious aristocrat, perhaps not without a touch of the Barbarian in him. He would have found Hamlet a wholly unintelligible person, who, in possession of his own thoughts, could be contented in a nutshell. When Shakspere wrote the *Two Gentlemen of Verona*, in which, with little dramatic propriety, the Duke of Milan celebrates "the force of heaven-bred poesy," we may reasonably suppose that the poet might not have been quite just to one who was indifferent to art. But now his self-mastery has increased, and therefore with unfeigned satisfaction he presents Theseus, the master of the world, who, having beauty and heroic strength in actual possession, does not need to summon them to occupy his imagination—the great chieftain to whom art is a very small concern of life, fit for a leisure hour between battle and battle. Theseus, who has nothing antique or Grecian about him, is an idealized study from the life. Perhaps he is idealized Essex, perhaps idealized Southampton. Perhaps some night a dramatic company was ordered to perform in presence of a great Elizabethan noble—we know not whom—who needed to entertain his guests, and there, in a moment of fine imaginative vision, the poet discovered Theseus.

[*From Weiss's "Wit, Humor, and Shakspeare."**]

All the scenes of the *Midsummer-Night's Dream* which depend upon the desire of the Athenian mechanicals to

* *Wit, Humor, and Shakspeare,* by John Weiss (Boston, 1876), p. 109 fol.

amuse their prince are merely comical when taken alone. The characters thus constructed, by passing into the serious portions of the play, infect it with the element of humour; for the simple earnestness of all their clownishness fraternizes in no offensive way with the more poetical moods of high society, and we feel the charm that equalizes all mankind. The pomp of a court is concentrated at a fustian play that is poorly propertied with bush, lantern, and a fellow daubed with lime.   Simpleness and duty tender this contrast, and it comes not amiss.   Their crude parody of the fate of Pyramus and Thisbe, done in perfect good faith, is a claim that humble love may have its fortunes too, as well as that of the proud and overconscious dames who have been roaming through the woods, sick with fancies.   What a delightful raillery it is!   Yes, we take the point: "The best in this kind are but shadows; and the worst are no worse, if imagination amend them."

It is also a suggestion of the subtlest humour when Titania summons her fairies to wait upon Bottom; for the fact is that the soul's airy and nimble fancies are constantly detailed to serve the donkeyism of this world.   "Be kind and courteous to this gentleman."   Divine gifts stick musk-roses in his sleek, smooth head.   The world is a peg that keeps all spiritual being tethered.   Watt agonizes to teach this *vis inertiæ* to drag itself by the car-load; Palissy starves for twenty years to enamel its platter; Franklin charms its house against thunder; Raphael contributes halos to glorify its ignorance of divinity; all the poets gather for its beguilement, hop in its walk and gambol before it, scratch its head, bring honey-bags, and light its farthing dip at glow-worms' eyes.   Bottom's want of insight is circled round by fulness of insight, his clumsiness by dexterity.   In matter of eating, he really prefers provender: "good hay, sweet hay, hath no fellow."   But how shrewdly Bottom manages this holding of genius to his service!   He knows how to send it to be oriented with the blossoms and the sweets, giving it the characteristic counsel not to fret itself too much in the action. . . .

The humour in this play meddles even with love; for that, too, must be the sport of circumstance and superior power, yet always continue to be the deepest motive of mankind. The juice of love's flower dropped on the eyelids of these distempered lovers makes the caprices of passion show and shift; love in idleness becomes love in earnest, as Puck distils the drops of marriage or of mischief. Titania herself is possessed with that common illusion which marries gracious qualities to absurd companionship. Says Puck,

> "Those things do best please me
> That befall preposterously."

But this is fleeting. Shakspeare soon breaks the spell in which some of his most delicate and sprightly verses have revelled. The whole play expresses humour on a revel, and brings into one human feeling the supernature, the caprice and gross mischance, the serious drift of life.

COIN OF ATHENS.

HIPPOLITA.

A MIDSUMMER-NIGHT'S DREAM.

DRAMATIS PERSONÆ.

THESEUS, Duke of Athens.
EGEUS, Father to Hermia.
LYSANDER, } in love with Hermia.
DEMETRIUS,
PHILOSTRATE, master of the revels to Theseus.
QUINCE, a carpenter.
SNUG, a joiner.
BOTTOM, a weaver.
FLUTE, a bellows-mender.
SNOUT, a tinker.
STARVELING, a tailor.

HIPPOLYTA, queen of the Amazons, betrothed to Theseus.

HERMIA, daughter to Egeus, in love with Lysander.
HELENA, in love with Demetrius.

OBERON, king of the fairies.
TITANIA, queen of the fairies.
PUCK, or Robin Goodfellow.
PEASEBLOSSOM, }
COBWEB,
MOTH, } fairies.
MUSTARDSEED, }
Other fairies attending their King and Queen.
Attendants on Theseus and Hippolyta.
SCENE: *Athens, and a wood near it.*

ATHENS.

ACT I.

SCENE I. *Athens. The Palace of Theseus.*

Enter THESEUS, HIPPOLYTA, PHILOSTRATE, *and* Attendants.

Theseus. Now, fair Hippolyta, our nuptial hour
Draws on apace ; four happy days bring in
'Another moon : but, O, methinks, how slow
This old moon wanes ! she lingers my desires,
Like to a step-dame or a dowager *widow endowed*
Long withering out a young man's revenue.

Hippolyta. Four days will quickly steep themselves in
      night ;
Four nights will quickly dream away the time ;

And then the moon, like to a silver bow
New-bent in heaven, shall behold the night
Of our solemnities. ____

    Theseus.   Go, Philostrate,
Stir up the Athenian youth to merriments;
Awake the pert and nimble spirit of mirth:
Turn melancholy forth to funerals;
The pale companion is not for our pomp.   [*Exit Philostrate.*
Hippolyta, I woo'd thee with my sword,
And won thy love, doing thee injuries;
But I will wed thee in another key,
With pomp, with triumph, and with revelling.

    Enter EGEUS, HERMIA, LYSANDER, *and* DEMETRIUS.

    Egeus. Happy be Theseus, our renowned duke!   20
    Theseus. Thanks, good Egeus: what's the news with
       thee?
    Egeus. Full of vexation come I, with complaint
Against my child, my daughter Hermia.—
Stand forth, Demetrius.—My noble lord,
This man hath my consent to marry her.—
Stand forth, Lysander:—and, my gracious duke,
This man hath bewitch'd the bosom of my child.—
Thou, thou, Lysander, thou hast given her rhymes
And interchang'd love-tokens with my child:
Thou hast by moonlight at her window sung
With feigning voice verses of feigning love,
And stolen the impression of her fantasy
With bracelets of thy hair, rings, gawds, conceits,
Knacks, trifles, nosegays, sweetmeats, messengers
Of strong prevailment in unharden'd youth.
With cunning hast thou filch'd my daughter's heart,
Turn'd her obedience, which is due to me,
To stubborn harshness:—and, my gracious duke,
Be it so she will not here before your grace

Henry V. is great hero [handwritten marginalia]

Consent to marry with Demetrius,   40
I beg the ancient privilege of Athens,
As she is mine, I may dispose of her;
Which shall be either to this gentleman
Or to her death, according to our law
Immediately provided in that case.

 Theseus. What say you, Hermia? be advis'd, fair maid:
To you your father should be as a god;
One that compos'd your beauties, yea, and one
To whom you are but as a form in wax
By him imprinted and within his power   50
To leave the figure or disfigure it.
Demetrius is a worthy gentleman.

 Hermia. So is Lysander. *key note to H's character* [handwritten marginalia]

 Theseus.   In himself he is;
But in this kind, wanting your father's voice,
The other must be held the worthier.

 Hermia. I would my father lock'd but with my eyes.

 Theseus. Rather your eyes must with his judgment look.

 Hermia. I do entreat your grace to pardon me.
I know not by what power I am made bold,
Nor how it may concern my modesty, *reflect upon life* [handwritten marginalia]   60
In such a presence here to plead my thoughts; *renounce under* [handwritten marginalia]
But I beseech your grace that I may know *vail* [handwritten marginalia]
The worst that may befall me in this case,
If I refuse to wed Demetrius.

 Theseus. Either to die the death, or to abjure
For ever the society of men.
Therefore, fair Hermia, question your desires;
Know of your youth, examine well your blood,
Whether, if you yield not to your father's choice,
You can endure the livery of a nun, *do some in that time* [handwritten marginalia]   70
For aye to be in shady cloister mew'd,
To live a barren sister all your life,
Chanting faint hymns to the cold fruitless moon.

Thrice blessed they that master so their blood,
To undergo such maiden pilgrimage;
But earthlier happy is the rose distill'd,
Than that which withering on the virgin thorn
Grows, lives, and dies in single blessedness.

Hermia. So will I grow, so live, so die, my lord,
Ere I will yield my virgin patent up
Unto his lordship whose unwished yoke   80
My soul consents not to give sovereignty.

    Theseus. Take time to pause; and, by the next new
        moon—
The sealing-day betwixt my love and me
For everlasting bond of fellowship—
Upon that day either prepare to die
For disobedience to your father's will,
Or else to wed Demetrius, as he would;
Or on Diana's altar to protest
For aye austerity and single life.   90

    Demetrius. Relent, sweet Hermia:—and, Lysander, yield
Thy crazed title to my certain right.

    Lysander. You have her father's love, Demetrius;
Let me have Hermia's: do you marry him.

    Egeus. Scornful Lysander! true, he hath my love,
And what is mine my love shall render him;
And she is mine, and all my right of her
I do estate unto Demetrius.

    Lysander. I am, my lord, as well deriv'd as he,
As well possess'd; my love is more than his;   100
My fortunes every way as fairly rank'd,
If not with vantage, as Demetrius';
And, which is more than all these boasts can be,
I am belov'd of beauteous Hermia:
Why should not I then prosecute my right?
Demetrius, I 'll avouch it to his head,
Made love to Nedar's daughter, Helena,

And won her soul; and she, sweet lady, dotes,
Devoutly dotes, dotes in idolatry,
Upon this spotted and inconstant man.   110

  Theseus. I must confess that I have heard so much,
And with Demetrius thought to have spoke thereof;
But, being over-full of self-affairs,
My mind did lose it.—But, Demetrius, come;
And come, Egeus; you shall go with me:
I have some private schooling for you both.—
For you, fair Hermia, look you arm yourself
To fit your fancies to your father's will;
Or else the law of Athens yields you up—
Which by no means we may extenuate—   120
To death, or to a vow of single life.—
Come, my Hippolyta: what cheer, my love?—
Demetrius and Egeus, go along:
I must employ you in some business
Against our nuptial, and confer with you
Of something nearly that concerns yourselves.

  Egeus. With duty and desire we follow you.
                    [*Exeunt all but Lysander and Hermia.*

  Lysander. How now, my love! why is your cheek so pale?
How chance the roses there do fade so fast?

  Hermia. Belike for want of rain, which I could well   130
Beteem them from the tempest of my eyes.

  Lysander. Ay me! for aught that I could ever read,
Could ever hear by tale or history,
The course of true love never did run smooth;
But, either it was different in blood,—

  Hermia. O cross! too high to be enthrall'd to low.

  Lysander. Or else misgraffed in respect of years,—

  Hermia. O spite! too old to be engag'd to young.

  Lysander. Or else it stood upon the choice of friends,—

  Hermia. O hell! to choose love by another's eyes.   140

  Lysander. Or, if there were a sympathy in choice,

War, death, or sickness did lay siege to it,
Making it momentany as a sound,
Swift as a shadow, short as any dream ;
Brief as the lightning in the collied night,
That, in a spleen, unfolds both heaven and earth,
And ere a man hath power to say ' Behold !'
The jaws of darkness do devour it up :
So quick bright things come to confusion.

    Hermia. If then true lovers have been ever cross'd,   150
It stands as an edict in destiny :
Then let us teach our trial patience,
Because it is a customary cross,
As due to love as thoughts and dreams and sighs,
Wishes and tears, poor fancy's followers.

    Lysander. A good persuasion : therefore, hear me, Hermia.
I have a widow aunt, a dowager
Of great revenue, and she hath no child :
From Athens is her house remote seven leagues ;
And she respects me as her only son.   160
There, gentle Hermia, may I marry thee ;
And to that place the sharp Athenian law
Cannot pursue us.   If thou lov'st me then,
Steal forth thy father's house to-morrow night ;
And in the wood, a league without the town,
Where I did meet thee once with Helena,
To do observance to a morn of May,
There will I stay for thee.

    Hermia.   My good Lysander !
I swear to thee, by Cupid's strongest bow,
By his best arrow with the golden head,   170
By the simplicity of Venus' doves,
By that which knitteth souls and prospers loves,
And by that fire which burn'd the Carthage queen,
When the false Troyan under sail was seen,
By all the vows that ever men have broke,

In number more than ever women spoke,
In that same place thou hast appointed me,
To-morrow truly will I meet with thee.

    Lysander. Keep promise, love. Look, here comes Helena.

Enter HELENA.

    Hermia. God speed fair Helena! whither away?   180
    Helena. Call you me fair? that fair again unsay.
Demetrius loves your fair: O happy fair!
Your eyes are lode-stars, and your tongue's sweet air
More tuneable than lark to shepherd's ear,
When wheat is green, when hawthorn buds appear.
Sickness is catching: O, were favour so,
Yours would I catch, fair Hermia, ere I go;
My ear should catch your voice, my eye your eye,
My tongue should catch your tongue's sweet melody.
Were the world mine, Demetrius being bated,   190
The rest I 'd give to be to you translated.
O, teach me how you look, and with what art
You sway the motion of Demetrius' heart.
    Hermia. I frown upon him, yet he loves me still.
    Helena. O that your frowns would teach my smiles such
        skill!
    Hermia. I give him curses, yet he gives me love.
    Helena. O that my prayers could such affection move!
    Hermia. The more I hate, the more he follows me.
    Helena. The more I love, the more he hateth me.
    Hermia. His folly, Helena, is no fault of mine.   200
    Helena. None, but your beauty: would that fault were mine!
    Hermia. Take comfort: he no more shall see my face;
Lysander and myself will fly this place.
Before the time I did Lysander see,
Seem'd Athens like a paradise to me:
O, then, what graces in my love do dwell,
That he hath turn'd a heaven into a hell!

Lysander. Helen, to you our minds we will unfold :
To-morrow night, when Phœbe doth behold
Her silver visage in the watery glass,   210
Decking with liquid pearl the bladed grass,
A time that lovers' flights doth still conceal,
Through Athens' gates have we devis'd to steal.

Hermia. And in the wood, where often you and I
Upon faint primrose-beds were wont to lie,
Emptying our bosoms of their counsel sweet,
There my Lysander and myself shall meet ;
And thence from Athens turn away our eyes,
To seek new friends and stranger companies.
Farewell, sweet playfellow : pray thou for us,   220
And good luck grant thee thy Demetrius !—
Keep word, Lysander : we must starve our sight
From lovers' food till morrow deep midnight.

Lysander. I will, my Hermia.—   [*Exit Hermia.*
                    Helena, adieu :
As you on him, Demetrius dote on you !   [*Exit.*

Helena. How happy some o'er other some can be !
Through Athens I am thought as fair as she ;
But what of that ?   Demetrius thinks not so ;
He will not know what all but he do know :
And as he errs, doting on Hermia's eyes,   230
So I, admiring of his qualities.
Things base and vile, holding no quantity,
Love can transpose to form and dignity.
Love looks not with the eyes, but with the mind ;
And therefore is wing'd Cupid painted blind :
Nor hath Love's mind of any judgment taste ;
Wings and no eyes figure unheedy haste :
And therefore is Love said to be a child,
Because in choice he is so oft beguil'd.
As waggish boys in game themselves forswear,   240
So the boy Love is perjur'd every where :

For ere Demetrius look'd on Hermia's eyne,
He hail'd down oaths that he was only mine ;
And when this hail some heat from Hermia felt,
So he dissolv'd, and showers of oaths did melt.
I will go tell him of fair Hermia's flight ;
Then to the wood will he to-morrow night
Pursue her ; and for this intelligence
If I have thanks, it is a dear expense :
But herein mean I to enrich my pain,   250
To have his sight thither and back again.   [*Exit.*

SCENE II. *Athens. Quince's House.*
Enter QUINCE, SNUG, BOTTOM, FLUTE, SNOUT, *and* STARVEL-
ING.

Quince. Is all our company here?

Bottom. You were best to call them generally, man by
man, according to the scrip.

Quince. Here is the scroll of every man's name, which is
thought fit, through all Athens, to play in our interlude before the duke and the duchess, on his wedding-day at night.

Bottom. First, good Peter Quince, say what the play treats
on, then read the names of the actors, and so grow to a point.

Quince. Marry, our play is, The most lamentable Comedy,
and most cruel Death of Pyramus and Thisby.   10

Bottom. A very good piece of work, I assure you, and a
merry. Now, good Peter Quince, call forth your actors by
the scroll. Masters, spread yourselves.

Quince. Answer as I call you. Nick Bottom, the weaver.

Bottom. Ready. Name what part I am for, and proceed.

Quince. You, Nick Bottom, are set down for Pyramus.

Bottom. What is Pyramus? a lover, or a tyrant?

Quince. A lover, that kills himself most gallant for love.

Bottom. That will ask some tears in the true performing
of it : if I do it, let the audience look to their eyes ; I will

move storms, I will condole in some measure.   To the rest.
—Yet my chief humour is for a tyrant : I could play Ercles
rarely, or a part to tear a cat in, to make all split.   23

> The raging rocks
> And shivering shocks
> Shall break the locks
>   Of prison gates ;
> And Phibbus' car
> Shall shine from far,
> And make and mar
>   The foolish Fates.   30

This was lofty !—Now name the rest of the players.—This is
Ercles' vein, a tyrant's vein ; a lover is more condoling.

Quince. Francis Flute, the bellows-mender.

Flute. Here, Peter Quince.

Quince. Flute, you must take Thisby on you.

Flute. What is Thisby ? a wandering knight ?

Quince. It is the lady that Pyramus must love.

Flute. Nay, faith, let not me play a woman ; I have a
beard coming.   40

Quince. That 's all one : you shall play it in a mask, and
you may speak as small as you will.

Bottom. An I may hide my face, let me play Thisby
too.   I 'll speak in a monstrous little voice : 'Thisne, Thisne,
—Ah Pyramus, my lover dear ! thy Thisby dear, and lady
dear !'

Quince. No, no ; you must play Pyramus : and, Flute, you
Thisby.

Bottom. Well, proceed.

Quince. Robin Starveling, the tailor.   50

Starveling. Here, Peter Quince.

Quince. Robin Starveling, you must play Thisby's mother.
—Tom Snout, the tinker.

Snout. Here, Peter Quince.

Quince. You, Pyramus' father : myself, Thisby's father.—

Snug, the joiner; you, the lion's part: and, I hope, here is a play fitted.

Snug. Have you the lion's part written? pray you, if it be, give it me, for I am slow of study.

Quince. You may do it extempore, for it is nothing but roaring. ₆₁

Bottom. Let me play the lion too: I will roar, that I will do any man's heart good to hear me; I will roar, that I will make the duke say, 'Let him roar again, let him roar again.'

Quince. An you should do it too terribly, you would fright the duchess and the ladies, that they would shriek; and that were enough to hang us all.

All. That would hang us, every mother's son.

Bottom. I grant you, friends, if that you should fright the ladies out of their wits, they would have no more discretion but to hang us: but I will aggravate my voice so that I will roar you as gently as any sucking dove; I will roar you an 't were any nightingale. ₇₃

Quince. You can play no part but Pyramus; for Pyramus is a sweet-faced man; a proper man, as one shall see in a summer's day; a most lovely gentleman-like man: therefore you must needs play Pyramus.

Bottom. Well, I will undertake it. What beard were I best to play it in?

Quince. Why, what you will.

Bottom. I will discharge it in either your straw-colour beard, your orange-tawny beard, your purple-in-grain beard, or your French-crown-colour beard, your perfect yellow. ₈₃

Quince. Some of your French crowns have no hair at all, and then you will play barefaced.—But, masters, here are your parts: and I am to entreat you, request you, and desire you, to con them by to-morrow night; and meet me in the palace wood, a mile without the town, by moonlight. There will we rehearse; for if we meet in the city, we shall be dogged with company, and our devices known. In the

meantime I will draw a bill of properties, such as our play
wants.   I pray you, fail me not.   92

obscurely

    Bottom. We will meet; and there we may rehearse most
obscenely and courageously.   Take pains; be perfect: adieu.

    Quince. At the duke's oak we meet.

    Bottom. Enough; hold or cut bow-strings.   [*Exeunt*

ACT II.

SCENE I. *A Wood near Athens.*

Enter, from opposite sides, a FAIRY *and* PUCK.

Puck. How now, spirit! whither wander you?
Fairy.   Over hill, over dale,
             Thorough bush, thorough brier,
           Over park, over pale,
             Thorough flood, thorough fire,
           I do wander every where,
           Swifter than the moon's sphere;
           And I serve the fairy queen,
           To dew her orbs upon the green.
           The cowslips tall her pensioners be:
           In their gold coats spots you see;
           Those be rubies, fairy favours.
           In those freckles live their savours.
I must go seek some dewdrops here,
And hang a pearl in every cowslip's ear.
Farewell, thou lob of spirits; I 'll be gone:
Our queen and all her elves come here anon.

10

Puck. The king doth keep his revels here to-night.
Take heed the queen come not within his sight;
For Oberon is passing fell and wrath,
Because that she as her attendant hath
A lovely boy, stolen from an Indian king;
She never had so sweet a changeling;
And jealous Oberon would have the child
Knight of his train, to trace the forests wild;
But she perforce withholds the loved boy,
Crowns him with flowers and makes him all her joy:
And now they never meet in grove or green,
By fountain clear, or spangled starlight sheen,
But they do square, that all their elves for fear
Creep into acorn-cups and hide them there.

Fairy. Either I mistake your shape and making quite,
Or else you are that shrewd and knavish sprite
Call'd Robin Goodfellow.   Are not you he
That frights the maidens of the villagery;
Skim milk, and sometimes labour in the quern,
And bootless make the breathless housewife churn;
And sometime make the drink to bear no barm;
Mislead night-wanderers, laughing at their harm?
Those that Hobgoblin call you and sweet Puck,
You do their work, and they shall have good luck:
Are not you he?

Puck.   Thou speak'st aright;
I am that merry wanderer of the night.
I jest to Oberon, and make him smile
When I a fat and bean-fed horse beguile,
Neighing in likeness of a filly foal:
And sometime lurk I in a gossip's bowl,
In very likeness of a roasted crab,
And when she drinks, against her lips I bob
And on her wither'd dewlap pour the ale.
The wisest aunt, telling the saddest tale,

Sometime for three-foot stool mistaketh me ;
Then slip I from her bum, down topples she,
And 'tailor' cries, and falls into a cough ;
And then the whole quire hold their hips and laugh,
And waxen in their mirth, and neeze, and swear
A merrier hour was never wasted there.
But, room, fairy ! here comes Oberon.
    Fairy. And here my mistress.   Would that he were gone !

Enter, from one side, OBERON, *with his train ; from the other,*
            TITANIA, *with hers.*

    Oberon. Ill met by moonlight, proud Titania.   60
    Titania. What, jealous Oberon !   Fairies, skip hence :
I have forsworn his bed and company.
    Oberon. Tarry, rash wanton : am not I thy lord ?
    Titania. Then I must be thy lady ; but I know
When thou hast stolen away from fairy land,
And in the shape of Corin sat all day,
Playing on pipes of corn, and versing love
To amorous Phillida.   Why art thou here,
Come from the farthest steep of India ?
But that, forsooth, the bouncing Amazon,   70
Your buskin'd mistress and your warrior love,
To Theseus must be wedded, and you come
To give their bed joy and prosperity.
    Oberon. How canst thou thus for shame, Titania,
Glance at my credit with Hippolyta,
Knowing I know thy love to Theseus ?
Didst thou not lead him through the glimmering night
From Perigenia, whom he ravished ?
And make him with fair Ægle break his faith,
With Ariadne and Antiopa ?   80
    Titania. These are the forgeries of jealousy :
And never, since the middle summer's spring,
Met we on hill, in dale, forest or mead,

By paved fountain or by rushy brook,
Or in the beached margent of the sea,
To dance our ringlets to the whistling wind,
But with thy brawls thou hast disturb'd our sport.
Therefore the winds, piping to us in vain,
As in revenge, have suck'd up from the sea
Contagious fogs; which falling in the land —
Hath every pelting river made so proud
That they have overborne their continents:
The ox hath therefore stretch'd his yoke in vain,
The ploughman lost his sweat, and the green corn
Hath rotted ere his youth attain'd a beard;
The fold stands empty in the drowned field,
And crows are fatted with the murrain flock;
The nine men's morris is fill'd up with mud,
And the quaint mazes in the wanton green
For lack of tread are undistinguishable:
The human mortals want their winter here;
No night is now with hymn or carol blest:
Therefore the moon, the governess of floods,
Pale in her anger, washes all the air,
That rheumatic diseases do abound:
And thorough this distemperature we see
The seasons alter: hoary-headed frosts
Fall in the fresh lap of the crimson rose,
And on old Hiems' thin and icy crown
An odorous chaplet of sweet summer buds
Is, as in mockery, set: the spring, the summer,
The childing autumn, angry winter, change
Their wonted liveries, and the mazed world,
By their increase, now knows not which is which.
And this same progeny of evils comes
From our debate, from our dissension;
We are their parents and original.

    Oberon. Do you amend it then; it lies in you:

Why should Titania cross her Oberon?
I do but beg a little changeling boy,   120
To be my henchman.

   Titania.   Set your heart at rest:
The fairy land buys not the child of me.
His mother was a votaress of my order:
And, in the spiced Indian air, by night,
Full often hath she gossip'd by my side,
And sat with me on Neptune's yellow sands,
Marking the embarked traders on the flood;
Which she with pretty and with swimming gait
Would imitate, and sail upon the land,
To fetch me trifles, and return again,   130
As from a voyage, rich with merchandise.
But she, being mortal, of that boy did die;
And for her sake do I rear up her boy,
And for her sake I will not part with him.

   Oberon. How long within this wood intend you stay?

   Titania. Perchance till after Theseus' wedding-day.
If you will patiently dance in our round
And see our moonlight revels, go with us;
If not, shun me, and I will spare your haunts.

   Oberon. Give me that boy, and I will go with thee.   140

   Titania. Not for thy fairy kingdom.—Fairies, away!
We shall chide downright, if I longer stay.

                   [*Exit Titania with her train.*

   Oberon. Well, go thy way: thou shalt not from this grove
Till I torment thee for this injury.—
My gentle Puck, come hither. Thou rememberest
Since once I sat upon a promontory,
And heard a mermaid on a dolphin's back
Uttering such dulcet and harmonious breath
That the rude sea grew civil at her song,
And certain stars shot madly from their spheres,   150
To hear the sea-maid's music.

Puck.   I remember.

Oberon. That very time I saw, but thou couldst not.
Flying between the cold moon and the earth,
Cupid all arm'd : a certain aim he took
At a fair vestal throned by the west,
And loos'd his love-shaft smartly from his bow,
As it should pierce a hundred thousand hearts ;
But I might see young Cupid's fiery shaft
Quench'd in the chaste beams of the watery moon,
And the imperial votaress passed on,   160
In maiden meditation, fancy-free.
Yet mark'd I where the bolt of Cupid fell :
It fell upon a little western flower,
Before milk-white, now purple with love's wound,
And maidens call it love-in-idleness.
Fetch me that flower ; the herb I show'd thee once :
The juice of it on sleeping eyelids laid
Will make or man or woman madly dote
Upon the next live creature that it sees.
Fetch me this herb ; and be thou here again   17o
Ere the leviathan can swim a league.

   Puck. I 'll put a girdle round about the earth
In forty minutes.   [*Exit.*

   Oberon.   Having once this juice,
I 'll watch Titania when she is asleep,
And drop the liquor of it in her eyes.
The next thing then she waking looks upon,
Be it on lion, bear, or wolf, or bull,
On meddling monkey, or on busy ape,
She shall pursue it with the soul of love ;
And ere I take this charm from off her sight,   18o
As I can take it with another herb,
I 'll make her render up her page to me.
But who comes here ?   I am invisible ;
And I will overhear their conference.

Enter DEMETRIUS, HELENA *following him.*

Demetrius. I love thee not, therefore pursue me not.
Where is Lysander and fair Hermia?
The one I 'll slay, the other slayeth me.
Thou told'st me they were stolen unto this wood;
And here am I, and wode within this wood,
Because I cannot meet my Hermia.   190
Hence, get thee gone, and follow me no more.
Helena. You draw me, you hard-hearted adamant;
But yet you draw not iron, for my heart
Is true as steel: leave you your power to draw,
And I shall have no power to follow you.
Demetrius. Do I entice you? do I speak you fair?
Or, rather, do I not in plainest truth
Tell you, I do not nor I cannot love you?
Helena. And even for that do I love you the more.
I am your spaniel; and, Demetrius,   200
'The more you beat me, I will fawn on you:
Use me but as your spaniel, spurn me, strike me,
Neglect me, lose me; only give me leave,
Unworthy as I am, to follow you.
What worser place can I beg in your love,—
And yet a place of high respect with me,—
Than to be used as you use your dog?
Demetrius. Tempt not too much the hatred of my spirit,
For I am sick when I do look on thee.
Helena. And I am sick when I look not on you.   210
Demetrius. You do impeach your modesty too much,
To leave the city and commit yourself
Into the hands of one that loves you not;
To trust the opportunity of night
And the ill counsel of a desert place
With the rich worth of your virginity.
Helena. Your virtue is my privilege for that.

It is not night when I do see your face,
Therefore I think I am not in the night ;
Nor doth this wood lack worlds of company,   220
For you in my respect are all the world :
Then how can it be said I am alone,
When all the world is here to look on me ?

    Demetrius. I 'll run from thee and hide me in the brakes,
And leave thee to the mercy of wild beasts.

    Helena. The wildest hath not such a heart as you.
Run when you will, the story shall be chang'd :
Apollo flies, and Daphne holds the chase ;
The dove pursues the griffin ; the mild hind
Makes speed to catch the tiger ; bootless speed,   230
When cowardice pursues and valour flies.

    Demetrius. I will not stay thy questions ; let me go :
Or, if thou follow me, do not believe
But I shall do thee mischief in the wood.

    Helena. Ay, in the temple, in the town, the field,
You do me mischief.   Fie, Demetrius !
Your wrongs do set a scandal on my sex :
We cannot fight for love, as men may do ;
We should be woo'd, and were not made to woo.

                          [Exit Demetrius.
I 'll follow thee and make a heaven of hell,   240
To die upon the hand I love so well.   *[Exit.*

    Oberon. Fare thee well, nymph : ere he do leave this grove,
Thou shalt fly him, and he shall seek thy love.—

Enter PUCK.

Hast thou the flower there ?   Welcome, wanderer.

    Puck. Ay, there it is.

    Oberon.   I pray thee, give it me.
I know a bank where the wild thyme blows,
Where oxlips and the nodding violet grows,
Quite over-canopied with luscious woodbine,

With sweet musk-roses and with eglantine :
There sleeps Titania sometime of the night,   250
Lull'd in these flowers with dances and delight ;
And there the snake throws her enamell'd skin,
Weed wide enough to wrap a fairy in :
And with the juice of this I 'll streak her eyes,
And make her full of hateful fantasies.
Take thou some of it, and seek through this grove :
A sweet Athenian lady is in love
With a disdainful youth : anoint his eyes ;
But do it when the next thing he espies
May be the lady.   Thou shalt know the man   260
By the Athenian garments he hath on.
Effect it with some care, that he may prove
More fond on her than she upon her love :
And look thou meet me ere the first cock crow.

    Puck. Fear not, my lord, your servant shall do so. [*Exeunt.*

SCENE II.   *Another Part of the Wood.*

Enter TITANIA, *with her train.*

  Titania. Come, now a roundel and a fairy song ;
Then, for the third part of a minute, hence ;
Some to kill cankers in the musk-rose buds,
Some war with rere-mice for their leathern wings,
To make my small elves coats, and some keep back
The clamorous owl that nightly hoots and wonders
At our quaint spirits.   Sing me now asleep ;
Then to your offices and let me rest.

Song.

  1 Fairy. *You spotted snakes with double tongue,*
     Thorny hedgehogs, be not seen ;   10
     Newts and blind-worms, do no wrong,
     Come not near our fairy queen.

Chorus. *Philomel, with melody*
　　　　Sing in our sweet lullaby;
　　　Lulla, lulla, lullaby, lulla, lulla, lullaby:
　　　　　Never harm,
　　　　　Nor spell nor charm,
　　　　Come our lovely lady nigh;
　　　　So, good night, with lullaby.

2 *Fairy.* *Weaving spiders, come not here;*　　　　　　20
　　　　Hence, you long-legg'd spinners, hence!
　　　　Beetles black, approach not near;
　　　　Worm nor snail, do no offence.
　Chorus. 　*Philomel, with melody,* etc.

1 *Fairy.* Hence, away! now all is well:
　　　　One aloof stand sentinel.
　　　　　　　[*Exeunt Fairies.　Titania sleeps.*

Enter OBERON, *and squeezes the flower on Titania's eyelids.*

Oberon. What thou seest when thou dost wake,
　　　Do it for thy true-love take;
　　　Love and languish for his sake:
　　　Be it ounce, or cat, or bear,　　　　　　30
　　　Pard, or boar with bristled hair,
　　　In thy eye that shall appear
　　　When thou wak'st, it is thy dear:
　　　Wake when some vile thing is near.　　　[*Exit.*

Enter LYSANDER *and* HERMIA.

Lysander. Fair love, you faint with wandering in the
　　　wood;
And to speak troth, I have forgot our way:
We'll rest us, Hermia, if you think it good,
And tarry for the comfort of the day.
　Hermia. Be it so, Lysander: find you out a bed;
For I upon this bank will rest my head.　　　　　　40

Lysander. One turf shall serve as pillow for us both;
One heart, one bed, two bosoms and one troth.

Hermia. Nay, good Lysander; for my sake, my dear,
Lie further off yet, do not lie so near.

Lysander. O, take the sense, sweet, of my innocence!
Love takes the meaning in love's conference.
I mean, that my heart unto yours is knit
So that but one heart we can make of it:
Two bosoms interchained with an oath;
So then two bosoms and a single troth.   50
Then by your side no bed-room me deny;
For lying so, Hermia, I do not lie.

Hermia. Lysander riddles very prettily:
Now much beshrew my manners and my pride,
If Hermia meant to say Lysander lied.
But, gentle friend, for love and courtesy
Lie further off; in human modesty,
Such separation as may well be said
Becomes a virtuous bachelor and a maid,
So far be distant; and, good night, sweet friend: 60
Thy love ne'er alter till thy sweet life end!

Lysander. Amen, amen, to that fair prayer, say I;
And then end life when I end loyalty!
Here is my bed: sleep give thee all his rest!

Hermia. With half that wish the wisher's eyes be press'd!
                                    [*They sleep.*

Enter PUCK.

Puck.   Through the forest have I gone,
           But Athenian found I none,
           On whose eyes I might approve
           This flower's force in stirring love.
           Night and silence.—Who is here?   70
           Weeds of Athens he doth wear:
           This is he, my master said,
           Despised the Athenian maid;

E

And here the maiden, sleeping sound,
On the dank and dirty ground.
Pretty soul! she durst not lie
Near this lack-love, this kill-courtesy.
Churl, upon thy eyes I throw
All the power this charm doth owe.
When thou wak'st, let love forbid   80
Sleep his seat on thy eyelid!
So awake when I am gone;
For I must now to Oberon.   [*Exit.*

Enter DEMETRIUS *and* HELENA, *running.*

Helena. Stay, though thou kill me, sweet Demetrius.
Demetrius. I charge thee, hence, and do not haunt me
    thus.
Helena. O, wilt thou darkling leave me? do not so.
Demetrius. Stay, on thy peril: I alone will go.   [*Exit.*
Helena. O, I am out of breath in this fond chase!
The more my prayer, the lesser is my grace.
Happy is Hermia, wheresoe'er she lies;   90
For she hath blessed and attractive eyes.
How came her eyes so bright? Not with salt tears:
If so, my eyes are oftener wash'd than hers.
No, no, I am as ugly as a bear;
For beasts that meet me run away for fear:
Therefore no marvel though Demetrius
Do, as a monster, fly my presence thus.
What wicked and dissembling glass of mine
Made me compare with Hermia's sphery eyne?—
But who is here? Lysander! on the ground!   100
Dead? or asleep? I see no blood, no wound.—
Lysander, if you live, good sir, awake.
    Lysander. [*Awaking.*] And run through fire I will for thy
        sweet sake.
Transparent Helena! Nature shows art,

That through thy bosom makes me see thy heart.
Where is Demetrius? O, how fit a word
Is that vile name to perish on my sword!
    Helena. Do not say so, Lysander; say not so.
What though he love your Hermia? Lord, what though?
Yet Hermia still loves you: then be content.   110
    Lysander. Content with Hermia! No; I do repent
The tedious minutes I with her have spent.
Not Hermia but Helena I love:
Who will not change a raven for a dove?
The will of man is by his reason sway'd,
And reason says you are the worthier maid.
Things growing are not ripe until their season:
So I, being young, till now ripe not to reason;
And touching now the point of human skill,
Reason becomes the marshal to my will   120
And leads me to your eyes, where I o'erlook
Love's stories written in love's richest book.
    Helena. Wherefore was I to this keen mockery born?
When at your hands did I deserve this scorn?
Is 't not enough, is 't not enough, young man,
That I did never, no, nor never can,
Deserve a sweet look from Demetrius' eye,
But you must flout my insufficiency?
Good troth, you do me wrong, good sooth, you do,
In such disdainful manner me to woo.   130
But fare you well: perforce I must confess
I thought you lord of more true gentleness.
O, that a lady, of one man refus'd,
Should of another therefore be abus'd!   [*Exit.*
    Lysander. She sees not Hermia.—Hermia, sleep thou
       there:
And never mayst thou come Lysander near!
For as a surfeit of the sweetest things
The deepest loathing to the stomach brings,

Or as the heresies that men do leave
Are hated most of those they did deceive,   140
So thou, my surfeit and my heresy,
Of all be hated, but the most of me!
And, all my powers, address your love and might
To honour Helen and to be her knight!   [*Exit.*

    Hermia. [*Awaking.*] Help me, Lysander, help me! do thy
      best
To pluck this crawling serpent from my breast!
Ay me, for pity! what a dream was here!
Lysander, look how I do quake with fear:
Methought a serpent eat my heart away,
And you sat smiling at his cruel prey.   150
Lysander! what, remov'd? Lysander! lord!
What, out of hearing? gone? no sound, no word?
Alack, where are you? speak, an if you hear;
Speak, of all loves! I swoon almost with fear.
No? then I well perceive you are not nigh:
Either death or you I 'll find immediately.   [*Exit.*

CUPID WHETTING HIS DARTS. FROM AN ANTIQUE GEM.

ACT III.

SCENE I. *The Wood. Titania lying asleep.*

Enter QUINCE, SNUG, BOTTOM, FLUTE, SNOUT, *and* STAR·
VELING.

Bottom. Are we all met?

Quince. Pat, pat; and here 's a marvellous convenient
place for our rehearsal. This green plot shall be our stage,

this hawthorn-brake our tiring-house; and we will do it in
action as we will do it before the duke.

Bottom. Peter Quince,—

Quince. What sayest thou, bully Bottom?

Bottom. There are things in this comedy of Pyramus
and Thisby that will never please. First, Pyramus must
draw a sword to kill himself; which the ladies cannot abide.
How answer you that?   11

Snout. By'r lakin, a parlous fear.

Starveling. I believe we must leave the killing out, when
all is done.

Bottom. Not a whit: I have a device to make all well.
Write me a prologue; and let the prologue seem to say, we
will do no harm with our swords, and that Pyramus is not
killed indeed; and, for the more better assurance, tell them
that I Pyramus am not Pyramus, but Bottom the weaver:
this will put them out of fear.   20

Quince. Well, we will have such a prologue; and it shall
be written in eight and six.

Bottom. No, make it two more; let it be written in eight
and eight.

Snout. Will not the ladies be afeard of the lion?

Starveling. I fear it, I promise you.

Bottom. Masters, you ought to consider with yourselves:
to bring in—God shield us!—a lion among ladies is a most
dreadful thing; for there is not a more fearful wild-fowl
than your lion living; and we ought to look to 't.   30

Snout. Therefore another prologue must tell he is not a
lion.

Bottom. Nay, you must name his name, and half his face
must be seen through the lion's neck: and he himself must
speak through, saying thus, or to the same defect,—'Ladies,'
—or 'Fair ladies,—I would wish you,'—or 'I would request
you,'—or 'I would entreat you,—not to fear, not to tremble:
my life for yours. If you think I come hither as a lion, it

were pity of my life: no, I am no such thing; I am a man
as other men are;' and there indeed let him name his name,
and tell them plainly he is Snug the joiner.   41

Quince. Well, it shall be so.   But there is two hard things;
that is, to bring the moonlight into a chamber; for, you know,
Pyramus and Thisby meet by moonlight.

Snout. Doth the moon shine that night we play our play?

Bottom. A calendar, a calendar! look in the almanac;
find out moonshine, find out moonshine.

Quince. Yes, it doth shine that night.

Bottom. Why, then may you leave a casement of the
great chamber window, where we play, open, and the moon
may shine in at the casement.   51

Quince. Ay; or else one must come in with a bush of
thorns and a lanthorn, and say he comes to disfigure, or to
present, the person of Moonshine.   Then, there is another
thing: we must have a wall in the great chamber; for Pyramus and Thisby, says the story, did talk through the chink
of a wall.

Snout. You can never bring in a wall.   What say you,
Bottom?   56

Bottom. Some man or other must present Wall: and let
him have some plaster, or some loam, or some rough-cast
about him, to signify wall; and let him hold his fingers thus,
and through that cranny shall Pyramus and Thisby whisper.

Quince. If that may be, then all is well.   Come, sit down,
every mother's son, and rehearse your parts.   Pyramus, you
begin: when you have spoken your speech, enter into that
brake; and so every one according to his cue.

Enter PUCK *behind.*

Puck. What hempen home-spuns have we swaggering here,
So near the cradle of the fairy queen?
What, a play toward?   I 'll be an auditor;   70
An actor too perhaps, if I see cause.

Quince. Speak, Pyramus.   Thisby, stand forth.

Bottom. Thisby, the flowers of odious savours sweet,—

Quince. Odours, odours.

Bottom. —— odours savours sweet:
So hath thy breath, my dearest Thisby dear.
But hark, a voice! stay thou but here awhile,
And by and by I will to thee appear.   [*Exit.*

Puck. A stranger Pyramus than e'er play'd here! [*Exit.*

Flute. Must I speak now?   80

Quince. Ay, marry, must you; for you must understand he
goes but to see a noise that he heard, and is to come again.

Flute. Most radiant Pyramus, most lily-white of hue,
Of colour like the red rose on triumphant brier,
Most brisky juvenal and eke most lovely Jew,
As true as truest horse that yet would never tire,
I 'li meet thee, Pyramus, at Ninny's tomb.

Quince. 'Ninus' tomb,' man: why, you must not speak
that yet; that you answer to Pyramus: you speak all your
part at once, cues and all.   Pyramus, enter: your cue is
past; it is, 'never tire.'   91

Flute. O,—As true as truest horse that yet would never tire.

Enter PUCK, *and* BOTTOM *with an ass's head.*

Bottom. If I were fair, Thisby, I were only thine.—

Quince. O monstrous! O strange! we are haunted.   Pray,
masters! fly, masters!   Help!
                 [*Exeunt Quince, Snug, Flute, Snout, and Starveling.*

Puck. I 'll follow you, I 'll lead you about a round,
Through bog, through bush, through brake, through brier:
Sometime a horse I 'll be, sometime a hound,
A hog, a headless bear, sometime a fire;
And neigh, and bark, and grunt, and roar, and burn,   100
Like horse, hound, hog, bear, fire, at every turn.   [*Exit.*

Bottom. Why do they run away? this is a knavery of them
to make me afeard.

Re-enter SNOUT.

Snout. O Bottom, thou art changed! what do I see on thee?   105

Bottom. What do you see? you see an ass-head of your own, do you?   [*Exit Snout.*

Re-enter QUINCE.

Quince. Bless thee, Bottom! bless thee! thou art trans-lated.   [*Exit.*

Bottom. I see their knavery: this is to make an ass of me; to fright me, if they could. But I will not stir from this place, do what they can: I will walk up and down here, and I will sing, that they shall hear I am not afraid.
                                                                        [*Sings.*

> The ousel cock so black of hue,
>   With orange-tawny bill,   115
>   The throstle with his note so true,
>   The wren with little quill,—

Titania. [*Awaking.*] What angel wakes me from my flow-ery bed?

Bottom. [Sings]
>   The finch, the sparrow, and the lark,
>   The plain-song cuckoo gray,   120
>   Whose note full many a man doth mark,
>   And dares not answer nay;—

for, indeed, who would set his wit to so foolish a bird? who would give a bird the lie, though he cry 'cuckoo' never so?

Titania. I pray thee, gentle mortal, sing again:
Mine ear is much enamour'd of thy note;
So is mine eye enthralled to thy shape;
And thy fair virtue's force perforce doth move me
On the first view to say, to swear, I love thee.   130

Bottom. Methinks, mistress, you should have little reason

for that : and yet, to say the truth, reason and love keep little company together now-a-days; the more the pity that some honest neighbours will not make them friends.   Nay, I can gleek upon occasion.

Titania. Thou art as wise as thou art beautiful.

Bottom. Not so, neither : but if I had wit enough to get out of this wood, I have enough to serve mine own turn.

Titania. Out of this wood do not desire to go :   140
Thou shalt remain here, whether thou wilt or no.
I am a spirit of no common rate :
The summer still doth tend upon my state ;
And I do love thee : therefore, go with me.
I 'll give thee fairies to attend on thee,
And they shall fetch thee jewels from the deep,
And sing while thou on pressed flowers dost sleep :
And I will purge thy mortal grossness so,
That thou shalt like an airy spirit go.
Peaseblossom! Cobweb! Moth! and Mustardseed!   150

Enter PEASEBLOSSOM, COBWEB, MOTH, *and* MUSTARDSEED.

Peaseblossom. Ready.

Cobweb.   And I.

Moth.   And I.

Mustardseed.   And I.

All.   Where shall we go?

Titania. Be kind and courteous to this gentleman ;
Hop in his walks, and gambol in his eyes ;
Feed him with apricocks and dewberries,
With purple grapes, green figs, and mulberries :
The honey-bags steal from the humble-bees,
And for night-tapers crop their waxen thighs,
And light them at the fiery glow-worm's eyes,
To have my love to bed and to arise ;
And pluck the wings from painted butterflies   160

To fan the moonbeams from his sleeping eyes.
Nod to him, elves, and do him courtesies.

Peaseblossom. Hail, mortal!

Cobweb. Hail!

Moth. Hail!

Mustardseed. Hail!

Bottom. I cry your worships mercy, heartily: I beseech
your worship's name.

Cobweb. Cobweb.

Bottom. I shall desire you of more acquaintance, good
Master Cobweb: if I cut my finger, I shall make bold with
you.—Your name, honest gentleman?   172

Peaseblossom. Peaseblossom.

Bottom. I pray you, commend me to Mistress Squash,
your mother, and to Master Peascod, your father. Good
Master Peaseblossom, I shall desire you of more acquaintance too.—Your name, I beseech you, sir?

Mustardseed. Mustardseed.

Bottom. Good Master Mustardseed, I know your patience
well: that same cowardly, giant-like ox-beef hath devoured
many a gentleman of your house. I promise you your kindred hath made my eyes water ere now. I desire you of
more acquaintance, good Master Mustardseed.   183

Titania. Come, wait upon him; lead him to my bower.
The moon methinks looks with a watery eye;
And when she weeps, weeps every little flower,
Lamenting some enforced chastity.
Tie up my love's tongue, bring him silently.   [*Exeunt*

SCENE II. *Another Part of the Wood.*

Enter OBERON.

Oberon. I wonder if Titania be awak'd;
Then, what it was that next came in her eye,
Which she must dote on in extremity.

Enter PUCK.

Here comes my messenger.—

How now, mad spirit!

What night-rule now about this haunted grove?

Puck. My mistress with a monster is in love.
Near to her close and consecrated bower,
While she was in her dull and sleeping hour,
A crew of patches, rude mechanicals,
That work for bread upon Athenian stalls,   10
Were met together to rehearse a play
Intended for great Theseus' nuptial day.
The shallowest thick-skin of that barren sort,
Who Pyramus presented, in their sport
Forsook his scene and enter'd in a brake:
When I did him at this advantage take,
An ass's nole I fixed on his head.
Anon his Thisbe must be answered,
And forth my mimic comes.   When they him spy,
As wild geese that the creeping fowler eye,
Or russet-pated choughs, many in sort,   20
Rising and cawing at the gun's report,
Sever themselves and madly sweep the sky,
So, at his sight, away his fellows fly;
And, at our stamp, here o'er and o'er one falls;
He murther cries, and help from Athens calls.
Their sense thus weak, lost with their fears thus strong,
Made senseless things begin to do them wrong;
For briers and thorns at their apparel snatch;
Some sleeves, some hats, from yielders all things catch.   30
I led them on in this distracted fear,
And left sweet Pyramus translated there;
When in that moment, so it came to pass,
Titania wak'd, and straightway lov'd an ass.

Oberon. This falls out better than I could devise.

But hast thou yet latch'd the Athenian's eyes
With the love-juice, as I did bid thee do?
 Puck. I took him sleeping,—that is finish'd too,—
And the Athenian woman by his side;
That, when he wak'd, of force she must be eyed.   40

Enter Hermia *and* Demetrius.

 Oberon. Stand close: this is the same Athenian.
 Puck. This is the woman, but not this the man.
 Demetrius. O, why rebuke you him that loves you so?
Lay breath so bitter on your bitter foe.
 Hermia. Now I but chide; but I should use thee worse,
For thou, I fear, hast given me cause to curse.
If thou hast slain Lysander in his sleep,
Being o'er shoes in blood, plunge in the deep,
And kill me too.
The sun was not so true unto the day   50
As he to me: would he have stolen away
From sleeping Hermia? I 'll believe as soon
This whole earth may be bor'd, and that the moon
May through the centre creep and so displease
Her brother's noontide with the Antipodes.
It cannot be but thou hast murther'd him;
So should a murtherer look, so dead, so grim.
 Demetrius. So should the murther'd look, and so should I,
Pierc'd through the heart with your stern cruelty;
Yet you, the murtherer, look as bright, as clear,   60
As yonder Venus in her glimmering sphere.
 Hermia. What 's this to my Lysander? where is he?
Ah, good Demetrius, wilt thou give him me?
 Demetrius. I had rather give his carcass to my hounds.
 Hermia. Out, dog! out, cur! thou driv'st me past the
  bounds
Of maiden's patience. Hast thou slain him, then?
Henceforth be never number'd among men!

O, once tell true, tell true, even for my sake!
Durst thou have look'd upon him being awake,
And hast thou kill'd him sleeping? O brave touch!   70
Could not a worm, an adder, do so much?
An adder did it; for with doubler tongue
Than thine, thou serpent, never adder stung.

    Demetrius. You spend your passion on a mispris'd mood:
I am not guilty of Lysander's blood;
Nor is he dead, for aught that I can tell.

    Hermia. I pray thee, tell me then that he is well.

    Demetrius. An if I could, what should I get therefore?

    Hermia. A privilege never to see me more.
And from thy hated presence part I so: 80
See me no more, whether he be dead or no.   [*Exit.*

    Demetrius. There is no following her in this fierce vein:
Here therefore for a while I will remain.
So sorrow's heaviness doth heavier grow
For debt that bankrupt sleep doth sorrow owe;
Which now in some slight measure it will pay,
If for his tender here I make some stay.

                [*Lies down and sleeps.*

    Oberon. What hast thou done? thou hast mistaken quite,
And laid the love-juice on some true-love's sight:
Of thy misprision must perforce ensue   90
Some true love turn'd, and not a false turn'd true.

    Puck. Then fate o'errules, that, one man holding troth,
A million fail, confounding oath on oath.

    Oberon. About the wood go swifter than the wind,
And Helena of Athens look thou find:
All fancy-sick she is and pale of cheer,
With sighs of love, that costs the fresh blood dear.
By some illusion see thou bring her here:
I'll charm his eyes against she do appear.

    Puck. I go, I go; look how I go,   100
Swifter than arrow from the Tartar's bow.   [*Exit.*

Oberon.	Flower of this purple dye,
	Hit with Cupid's archery,
	Sink in apple of his eye.
	When his love he doth espy,
	Let her shine as gloriously
	As the Venus of the sky.
	When thou wak'st, if she be by,
	Beg of her for remedy.

Re-enter PUCK.

Puck.	Captain of our fairy band,	110
	Helena is here at hand;	
	And the youth, mistook by me,	
	Pleading for a lover's fee.	
	Shall we their fond pageant see?	
	Lord, what fools these mortals be!	
Oberon.	Stand aside: the noise they make	
	Will cause Demetrius to awake.	
Puck.	Then will two at once woo one:	
	That must needs be sport alone;	
	And those things do best please me	120
	That befall preposterously.	

Enter LYSANDER *and* HELENA.

Lysander. Why should you think that I should woo in
    scorn?
Scorn and derision never come in tears:
Look, when I vow I weep; and vows so born,
    In their nativity all truth appears.
How can these things in me seem scorn to you,
Bearing the badge of faith, to prove them true?
    Helena. You do advance your cunning more and more.
    When truth kills truth, O devilish-holy fray!
These vows are Hermia's: will you give her o'er?   130
    Weigh oath with oath, and you will nothing weigh:

Your vows to her and me, put in two scales,
Will even weigh, and both as light as tales.

    Lysander. I had no judgment when to her I swore.

    Helena. Nor none, in my mind, now you give her o'er.

    Lysander. Demetrius loves her, and he loves not you.

    Demetrius. [*Awaking.*] O Helen, goddess, nymph, perfect,
        divine !

To what, my love, shall I compare thine eyne ?
Crystal is muddy.   O, how ripe in show
Thy lips, those kissing cherries, tempting grow !   140
That pure congealed white, high Taurus' snow,
Fann'd with the eastern wind, turns to a crow
When thou hold'st up thy hand.   O, let me kiss
This princess of pure white, this seal of bliss !

    Helena. O spite ! O hell ! I see you all are bent
To set against me for your merriment :
If you were civil and knew courtesy,
You would not do me thus much injury.
Can you not hate me, as I know you do,
But you must join in souls to mock me too?   150
If you were men, as men you are in show,
You would not use a gentle lady so ;
To vow, and swear, and superpraise my parts,
When I am sure you hate me with your hearts.
You both are rivals, and love Hermia ;
And now both rivals, to mock Helena.
A trim exploit, a manly enterprise,
To conjure tears up in a poor maid's eyes
With your derision ! none of noble sort
Would so offend a virgin, and extort   160
A poor soul's patience, all to make you sport.

    Lysander. You are unkind, Demetrius ; be not so ;
For you love Hermia ; this you know I know :
And here, with all good will, with all my heart,
In Hermia's love I yield you up my part :

And yours of Helena to me bequeath,
Whom I do love, and will do till my death.

   Helena. Never did mockers waste more idle breath.

   Demetrius. Lysander, keep thy Hermia; I will none:
If e'er I lov'd her, all that love is gone.   170
My heart to her but as guest-wise sojourn'd,
And now to Helen is it home return'd,
There to remain.

   Lysander.   Helen, it is not so.

   Demetrius. Disparage not the faith thou dost not know,
Lest, to thy peril, thou aby it dear.
Look, where thy love comes; yonder is thy dear.

            Enter HERMIA.

   Hermia. Dark night, that from the eye his function takes,
The ear more quick of apprehension makes;
Wherein it doth impair the seeing sense,
It pays the hearing double recompense.   180
Thou art not by mine eye, Lysander, found;
My ear, I thank it, brought me to thy sound.
But why unkindly didst thou leave me so?

   Lysander. Why should he stay, whom love doth press to go?

   Hermia. What love could press Lysander from my side?

   Lysander. Lysander's love, that would not let him bide;
Fair Helena, who more engilds the night
Than all yon fiery oes and eyes of light.
Why seek'st thou me? could not this make thee know,
The hate I bear thee made me leave thee so?   190

   Hermia. You speak not as you think: it cannot be.

   Helena. Lo, she is one of this confederacy!
Now I perceive they have conjoin'd all three
To fashion this false sport in spite of me.
Injurious Hermia! most ungrateful maid!
Have you conspir'd, have you with these contriv'd
To bait me with this foul derision?

Is all the counsel that we two have shar'd,
The sisters' vows, the hours that we have spent,
When we have chid the hasty-footed time   200
For parting us,—O, is all forgot?
All school-days' friendship, childhood innocence?
We, Hermia, like two artificial gods,
Have with our needles created both one flower,
Both on one sampler, sitting on one cushion,
Both warbling of one song, both in one key,
As if our hands, our sides, voices, and minds,
Had been incorporate.   So we grew together,
Like to a double cherry, seeming parted,
But yet an union in partition,   210
Two lovely berries moulded on one stem;   •
So, with two seeming bodies, but one heart;
Two of the first, like coats in heraldry
Due but to one and crowned with one crest.
And will you rent our ancient love asunder,
To join with men in scorning your poor friend?
It is not friendly, 't is not maidenly:
Our sex, as well as I, may chide you for it,
Though I alone do feel the injury.
    Hermia. I am amazed at your passionate words.   220
I scorn you not: it seems that you scorn me.
    Helena. Have you not set Lysander, as in scorn,
To follow me and praise my eyes and face?
And made your other love, Demetrius,
Who even but now did spurn me with his foot,
To call me goddess, nymph, divine and rare,
Precious, celestial?   Wherefore speaks he this
To her he hates? and wherefore doth Lysander
Deny your love, so rich within his soul,
And tender me, forsooth, affection,   230
But by your setting on, by your consent?
What though I be not so in grace as you,

So hung upon with love, so fortunate,
But miserable most, to love unlov'd?
This you should pity rather than despise.

    Hermia. I understand not what you mean by this.

    Helena. Ay, do, persever, counterfeit sad looks,
Make mouths upon me when I turn my back;
Wink each at other; hold the sweet jest up:
This sport, well carried, shall be chronicled.   140
If you have any pity, grace, or manners,
You would not make me such an argument.
But fare ye well: 't is partly my own fault,
Which death or absence soon shall remedy.

    Lysander. Stay, gentle Helena; hear my excuse:
My love, my life, my soul, fair Helena!

    Helena. O excellent!

    Hermia.   Sweet, do not scorn her so.

    Demetrius. If she cannot entreat, I can compel.

    Lysander. Thou canst compel no more than she entreat:
Thy threats have no more strength than her weak prayers.—
Helen, I love thee; by my life, I do: 251
I swear by that which I will lose for thee,
To prove him false that says I love thee not.

    Demetrius. I say I love thee more than he can do.

    Lysander. If thou say so, withdraw, and prove it too.

    Demetrius. Quick, come!

    Hermia.   Lysander, whereto tends all this?

    Lysander. Away, you Ethiope!

    Demetrius.   No, no, sir;
Seem to break loose; take on as you would follow,
But yet come not: you are a tame man, go!

    Lysander. Hang off, thou cat, thou burr! vile thing, let
    loose,   260
Or I will shake thee from me like a serpent!

    Hermia. Why are you grown so rude? what change is this?
Sweet love,—

Lysander.   Thy love! out, tawny Tartar, out!
Out, loathed medicine! hated potion, hence!
Hermia. Do you not jest?
Helena.   Yes, sooth; and so do you.
Lysander. Demetrius, I will keep my word with thee.
Demetrius. I would I had your bond, for I perceive
A weak bond holds you: I 'll not trust your word.
    Lysander. What, should I hurt her, strike her, kill her
        dead?
Although I hate her, I 'll not harm her so.   270
    Hermia. What, can you do me greater harm than hate?
Hate me! wherefore? O me! what news, my love!
Am not I Hermia? are not you Lysander?
I am as fair now as I was erewhile.
Since night you lov'd me; yet since night you left me:
Why, then you left me—O, the gods forbid!—
In earnest, shall I say?
    Lysander.   Ay, by my life;
And never did desire to see thee more.
Therefore be out of hope, of question, of doubt;
Be certain, nothing truer; 't is no jest   280
That I do hate thee, and love Helena.
    Hermia. O me! you juggler! you canker-blossom!
You thief of love! what, have you come by night
And stolen my love's heart from him?
    Helena.   Fine, i' faith!
Have you no modesty, no maiden shame,
No touch of bashfulness? What, will you tear
Impatient answers from my gentle tongue?
Fie, fie! you counterfeit, you puppet, you!
    Hermia. Puppet! why so? ay, that way goes the game.
Now I perceive that she hath made compare   290
Between our statures; she hath urg'd her height;
And with her personage, her tall personage,
Her height, forsooth, she hath prevail'd with him.

And are you grown so high in his esteem,
Because I am so dwarfish and so low?
How low am I, thou painted maypole? speak;
How low am I?   I am not yet so low
But that my nails can reach unto thine eyes.

 Helena. I pray you, though you mock me, gentlemen,
Let her not hurt me: I was never curst;   300
I have no gift at all in shrewishness;
I am a right maid for my cowardice:
Let her not strike me.   You perhaps may think,
Because she is something lower than myself,
That I can match her.

 Hermia.   Lower! hark, again.

 Helena. Good Hermia, do not be so bitter with me.
I evermore did love you, Hermia,
Did ever keep your counsels, never wrong'd you;
Save that, in love unto Demetrius,
I told him of your stealth unto this wood.   310
He follow'd you; for love I follow'd him;
But he hath chid me hence, and threaten'd me
To strike me, spurn me, nay, to kill me too:
And now, so you will let me quiet go,
To Athens will I bear my folly back,
And follow you no further.   Let me go:
You see how simple and how fond I am.

 Hermia. Why, get you gone: who is 't that hinders you?

 Helena. A foolish heart, that I leave here behind.

 Hermia. What, with Lysander?

 Helena.   With Demetrius. 320

 Lysander. Be not afraid; she shall not harm thee, Helena.

 Demetrius. No, sir, she shall not, though you take her part.

 Helena. O, when she's angry, she is keen and shrewd!
She was a vixen when she went to school;
And though she be but little, she is fierce.

 Hermia. Little again! nothing but low and little!

Why will you suffer her to flout me thus?
Let me come to her.

   Lysander.   Get you gone, you dwarf;
You minimus, of hindering knot-grass made;
You bead, you acorn.

   Demetrius.   You are too officious   330
In her behalf that scorns your services.
Let her alone: speak not of Helena;
Take not her part; for if thou dost intend
Never so little show of love to her,
Thou shalt aby it.

   Lysander.   Now she holds me not;
Now follow, if thou dar'st, to try whose right,
Of thine or mine, is most in Helena.

   Demetrius. Follow! nay, I'll go with thee, cheek by jole.

                [Exeunt Lysander and Demetrius.

   Hermia. You, mistress, all this coil is long of you:
Nay, go not back.

   Helena.   I will not trust you, I,   340
Nor longer stay in your curst company.
Your hands than mine are quicker for a fray,
My legs are longer, though, to run away.   *[Exit.*

   Hermia. I am amaz'd, and know not what to say.   *[Exit.*

   Oberon. This is thy negligence; still thou mistak'st,
Or else committ'st thy knaveries wilfully.

   Puck. Believe me, king of shadows, I mistook.
Did not you tell me I should know the man
By the Athenian garments he had on?
And so far blameless proves my enterprise,   350
That I have 'nointed an Athenian's eyes;
And so far am I glad it so did sort,
As this their jangling I esteem a sport.

   Oberon. Thou see'st these lovers seek a place to fight:
Hie therefore, Robin, overcast the night;
The starry welkin cover thou anon

With drooping fog as black as Acheron,
And lead these testy rivals so astray
As one come not within another's way.
Like to Lysander sometime frame thy tongue,   360
Then stir Demetrius up with bitter wrong;
And sometime rail thou like Demetrius;
And from each other look thou lead them, thus,
Till o'er their brows death-counterfeiting sleep
With leaden legs and batty wings doth creep:
Then crush this herb into Lysander's eye;
Whose liquor hath this virtuous property,
To take from thence all error with his might,
And make his eyeballs roll with wonted sight.
When they next wake, all this derision   370
Shall seem a dream and fruitless vision,
And back to Athens shall the lovers wend,
With league whose date till death shall never end.
Whiles I in this affair do thee employ,
I 'll to my queen and beg her Indian boy;
And then I will her charmed eye release
From monster's view, and all things shall be peace.

   Puck. My fairy lord, this must be done with haste;
For night's swift dragons cut the clouds full fast,
And yonder shines Aurora's harbinger,   380
At whose approach, ghosts, wandering here and there,
Troop home to churchyards: damned spirits all,
That in crossways and floods have burial,
Already to their wormy beds are gone;
For fear lest day should look their shames upon,
They wilfully themselves exile from light,
And must for aye consort with black-brow'd night.

   Oberon. But we are spirits of another sort:
I with the morning's love have oft made sport,
And, like a forester, the groves may tread,   390
Even till the eastern gate, all fiery-red,

Opening on Neptune with fair blessed beams,
Turns into yellow gold his salt green streams.
But, notwithstanding, haste; make no delay:
We may effect this business yet ere day.   [*Exit.*

    Puck.   Up and down, up and down,
            I will lead them up and down:
            I am fear'd in field and town:
            Goblin, lead them up and down.
Here comes one.   400

Enter LYSANDER.

    Lysander. Where art thou, proud Demetrius? speak thou
        now.
    Puck. Here, villain; drawn and ready.   Where art thou?
    Lysander. I will be with thee straight.
    Puck.   Follow me, then,
To plainer ground.   [*Exit Lysander, as following the voice.*

Enter DEMETRIUS.

    Demetrius.   Lysander! speak again:
Thou runaway, thou coward, art thou fled?
Speak!   In some bush?   Where dost thou hide thy head?
    Puck. Thou coward, art thou bragging to the stars,
Telling the bushes that thou look'st for wars,
And wilt not come?   Come, recreant; come, thou child;
I 'll whip thee with a rod: he is defil'd   410
That draws a sword on thee.
    Demetrius.   Yea, art thou there?
    Puck. Follow my voice: we 'll try no manhood here.
                      [*Exeunt*

Enter LYSANDER.

    Lysander. He goes before me and still dares me on:
When I come where he calls, then he is gone.
The villain is much lighter-heel'd than I:
I follow'd fast, but faster he did fly;

That fallen am I in dark uneven way,
And here will rest me. [*Lies down.*] Come, thou gentle
    day!
For if but once thou show me thy grey light,
I 'll find Demetrius and revenge this spite.   [*Sleeps.*

Enter PUCK *and* DEMETRIUS.

Puck. Ho, ho, ho! Coward, why comest thou not?   421
Demetrius. Abide me, if thou dar'st; for well I wot
Thou runn'st before me, shifting every place,
And dar'st not stand, nor look me in the face.
Where art thou now?
    Puck.   Come hither: I am here.
    Demetrius. Nay, then, thou mock'st me. Thou shalt buy
    this dear,
If ever I thy face by daylight see:
Now, go thy way. Faintness constraineth me
To measure out my length on this cold bed.
By day's approach look to be visited. [*Lies down and sleeps.*

Enter HELENA.

Helena. O weary night, O long and tedious night,   431
    Abate thy hours! Shine comforts from the east,
That I may back to Athens by daylight,
    From these that my poor company detest:
And sleep, that sometime shuts up sorrow's eye.
Steal me awhile from mine own company.
                      [*Lies down and sleeps.*
    Puck.   Yet but three? Come one more;
      Two of both kinds makes up four.
      Here she comes, curst and sad:
      Cupid is a knavish lad,   440
      Thus to make poor females mad.

Enter HERMIA.

Hermia. Never so weary, never so in woe,
   Bedabbled with the dew and torn with briers,
I can no further crawl, no further go;
   My legs can keep no pace with my desires.
Here will I rest me till the break of day.
Heavens shield Lysander, if they mean a fray!
                                   [*Lies down and sleeps.*

Puck.   On the ground
                  Sleep sound:
                  I 'll apply   450
                  To your eye,
            Gentle lover, remedy.
                  [*Squeezing the juice on Lysander's eyes.*
                  When thou wak'st,
                  Thou tak'st
                  True delight
                  In the sight
            Of thy former lady's eye:
            And the country proverb known,
            That every man should take his own,
            In your waking shall be shown: 460
                  Jack shall have Jill;
                  Nought shall go ill;
The man shall have his mare again, and all shall be well.
                                          [*Exit.*

ACT IV.

SCENE I. *The Same.* LYSANDER, DEMETRIUS, HELENA, *and* HERMIA *lying asleep.*

Enter TITANIA *and* BOTTOM; PEASEBLOSSOM, COBWEB, MOTH, MUSTARDSEED, *and other Fairies attending;* OBERON *behind unseen.*

Titania. Come, sit thee down upon this flowery bed,
While I thy amiable cheeks do coy,
And stick musk-roses in thy sleek smooth head,
And kiss thy fair large ears, my gentle joy.

Bottom. Where 's Peaseblossom?

Peaseblossom. Ready.

Bottom. Scratch my head, Peaseblossom. Where's Mounsieur Cobweb?

Cobweb. Ready.   9

Bottom. Mounsieur Cobweb, good mounsieur, get you your weapons in your hand, and kill me a red-hipped humble-bee on the top of a thistle; and, good mounsieur, bring me the honey-bag. Do not fret yourself too much in the action, mounsieur; and, good mounsieur, have a care the honey-bag break not; I would be loath to have you overflown with a honey-bag, signior. Where 's Mounsieur Mustardseed?

Mustardseed. Ready.

Bottom. Give me your neaf, Mounsieur Mustardseed. Pray you, leave your courtesy, good mounsieur.

Mustardseed. What 's your will?   20

Bottom. Nothing, good mounsieur, but to help Cavalery Cobweb to scratch.   I must to the barber's, mounsieur; for methinks I am marvellous hairy about the face; and I am such a tender ass, if my hair do but tickle me I must scratch.

Titania. What, wilt thou hear some music, my sweet love?

Bottom. I have a reasonable good ear in music.   Let's have the tongs and the bones.

Titania. Or say, sweet love, what thou desirest to eat.

Bottom. Truly, a peck of provender: I could munch your good dry oats.   Methinks I have a great desire to a bottle of hay: good hay, sweet hay, hath no fellow.   31

Titania. I have a venturous fairy that shall seek
The squirrel's hoard, and fetch thee new nuts.

Bottom. I had rather have a handful or two of dried peas. But, I pray you, let none of your people stir me: I have an exposition of sleep come upon me.

Titania. Sleep thou, and I will wind thee in my arms.
Fairies, be gone, and be all ways away.   [*Exeunt fairies.*
So doth the woodbine the sweet honeysuckle
Gently entwist; the female ivy so
Enrings the barky fingers of the elm.   40
O, how I love thee! how I dote on thee!   [*They sleep.*

Enter PUCK.

Oberon. [*Advancing.*] Welcome, good Robin. See'st thou
          this sweet sight?
Her dotage now I do begin to pity:
For, meeting her of late behind the wood,
Seeking sweet favours for this hateful fool,
I did upbraid her and fall out with her.
For she his hairy temples then had rounded
With coronet of fresh and fragrant flowers;
And that same dew, which sometime on the buds   50
Was wont to swell like round and orient pearls,
Stood now within the pretty flowerets' eyes

Like tears that did their own disgrace bewail.
When I had at my pleasure taunted her
And she in mild terms begg'd my patience,
I then did ask of her her changeling child;
Which straight she gave me, and her fairy sent
To bear him to my bower in fairy land.
And now I have the boy, I will undo
This hateful imperfection of her eyes: 60
And, gentle Puck, take this transformed scalp
From off the head of this Athenian swain;
That, he awaking when the other do,
May all to Athens back again repair
And think no more of this night's accidents
But as the fierce vexation of a dream.
But first I will release the fairy queen.
         Be as thou wast wont to be;
         See as thou wast wont to see:
         Dian's bud o'er Cupid's flower   70
         Hath such force and blessed power.
Now, my Titania; wake you, my sweet queen.
    Titania. My Oberon! what visions have I seen!
Methought I was enamour'd of an ass.
    Oberon. There lies your love.
    Titania.   How came these things to pass?
O, how mine eyes do loathe his visage now!
    Oberon. Silence awhile.—Robin, take off this head.—
Titania, music call; and strike more dead
Than common sleep of all these five the sense.
    Titania. Music, ho! music, such as charmeth sleep!   80
                                        [*Music, still.*
    Puck. Now, when thou wak'st, with thine own fool's eyes
         peep.
    Oberon. Sound, music! Come, my queen, take hands
         with me,
And rock the ground whereon these sleepers be.

Now thou and I are new in amity,
And will to-morrow midnight solemnly
Dance in Duke Theseus' house triumphantly,
And bless it to all fair posterity.
There shall the pairs of faithful lovers be
Wedded, with Theseus, all in jollity.

Puck.   Fairy king, attend, and mark:
            I do hear the morning lark.   90

Oberon. Then, my queen, in silence sad,
            Trip we after the night's shade:
            We the globe can compass soon,
            Swifter than the wandering moon.

Titania. Come, my lord, and in our flight
            Tell me how it came this night
            That I sleeping here was found
            With these mortals on the ground.   [*Exeunt.*
                                    [*Horns winded within.*

Enter THESEUS, HIPPOLYTA, EGEUS, *and train.*

Theseus. Go, one of you, find out the forester;   100
For now our observation is perform'd;
And since we have the vaward of the day,
My love shall hear the music of my hounds.—
Uncouple in the western valley; let them go!—
Dispatch, I say, and find the forester.— [*Exit an Attendant.*
We will, fair queen, up to the mountain's top
And mark the musical confusion
Of hounds and echo in conjunction.

Hippolyta. I was with Hercules and Cadmus once,
When in a wood of Crete they bay'd the bear   110
With hounds of Sparta: never did I hear
Such gallant chiding; for, besides the groves,
The skies, the fountains, every region near
Seem'd all one mutual cry.   I never heard
So musical a discord, such sweet thunder.

Theseus. My hounds are bred out of the Spartan kind,
So flew'd, so sanded, and their heads are hung
With ears that sweep away the morning dew;
Crook-kneed, and dew-lapp'd like Thessalian bulls;
Slow in pursuit, but match'd in mouth like bells,   120
Each under each. A cry more tuneable
Was never holla'd to, nor cheer'd with horn,
In Crete, in Sparta, nor in Thessaly:
Judge when you hear.—But, soft! what nymphs are these?

Egeus. My lord, this is my daughter here asleep;
And this, Lysander; this Demetrius is;
This Helena, old Nedar's Helena:
I wonder of their being here together.

Theseus. No doubt they rose up early to observe
The rite of May; and, hearing our intent,   130
Came here in grace of our solemnity.—
But speak, Egeus; is not this the day
That Hermia should give answer of her choice?

Egeus. It is, my lord.

Theseus. Go, bid the huntsmen wake them with their
horns.

> [*Horns and shout within. Lysander, Demetrius,
> Helena, and Hermia wake and start up.*

Good morrow, friends. Saint Valentine is past:
Begin these wood-birds but to couple now?

Lysander. Pardon, my lord.

Theseus.   I pray you all, stand up.
I know you two are rival enemies:
How comes this gentle concord in the world,   140
That hatred is so far from jealousy,
To sleep by hate, and fear no enmity?

Lysander. My lord, I shall reply amazedly,
Half sleep, half waking: but as yet, I swear,
I cannot truly say how I came here;
But, as I think,—for truly would I speak,

And now I do bethink me, so it is,—
I came with Hermia hither: our intent
Was to be gone from Athens, where we might,
Without the peril of the Athenian law—   150
  Egeus. Enough, enough, my lord; you have enough:
I beg the law, the law, upon his head.
They would have stolen away; they would, Demetrius,
Thereby to have defeated you and me,
You of your wife and me of my consent,
Of my consent that she should be your wife.
  Demetrius. My lord, fair Helen told me of their stealth,
Of this their purpose hither to this wood;
And I in fury hither follow'd them,
Fair Helena in fancy following me.   160
But, my good lord, I wot not by what power,—
But by some power it is,—my love to Hermia,
Melted as the snow, seems to me now
As the remembrance of an idle gawd)
Which in my childhood I did dote upon:
And all the faith, the virtue of my heart,
The object and the pleasure of mine eye,
Is only Helena.   To her, my lord,
Was I betroth'd ere I saw Hermia:
But, like in sickness, did I loathe this food;   170
But, as in health, come to my natural taste,
Now I do wish it, love it, long for it,
And will for evermore be true to it.
  Theseus. Fair lovers, you are fortunately met:
Of this discourse we more will hear anon.
Egeus, I will overbear your will;
For in the temple, by and by, with us
These couples shall eternally be knit:
And, for the morning now is something worn,
Our purpos'd hunting shall be set aside.   180
Away with us to Athens: three and three,

We 'll hold a feast in great solemnity.——
Come, Hippolyta.

            [*Exeunt Theseus, Hippolyta, Egeus, and train.*

  Demetrius. These things seem small and undistinguish-
     able,
Like far-off mountains turned into clouds.

  Hermia. Methinks I see these things with parted eye,
When every thing seems double.

  Helena.   So methinks:
And I have found Demetrius like a jewel,
Mine own, and not mine own.

  Demetrius.   Are you sure
That we are awake? It seems to me   190
That yet we sleep, we dream. Do not you think
The duke was here, and bid us follow him?

  Hermia. Yea; and my father.

  Helena.   And Hippolyta.

  Lysander. And he did bid us follow to the temple.

  Demetrius. Why, then, we are awake: let 's follow him;
And by the way let us recount our dreams.   [*Exeunt.*

  Bottom. [*Awaking.*] When my cue comes, call me, and I
will answer: my next is, 'Most fair Pyramus.' Heigh-ho!
Peter Quince! Flute, the bellows-mender! Snout, the tinker! Starveling! God's my life, stolen hence, and left me
asleep! I have had a most rare vision. I have had a
dream, past the wit of man to say what dream it was: man
is but an ass, if he go about to expound this dream. Methought I was—there is no man can tell what. Methought
I was,—and methought I had,—but man is but a patched
fool, if he will offer to say what methought I had. The eye
of man hath not heard, the ear of man hath not seen, man's
hand is not able to taste, his tongue to conceive, nor his
heart to report, what my dream was. I will get Peter Quince
to write a ballad of this dream: it shall be called Bottom's
Dream, because it hath no bottom; and I will sing it in the

latter end of a play, before the duke : peradventure, to make
it the more gracious, I shall sing it at her death.   [*Exit.*

SCENE II. *Athens.   Quince's House.*

Enter QUINCE, FLUTE, SNOUT, *and* STARVELING.

Quince. Have you sent to Bottom's house? is he come
home yet?

Starveling. He cannot be heard of.   Out of doubt he is
transported.

Flute. If he come not, then the play is marred: it goes
not forward, doth it ?

Quince. It is not possible : you have not a man in all
Athens able to discharge Pyramus but he.

Flute. No, he hath simply the best wit of any handicraft
man in Athens.   10

Quince. Yea, and the best person too ; and he is a very
paramour for a sweet voice.

Flute. You must say paragon : a paramour is, God bless
us, a thing of naught.

Enter SNUG.

Snug. Masters, the duke is coming from the temple, and
there is two or three lords and ladies more married : if our
sport had gone forward, we had all been made men.

Flute. O, sweet bully Bottom ! Thus hath he lost sixpence
a day during his life ; he could not have scaped sixpence
a day : an the duke had not given him sixpence a day for
playing Pyramus, I 'll be hanged ; he would have deserved
it : sixpence a day in Pyramus, or nothing.   22

Enter BOTTOM.

Bottom. Where are these lads ? where are these hearts?

Quince. Bottom ! O most courageous day ! O most happy hour !

Bottom. Masters, I am to discourse wonders : but ask me not what ; for if I tell you, I am no true Athenian.   I will tell you every thing, right as it fell out.

Quince. Let us hear, sweet Bottom.   29

Bottom. Not a word of me.   All that I will tell you is, that the duke hath dined.   Get your apparel together, good strings to your beards, new ribbons to your pumps ; meet presently at the palace ; every man look o'er his part ; for the short and the long is, our play is preferred.   In any case, let Thisby have clean linen ; and let not him that plays the lion pare his nails, for they shall hang out for the lion's claws.   And, most dear actors, eat no onions nor garlic, for we are to utter sweet breath ; and I do not doubt but to hear them say, it is a sweet comedy.   No more words : away ! go, away !   [*Exeunt.*

AN AMAZON.

STATUE OF THESEUS, FROM THE PEDIMENT OF THE PARTHENON.

ACT V.

SCENE I. *Athens. The Palace of Theseus.*

Enter THESEUS, HIPPOLYTA, PHILOSTRATE, Lords, *and*
Attendants.

Hippolyta. 'T is strange, my Theseus, that these lovers
  speak of.

Theseus. More strange than true: I never may believe
These antique fables, nor these fairy toys.
Lovers and madmen have such seething brains,
Such shaping fantasies, that apprehend
More than cool reason ever comprehends.
The lunatic, the lover, and the poet
Are of imagination all compact:
One sees more devils than vast hell can hold,
That is, the madman: the lover, all as frantic,
Sees Helen's beauty in a brow of Egypt:
The poet's eye, in a fine frenzy rolling,
Doth glance from heaven to earth, from earth to heaven;
And as imagination bodies forth

10

The forms of things unknown, the poet's pen
Turns them to shapes, and gives to airy nothing
A local habitation and a name.
Such tricks hath strong imagination,
That, if it would but apprehend some joy,
It comprehends some bringer of that joy;   20
Or in the night, imagining some fear,
How easy is a bush suppos'd a bear!
   Hippolyta. But all the story of the night told over,
And all their minds transfigur'd so together,
More witnesseth than fancy's images,
And grows to something of great constancy,
But, howsoever, strange and admirable.
   Theseus. Here come the lovers, full of joy and mirth.

   Enter LYSANDER, DEMETRIUS, HERMIA, *and* HELENA.

Joy, gentle friends! joy and fresh days of love
Accompany your hearts!
   Lysander.   More than to us   30
Wait in your royal walks, your board, your bed!
   Theseus. Come now; what masques, what dances shall we
      have,
To wear away this long age of three hours
Between our after-supper and bed-time?
Where is our usual manager of mirth?
What revels are in hand? Is there no play,
To ease the anguish of a torturing hour?
Call Philostrate.
   Philostrate.   Here, mighty Theseus.
   Theseus. Say, what abridgment have you for this evening?
What masque? what music?   How shall we beguile   40
The lazy time, if not with some delight?
   Philostrate. There is a brief how many sports are ripe:
Make choice of which your highness will see first.
                       [Giving a paper.

Theseus. [Reads] '*The battle with the Centaurs, to be sung
By an Athenian eunuch to the harp.*'
We 'll none of that: that have I told my love,
In glory of my kinsman Hercules.
[Reads] '*The riot of the tipsy Bacchanals,
Tearing the Thracian singer in their rage.*'
That is an old device; and it was play'd
When I from Thebes came last a conqueror.
[Reads] '*The thrice three Muses mourning for the death
Of Learning, late deceas'd in beggary.*'   50
That is some satire, keen and critical,
Not sorting with a nuptial ceremony.
[Reads] '*A tedious brief scene of young Pyramus
And his love Thisbe; very tragical mirth.*'
Merry and tragical! tedious and brief!
That is, hot ice and wondrous strange snow.
How shall we find the concord of this discord?   60
    Philostrate. A play there is, my lord, some ten words long,
Which is as brief as I have known a play;
But by ten words, my lord, it is too long,
Which makes it tedious; for in all the play
There is not one word apt, one player fitted.
And tragical, my noble lord, it is;
For Pyramus therein doth kill himself:
Which, when I saw rehears'd, I must confess,
Made mine eyes water; but more merry tears
The passion of loud laughter never shed.   70
    Theseus. What are they that do play it?
    Philostrate. Hard-handed men that work in Athens here,
Which never labour'd in their minds till now,
And now have toil'd their unbreath'd memories
With this same play, against your nuptial.
    Theseus. And we will hear it.
    Philostrate.   No, my noble lord;
It is not for you: I have heard it over,

And it is nothing, nothing in the world,
Unless you can find sport in their intents,
Extremely stretch'd and conn'd with cruel pain,   80
To do you service.

    Theseus.   I will hear that play;
For never any thing can be amiss,
When simpleness and duty tender it.
Go, bring them in: and take your places, ladies.

                         [*Exit Philostrate.*

    Hippolyta. I love not to see wretchedness o'ercharg'd,
And duty in his service perishing.

    Theseus. Why, gentle sweet, you shall see no such thing.

    Hippolyta. He says they can do nothing in this kind.

    Theseus. The kinder we, to give them thanks for nothing.
Our sport shall be to take what they mistake: 90
And what poor duty cannot do, noble respect
Takes it in might, not merit.
Where I have come, great clerks have purposed
To greet me with premeditated welcomes;
Where I have seen them shiver and look pale,
Make periods in the midst of sentences,
Throttle their practis'd accent in their fears,
And in conclusion dumbly have broke off,
Not paying me a welcome.   Trust me, sweet,
Out of this silence yet I pick'd a welcome;   100
And in the modesty of fearful duty
I read as much as from the rattling tongue
Of saucy and audacious eloquence.
Love, therefore, and tongue-tied simplicity
In least speak most, to my capacity.

                Enter PHILOSTRATE.

    Philostrate. So please your grace, the Prologue is address'd.
    Theseus. Let him approach.   [*Flourish of trumpets.*

Enter QUINCE *for the* Prologue.

Prologue. If we offend, it is with our good will.
  That you should think, we come not to offend,
But with good will   To show our simple skill,   110
  That is the true beginning of our end.
Consider then we come but in despite.
  We do not come as minding to content you,
Our true intent is.   All for your delight
  We are not here.   That you should here repent you,
The actors are at hand, and by their show
You shall know all that you are like to know.

Theseus. This fellow doth not stand upon points.

Lysander. He hath rid his prologue like a rough colt; he
knows not the stop.   A good moral, my lord: it is not enough
to speak, but to speak true.   121

Hippolyta. Indeed he hath played on his prologue like a
child on a <u>recorder</u>; a sound, but not in government.

Theseus. His speech was like a tangled chain; nothing
impaired, but all disordered.   Who is next?

Enter PYRAMUS *and* THISBE, WALL, MOONSHINE, *ana* LION.

Prologue. Gentles, perchance you wonder at this show;
  But wonder on, till truth make all things plain.
This man is Pyramus, if you would know;
  This beauteous lady Thisby is certain.
This man, with lime and rough-cast, doth present   130
  Wall, that vile Wall which did these lovers sunder;
And through Wall's chink, poor souls, they are content
  To whisper; at the which let no man wonder.
This man, with lanthorn, dog, and bush of thorn,
  Presenteth Moonshine; for, if you will know,
By moonshine did these lovers think no scorn
  To meet at Ninus' tomb, there, there to woo.
This grisly beast, which Lion hight by name,
  The trusty Thisby, coming first by night,

Did scare away, or rather did affright ;   140
And, as she fled, her mantle she did fall,
  Which Lion vile with bloody mouth did stain.
Anon comes Pyramus, sweet youth and tall,
  And finds his trusty Thisby's mantle slain :
Whereat, with blade, with bloody blameful blade,
  He bravely broach'd his boiling bloody breast ;
And Thisby, tarrying in mulberry shade,
  His dagger drew, and died.   For all the rest,
Let Lion, Moonshine, Wall, and lovers twain
At large discourse, while here they do remain.   150

      [*Exeunt Prologue, Thisbe, Lion, and Moonshine.*

Theseus. I wonder if the lion be to speak.

Demetrius. No wonder, my lord : one lion may, when many
    asses do.

Wall. In this same interlude it doth befall
That I, one Snout by name, present a wall ;
And such a wall, as I would have you think,
That had in it a crannied hole or chink,
Through which the lovers, Pyramus and Thisby,
Did whisper often very secretly.
This loam, this rough-cast, and this stone doth show
That I am that same wall : the truth is so ;   160
And this the cranny is, right and sinister,
Through which the fearful lovers are to whisper.

   Theseus. Would you desire lime and hair to speak better ?

   Demetrius. It is the wittiest partition that ever I heard
discourse, my lord.

   Theseus. Pyramus draws near the wall : silence !

          Enter PYRAMUS.

   Pyramus. O grim-look'd night ! O night with hue so black !
O night, which ever art when day is not !
O night, O night ! alack, alack, alack,
  I fear my Thisby's promise is forgot !   170
And thou, O wall, O sweet, O lovely wall,
  That stand'st between her father's ground and mine !

Thou wall, O wall, O sweet and lovely wall,
  Show me thy chink, to blink through with mine eyne !

[Wall holds up his fingers.

Thanks, courteous wall : Jove shield thee well for this !
  But what see I ?   No Thisby do I see.
O wicked wall, through whom I see no bliss !
  Curst be thy stones for thus deceiving me !

  Theseus. The wall, methinks, being sensible, should curse
again.   180

  Pyramus. No, in truth, sir, he should not. ' Deceiving me'
is Thisby's cue : she is to enter now, and I am to spy her
through the wall.   You shall see, it will fall pat as I told you.
Yonder she comes.

Enter THISBE.

  Thisbe. O wall, full often hast thou heard my moans,
  For parting my fair Pyramus and me !
My cherry lips have often kiss'd thy stones,
  Thy stones with lime and hair knit up in thee.

  Pyramus. I see a voice : now will I to the chink,
To spy an I can hear my Thisby's face.   190
Thisby !

  Thisbe. My love thou art, my love I think.

  Pyramus. Think what thou wilt, I am thy lover's grace ;
And, like Limander, am I trusty still.

  Thisbe. And I like Helen, till the Fates me kill.

  Pyramus. Not Shafalus to Procrus was so true.

  Thisbe. As Shafalus to Procrus, I to you.

  Pyramus. O, kiss me through the hole of this vile wall !

  Thisbe. I kiss the wall's hole, not your lips at all.

  Pyramus. Wilt thou at Ninny's tomb meet me straightway ?

  Thisbe. Tide life, tide death, I come without delay.   200

[Exeunt Pyramus and Thisbe.

  Wall. Thus have I, Wall, my part discharged so ;
And, being done, thus Wall away doth go.   *[Exit.*

  Theseus. Now is the mural down between the two neighbours.

Demetrius. No remedy, my lord, when walls are so wilful to hear without warning.

Hippolyta. This is the silliest stuff that ever I heard.

Theseus. The best in this kind are but shadows; and the worst are no worse, if imagination amend them.

Hippolyta. It must be your imagination then, and not theirs.   211

Theseus. If we imagine no worse of them than they of themselves, they may pass for excellent men.   Here come two noble beasts in, a man and a lion.

Enter LION *and* MOONSHINE.

Lion. You, ladies, you, whose gentle hearts do fear
The smallest monstrous mouse that creeps on floor,
May now perchance both quake and tremble here,
    When lion rough in wildest rage doth roar.
Then know that I, one Snug the joiner, am
A lion fell, nor else no lion's dam ;   220
For if I should as lion come in strife
Into this place, 't were pity of my life.

Theseus. A very gentle beast, and of a good conscience.

Demetrius. The very best at a beast, my lord, that e'er I saw.

Lysander. This lion is a very fox for his valour.

Theseus. True ; and a goose for his discretion.

Demetrius. Not so, my lord ; for his valour cannot carry his discretion, and the fox carries the goose.

Theseus. His discretion, I am sure, cannot carry his valour, for the goose carries not the fox.   It is well: leave it to his discretion, and let us listen to the moon.   232

Moon. This lanthorn doth the horned moon present ;—

Demetrius. He should have worn the horns on his head.

Theseus. He is no crescent, and his horns are invisible within the circumference.

Moon. This lanthorn doth the horned moon present ;
Myself the man i' the moon do seem to be.

Theseus. This is the greatest error of all the rest. The man should be put into the lanthorn. How is it else the man i' the moon? 　　241

Demetrius. He dares not come there for the candle; for, you see, it is already in snuff.

Hippolyta. I am aweary of this moon: would he would change!

Theseus. It appears, by his small light of discretion, that he is in the wane; but yet, in courtesy, in all reason, we must stay the time.

Lysander. Proceed, Moon.

Moon. All that I have to say is to tell you that the lanthorn is the moon; I, the man i' the moon; this thorn-bush, my thorn-bush; and this dog, my dog. 　　252

Demetrius. Why, all these should be in the lanthorn: for they are in the moon. But silence! here comes Thisbe.

Enter THISBE.

Thisbe. This is old Ninny's tomb. Where is my love?

Lion. [*Roaring.*] Oh——　　　　　　　　 [*Thisbe runs off.*

Demetrius. Well roared, Lion.

Theseus. Well run, Thisbe.

Hippolyta. Well shone, Moon. Truly, the moon shines with a good grace. 　　[*The Lion shakes Thisbe's mantle, and exit.*

Theseus. Well moused, Lion. 　　260

Demetrius. And then came Pyramus.

Lysander. And so the lion vanished.

Enter PYRAMUS.

Pyramus. Sweet Moon, I thank thee for thy sunny beams:
I thank thee, Moon, for shining now so bright;
For, by thy gracious, golden, glittering gleams,
I trust to take of truest Thisby sight.
　　　　　But stay, O spite!
　　　　　But mark, poor knight,

What dreadful dole is here !
   Eyes, do you see ?   270
   How can it be ?
O dainty duck ! O dear !
   Thy mantle good,
     What, stained with blood !
Approach, ye Furies fell !
   O Fates, come, come,
   Cut thread and thrum ;
Quail, crush, conclude, and quell !

Theseus. This passion, and the death of a dear friend,
would go near to make a man look sad.   280

Hippolyta. Beshrew my heart, but I pity the man.

Pyramus. O wherefore, Nature, didst thou lions frame ?
Since lion vile hath here deflower'd my dear :
Which is—no, no—which was the fairest dame
That liv'd, that lov'd, that lik'd, that look'd with cheer.
     Come, tears, confound ;
     Out, sword, and wound
     The pap of Pyramus ;
     Ay, that left pap,
     Where heart doth hop :   *[Stabs himself.*
Thus die I, thus, thus, thus.   291
     Now am I dead,
     Now am I fled ;
My soul is in the sky :
     Tongue, lose thy light !
     Moon, take thy flight !   *[Exit Moonshine.*
Now die, die, die, die, die.   *[Dies.*

Demetrius. No die, but an ace, for him ; for he is but one.

Lysander. Less than an ace, man ; for he is dead ; he is
nothing.   300

Theseus. With the help of a surgeon he might yet recover,
and prove an ass.

Hippolyta. How chance Moonshine is gone before Thisbe
comes back and finds her lover ?

Theseus. She will find him by starlight.   Here she comes; and her passion ends the play.

Re-enter THISBE.

Hippolyta. Methinks she should not use a long one for such a Pyramus : I hope she will be brief.

Demetrius. A mote will turn the balance, which Pyramus, which Thisbe, is the better : he for a man, God warrant us; she for a woman, God bless us.   311

Lysander. She hath spied him already with those sweet eyes.

Demetrius. And thus she moans, videlicet :—

Thisbe.   Asleep, my love ?
                What, dead, my dove ?
            O Pyramus, arise !
                Speak, speak.   Quite dumb ?
                Dead, dead ?   A tomb
        Must cover thy sweet eyes.   320
                These lily lips,
                This cherry nose,
            These yellow cowslip cheeks,
                Are gone, are gone.
                Lovers, make moan !
        His eyes were green as leeks.
                O Sisters Three,
                Come, come to me,
            With hands as pale as milk ;
                Lay them in gore,   330
                Since you have shore
        With shears his thread of silk.
                Tongue, not a word :
                Come, trusty sword ;
        Come, blade, my breast imbrue :   [*Stabs herself.*
                And, farewell, friends !
            Thus Thisby ends :
        Adieu, adieu, adieu !   [*Dies.*

Theseus. Moonshine and Lion are left to bury the dead.

Demetrius. Ay, and Wall too. 340

Bottom. [*Starting up.*] No, I assure you; the wall is down that parted their fathers. Will it please you to see the epilogue, or to hear a Bergomask dance between two of our company?

Theseus. No epilogue, I pray you; for your play needs no excuse. Never excuse; for when the players are all dead, there need none to be blamed. Marry, if he that writ it had played Pyramus and hanged himself in Thisbe's garter, it would have been a fine tragedy; and so it is, truly, and very notably discharged. But, come, your Bergomask: let your epilogue alone. [*A dance.*

The iron tongue of midnight hath told twelve: 352
Lovers, to bed; 't is almost fairy time.
I fear we shall out-sleep the coming morn
As much as we this night have overwatch'd.
This palpable-gross play hath well beguil'd
The heavy gait of night. Sweet friends, to bed.
A fortnight hold we this solemnity,
In nightly revels and new jollity. [*Exeunt.*

Enter PUCK.

Puck. Now the hungry lion roars, 360
   And the wolf behowls the moon;
Whilst the heavy ploughman snores,
   All with weary task fordone.
Now the wasted brands do glow,
   Whilst the screech-owl, screeching loud,
Puts the wretch that lies in woe
   In remembrance of a shroud.
Now it is the time of night
   That the graves, all gaping wide,
Every one lets forth his sprite, 370
   In the church-way paths to glide:

> And we fairies, that do run
>   By the triple Hecate's team,
> From the presence of the sun,
>   Following darkness like a dream,
> Now are frolic; not a mouse
> Shall disturb this hallow'd house:
> I am sent with broom before,
> To sweep the dust behind the door.

Enter OBERON *and* TITANIA *with their train.*

Oberon. Through the house give glimmering light,   380
>   By the dead and drowsy fire:
> Every elf and fairy sprite
>   Hop as light as bird from brier;
> And this ditty, after me,
> Sing, and dance it trippingly.

Titania. First, rehearse your song by rote,
> To each word a warbling note:
> Hand in hand, with fairy grace,
> Will we sing, and bless this place.

>   [*Song and dance.*

Oberon. Now, until the break of day,   390
> Through this house each fairy stray.
> To the best bride-bed will we,
> Which by us shall blessed be:
> So shall all the couples three
> Ever true in loving be;
> And the blots of Nature's hand
> Shall not in their issue stand;
> Never mole, hare-lip, nor scar,
> Nor mark prodigious, such as are
> Despised in nativity,   400
> Shall upon their children be.
> With this field-dew consecrate,
> Every fairy take his gait;

And each several chamber bless,
Through this palace, with sweet peace;
And the owner of it blest
Ever shall in safety rest.
Trip away; make no stay;
Meet me all by break of day.
　　　　　　[Exeunt Oberon, Titania, and train.

Puck.　If we shadows have offended,　　　410
Think but this, and all is mended,
That you have but slumber'd here
While these visions did appear.
And this weak and idle theme,
No more yielding but a dream,
Gentles, do not reprehend:
If you pardon, we will mend.
And, as I am an honest Puck,
If we have unearned luck
Now to scape the serpent's tongue,　　　420
We will make amends ere long;
Else the Puck a liar call:
So, good night unto you all.
Give me your hands, if we be friends,
And Robin shall restore amends.　　　*[Exit.*

THE VENUS OF MILO.

NOTES.

ABBREVIATIONS USED IN THE NOTES.

Abbott (or Gr.), Abbott's *Shakespearian Grammar* (third edition).
A. S., Anglo-Saxon.
A. V., Authorized Version of the Bible (1611).
B. and F., Beaumont and Fletcher.
B. J., Ben Jonson.
Camb. ed., "Cambridge edition" of *Shakespeare*, edited by Clark and Wright.
Cf. (*confer*), compare.
Coll., Collier.
Coll. MS., Manuscript Corrections of Second Folio, edited by Collier.
D., Dyce.
H., Hudson.
Hen. VIII. (followed by reference to *page*), Rolfe's edition of *Henry VIII.*
Id. (*idem*), the same.
J. C. (followed by reference to *page*), Rolfe's edition of *Julius Cæsar.*
J. H., John Hunter's edition of *Midsummer-Night's Dream* (London, 1874).
K., Knight.
Macb. (followed by reference to *page*), Rolfe's edition of *Macbeth.*
Mer., Rolfe's edition of *The Merchant of Venice.*
Nares, *Glossary*, edited by Halliwell and Wright (London, 1859).
Prol., Prologue.
Rich. II. (followed by reference to *page*), Rolfe's edition of *Richard II.*
S., Shakespeare.
Schmidt, A. Schmidt's *Shakespeare-Lexicon* (Berlin, 1874).
Sr., Singer.
St., Staunton.
Temp. (followed by reference to *page*), Rolfe's edition of *The Tempest.*
Theo., Theobald.
V., Verplanck.
W., White.
Walker, Wm. Sidney Walker's *Critical Examination of the Text of Shakespeare* (London, 1860).
Warb., Warburton.
Wb., Webster's Dictionary (revised quarto edition of 1864).
Worc., Worcester's Dictionary (quarto edition).

The abbreviations of the names of Shakespeare's Plays will be readily understood; as *T. N.* for *Twelfth Night, Cor.* for *Coriolanus,* 3 *Hen. VI.* for *The Third Part of King Henry the Sixth*, etc. *P. P.* refers to *The Passionate Pilgrim; V. and A.* to *Venus and Adonis; L. C.* to *Lover's Complaint;* and *Sonn.* to the *Sonnets.*

NOTES.

PANATHENAIC PROCESSION. FROM THE FRIEZE OF THE PARTHENON.

INTRODUCTION.

CHAUCER'S *Knightes Tale* and the story of "Thisbe of Babylon" in his *Legende of Goode Women*, and Golding's translation of Ovid's *Metamorphoses*, were all well known to Shakespeare, and, as already stated (p. 14 above), furnished materials for this play.

The *Knightes Tale*, from which the poet drew very little, opens thus:

> "Whilom, as olde stories tellen us,
> Ther was a duk that highte Theseus;
> Of Athenes he was lord and governour,
> And in his tyme swich a conquerour,
> That gretter was ther non under the sonne.
> Ful many a riche contré hadde he wonne;
> That with his wisdam and his chivalrie
> He conquered al the regne of Femynye,*
> That whilom was i-cleped Cithea;
> And weddede the queen Ipolita,
> And brought hire hoom with him in his contré,
> With moche glorie and gret solempnité,
> And eek hire yonge suster Emelye.
> And thus with victorie and with melodye

---

* The kingdom of the Amazons. The name is formed from the Latin *femina*. In the next line *Cithea* = Scythia.

> Lete I this noble duk to Athenes ryde,
> And al his ost, in armes him biside.
> And certes, if it nere to long to heere,
> I wolde han told you fully the manere,
> How wonnen was the regne of Femynye
> By Theseus, and by his chivalrye;
> And of the grete bataille for the nones
> Bytwix Athenes and the Amazones;
> And how asegid* was Ypolita,
> The faire hardy quyen of Cithea;
> And of the feste that was at hire weddynge,
> And of the tempest at hire hoom comynge;
> But al that thing I most as now forbere."

Halliwell suggests that the following passage (*C. T.* 2961–2966) may have furnished Shakespeare with the idea of introducing an interlude into the play:

> "ne how the Grekes pleye
> The wake-pleyes,† kepe I nat to seye;
> Who wrastleth best naked, with oyle enoynt,
> Ne who that bar him best in no disjoynt.
> I wole not telle eek how that they ben goon
> Home til Athenes whan the pley is doon."

He also quotes lines 2702–2704:

> "Duk Theseus, and al his companye,
> Is comen hom to Athenes his cité,
> With alle blys and gret solempnité,"

which he believes to bear more than an accidental resemblance to what Theseus says, iv. 1. 181, 182:

> "Away with us to Athens: three and three,
> We 'll hold a feast in great solemnity."

In the Legende of Thisbe of Babylon (lines 756, 757) we read

> "Thus wolde they seyn: Allas, thou wikked walle!
> Thurgh thyne envye thou us lettest alle;"

which Halliwell compares with Pyramus's address to Wall, v. 1. 181:

> "O wicked wall, through whom I see no bliss!"

There are many similarities between the tale of Pyramus and Thisbe as related in Golding's *Ovid* and Shakespeare's interlude. We give the former in full from Halliwell's Introduction to the play:

> "Within the towne (of whose huge walles so monstrous high and thicke,
> The fame is given Semiramis for making them of bricke.)
> Dwelt hard together two young folke in houses joynde so nere,
> That under all one roofe well nie both twaine convayed were.
> The name of him was *Pyramus*, and Thisbe called was she;
> So faire a man in all the East was none alive as he,
> Nor nere a woman, mayde, nor wife, in beautie like to her.
> This neigh-brod bred acquaintance first, this neigh-brod first did ster
> The secret sparkes: this neigh-brod first an entrance in did show
> For love, to come to that to which it afterward did grow.
> And if that right had taken place, they had beene man and wife;
> But still their parents went about to let which (for their life)
> They could not let. For both their hearts with equal flame did burne;

---

* Besieged.   † Wake-plays, or funeral games.

No man was privie to their thoughts.   And for to serve their turne,
Instead of talke they used signes: the closlier they supprest
The fire of love, the fiercer still it raged in their brest.
The wall that parted house from house had riven therein a cranie,
Which shroonke at making of the wall: this fault not markt of anie
Of many hundred yeeres before (what doth not love espie?)
These lovers first of all found out, and made a way whereby
To talke together secretly, and through the same did go
Their loving whisprings very light and safely to and fro.
Now, as at one side *Pyramus*, and *Thisbe* on the tother,
Stood often drawing one of them the pleasant breath from other:
O thou envious wall (they sayed), why letst thou lovers thus;
What matter were it if that thou permitted both of us
In armes each other to embrace: or if thou think that this
Were over-much, yet mightest thou at least make roome to kisse.
And yet thou shalt not finde us churles: we thinke our selves in det,
For the same piece of curtesie, in vouching safe to let
Our sayings to our friendly eares thus freely come and go.
Thus having where they stood in vaine complained of their wo,
When night drew neare they bad adue, and ech gave kisses sweete,
Unto the parget on their side the which did never meete.
Next morning with her cheerefull light had driven the starres aside,
And Phœbus with his burning beames the dewie grasse had dride,
These lovers at their wonted place to meet without the towne,
Where, after much complaint and mone they covenanted to get
Away from such as watched them, and in the evening late
To steale out of their father's house, and eke the citie gate.
And to th' intent that in the fields they strayd not up and downe,
They did agree at Ninus Tombe to meet without the towne,
And tary underneath a tree that by the same did grow:
Which was a faire high mulberie with fruite as white as snow,
Hard by a coole and trickling spring.   This bargaine pleased them both
And so day-light (which to their thought away but slowly goth)
Did in the ocian fall to rest, and night from thence did rise.
As soone as darkenesse once was come, straight *Thisbe* did devise
A shift to winde her out of doores, that none that were within
Perceived her: and muffling her with clothes about her chin,
That no man might discerne her face, to Ninus Tombe she came
Unto the tree: and set her downe there underneath the same.
Love made her bold.   But see the chance; there comes besmerde with blood
About the chappes, a lyonesse all foming from the wood,
From slaughter lately made of kine, to staunch her bloody thirst
With water of the foresaid spring.   Whom Thisbe spying first,
Afarre by moone-light, thereupon with fearfull steps gan flie,
And in a darke and yrkesome cave did hide herselfe thereby.
And as she fled away for haste she let her mantle fall,
The which for feare she left behinde not looking backe at all.
Now when the cruell lyonesse her thirst had staunched well,
In going to the wood she found the slender weede that fell
From Thisbe, which with bloodie teeth in peeces he did teare:
The night was somewhat further spent ere Pyramus came there,
Who seeing in the suttle sand the print of lyon's paw,
Waxt pale for feare.   But when also the bloodie cloke he saw
All rent and torne: one night (he sayed) shall lovers two confound,
Of which long life deserved she of all that live on ground;
My soule deserves of this mischaunce the perill for to beare.
I, wretch, have been the death of thee, which to this place of feare
Did cause thee in the night to come, and came not there before.
My wicked lims and wretched guts, with cruell teeth therefore,
Devoure ye, O ye lyons all, that in this rocke doe dwell.
But cowards use to wish for death.   The slender weede that fell
From Thisbe up he takes, and straight doth beare it to the tree,
Which was appointed erst the place of meeting for to bee.

And when he had bewept, and kist the garment which he knew,
Receive thou my blood too (quoth he) ; and therewithall he drew
His sword, the which among his guts he thrust, and by and bie
Did draw it from the bleeding wound, beginning for to die,
And cast himselfe upon his backe ; the blood did spinne on hie,
As when a conduite pipe is crackt, the water bursting out
Doth shote it selfe a great way off, and pierse the ayre about,
The leaves that were upon the tree besprinkled with his blood,
Were died black. The roote also bestained as it stood,
A deepe dark purple colour straight upon the berries cast.
Anon scarce ridded of her feare with which she was agast,
For doubt of disapoynting him comes *Thisbe* forth in hast,
And for her lover lookes about, rejoycing for to tell
How hardly she had scapt that night the danger that befell.
And as she knew right well the place and facion of the tree,
(As which she saw so late before :) even so when she did see
The colour of the berries turn'd, she was uncertaine whither
It were the tree at which they both agreed to meet togither.
While in this doubtfull stound she stood, she cast her eye aside,
And there beweltred in his blood hir lover she espide,
Lie sprawling with his dying lims : at which she started backe,
And looked pale as any box, a shuddring through her stracke,
Even like the sea which suddenly with whissing noyse doth move,
When with a little blast of wind it is but toucht above.
But when approching nearer him she knew it was her love,
She beate her brest, she shriked out, she tare her golden heares,
And taking him betweene her armes did wash his woundes with **teares.**
She meynd her weeping with his blood, and kissing all his face,
(Which now became as cold as yse) she cryde in wofull case,
Alas, what chaunce my *Pyramus* hath parted thee and mee !
Make answere, O my *Pyramus* ; it is thy *Thisb.* even shee
Whom thou doost love most hartily, that speaketh unto thee,
Give eare and raise thy heavie head. He hearing *Thisbes* name,
Lift up his dying eyes, and having seene her, closd the same.
But when she knew her mantle there, and saw his scaberd lie
Without the sworde : Unhappy man, thy love hath made thee die :
Thy love (she said) hath made thee slea thyselfe. This hand of mine
Is strong inough to doe the like. My love no lesse than thine
Shall give me force to worke my wound, I will pursue thee dead,
And wretched woman as I am, it shall of me be sed
That like as of thy death I was the onely cause and blame,
So am I thy companion eke and partner in the same.
For death which onely could alas ! asunder part us twaine,
Shall never so dissever us but we will meete againe.
And you the parents of us both, most wretched folke alive,
Let this request that I shall make in both our names belive,
Intreate you to permit, that we whom chaste and stedfast love,
And whom even death hath joyned in one, may as it doth behove
In one grave be together layd. And thou, unhappie tree,
Which shouldest now the corse of one, and shalt anon through mee
Shroude two, of this same slaughter hold the sicker sinnes for ay,
Blacke be the colour of thy fruite and mourning like alway,
Such as the murder of us twaine may evermore bewray.
This said, she tooke the sword yet warme with slaughter of her love,
And setting it beneath her brest did to the heart it shove.
Her prayer with the Gods and with their parents tooke effect,
For when the fruite is thoroughly ripe, the berrie is bespect
With colour tending to a blacke. And that which after fire
Remained, rested in one tombe, as *Thisbe* did desire."

The " Life of Theseus" in North's *Plutarch* has also been mentioned
as one of the sources from which Shakespeare drew some small part of

his material. The only passages that can be cited as illustrating the play are the following :

"And so going on further, in the straits of Peloponnesus he killed another [robber], called Sinnis, surnamed Pityocamtes, that is to say, a wreather or bower of pine-apple trees : whom he put to death in that self cruel manner that Sinnis had slain many other travellers before. . . . This Sinnis had a goodly fair daughter called Perigouna, which fled away when she saw her father slain ; whom he followed and sought all about. But she had hidden herself in a grove full of certain kinds of wild pricking rushes called *stœbe*, and wild sperage, which she simply like a child intreated to hide her, as if they had heard, and had sense to understand her : promising them with an oath, that if they saved her from being found, she would never cut them down, nor burn them. But Theseus finding her, called her, and sware by his faith he would use her gently, and do her no hurt, nor displeasure at all. Upon which promise she came out of the bush, and bare unto him a goodly boy, which was called Menalippus. . . .

"Furthermore, after he was arrived in Creta, he slew there the Minotaur (as the most part of ancient authors do write) by the means and help of Ariadne : who being fallen in fancy with him, did give him a clue of thread, by the help whereof she taught him, how he might easily wind out of the turnings and crancks of the labyrinth. . . . They report many other things also touching this matter, and specially of Ariadne : but there is no troth nor certainty in it. For some say, that Ariadne hung herself for sorrow, when she saw that Theseus had cast her off. Others write, that she was transported by mariners into the ile of Naxos, where she was married unto Œnarus the priest of Bacchus : and they think that Theseus left her, because he was in love with another, as by these verses should appear :

> Ægles, the nymph, was loved of Theseus,
> Who was the daughter of Panopeus. . . .

"Touching the voyage he made by the sea Major, Philochorus, and some other hold opinion, that he went thither with Hercules against the Amazons : and that to honour his valiantness, Hercules gave him Antiopa the Amazon. But the more part of the other historiographers, namely, Hellanicus, Pherecides, and Herodotus, do write, that Theseus went thither alone, after Hercules' voyage, and that he took this Amazon prisoner : which is likeliest to be true. For we do not find that any other who went this journey with him, had taken any Amazon prisoner beside himself. Bion also the historiographer, this notwithstanding, saith, that he brought her away by deceit and stealth. For the Amazons (saith he) naturally loving men, did not fly at all when they saw them land in their country, but sent them presents, and that Theseus enticed her to come into his ship, who brought him a present : and so soon as she was aboard, he hoised his sail, and so carried her away. . . .

"Now, whether they [the Amazons] came by land from so far a country, or that they passed over an arm of the sea, which is called Bosphorus Cimmericus, being frozen as Hellanicus saith : it is hardly to be credited. But that they camped within the precinct of the very city

itself, the names of the places which continue yet to this present day do
witness it, and the graves also of the women which died there.   But so
it is, that both armies lay a great time one in the face of the other, ere
they came to battle.   Howbeit at the length Theseus, having first made
sacrifice unto Fear the goddess, according to the counsel of a prophecy
he had received, he gave them battle in the month of August, on the
same day in the which the Athenians do even at this present solemnise
the feast which they call Boedromia. . . . Afterwards, at the end of four
months, peace was taken between them by means of one of the women
called Hippolyta.   For this historiographer calleth the Amazon which
Theseus married, Hippolyta, and not Antiopa."

Halliwell points out certain " anachronisms " in the play :—
" For instance, Theseus marries Hippolyta on the night of the new
moon ; but how does this agree with the discourse of the clowns (iii. 1.
45–51) at the rehearsal ?
" Again, the period of action is four days, concluding with the night of
the new moon.   But Hermia and Lysander receive the edict of Theseus
four days before the new moon ; they fly from Athens 'to-morrow
night ;' they become the sport of the fairies, along with Helena and
Demetrius, *during one night only*, for Oberon accomplishes all in one
night, before 'the first cock crows ;' and the lovers are discovered by
Theseus the morning before that which would have rendered this portion
of the plot chronologically consistent.   For, although Oberon, addressing
his queen, says,

> 'Now thou and I are new in amity ;
> And will, *to-morrow midnight*, solemnly,
> Dance in Duke Theseus' house triumphantly,'

yet Theseus, when he discovers the lovers, asks Egeus,

> 'is not this the day
> That Hermia should give answer of her choice?'

and the answer of Egeus, 'It is, my Lord,' coupled with what Theseus
says to Hermia, i. 1. 83 fol.—

> 'Take time to pause ; and by the next new moon,' etc.—

proves that the action of the remaining part of the play is not intended
to consist of two days.
" The preparation and rehearsal of the interlude present similar in-
consistencies.   In i. 2. 9–55, Quince is the only one who has any
knowledge of the 'most lamentable comedy, and most cruel death of
Pyramus and Thisby,' and he selects actors for Thisby's mother, Pyramus's father, and Thisby's father, none of whom appear in the interlude
itself.   In iii. 1. 73–93, we have the commencement of the play in
rehearsal, none of which appears in the piece itself.   Again, the play
could have been but partially rehearsed once ; for Bottom only returns
in time to advise 'every man look o'er his part ;' and immediately before
his companions were lamenting the failure of their 'sport.'   How then
could the 'merry tears' of Philostrate be shed at its rehearsal ?"

"And in the wood where often you and I
Upon faint primrose beds were wont to lie" (i. 1. 214).

ACT I.

SCENE I.—The opening lines appear in Fisher's quarto as follows:

"Now faire *Hippolita*, our nuptiall hower
Draws on apase: fower happy daies bring in
An other Moone: but oh, me thinks, how slow

> This old Moone waues! She lingers my desires,
> Like to a Stepdame, or a dowager,
> Long withering out a yong mans reuenewe.
>   *Hip.* Fower daies will quickly steepe themselues in night:
> Fower nights will quickly dreame away the time:
> And then the Moone, like to a siluer bowe,
> Now bent in heauen, shall beholde the night
> Of our solemnities.
>   *The.* Goe *Philostrate,*
> Stirre vp the *Athenian* youth to merriments,
> Awake the peart and nimble spirit of mirth,
> Turne melancholy foorth to funerals:
> The pale companion is not for our pomp.
> *Hyppolita,* I woo'd thee with my sword,
> And wonne thy loue, doing thee iniuries:
> But I will wed thee in another key,
> With pompe, with triumph, and with reueling."

In the 1st folio they read thus:

> "Now faire Hippolita, our nuptiall houre
> Drawes on apace: foure happy daies bring in
> Another Moon: but oh, me thinkes, how slow
> This old Moon wanes; She lingers my desires
> Like to a Step-dame, or a Dowager,
> Long withering out a yong mans reuennew.
>   *Hip.* Foure daies wil quickly steep thēselues in nights
> Foure nights wil quickly dreame away the time:
> And then the Moone, like to a siluer bow,
> Now bent in heauen, shal behold the night
> Of our solemnities.
>   *The.* Go *Philostrate,*
> Stirre vp the Athenian youth to merriments,
> Awake the pert and nimble spirit of mirth,
> Turne melancholy forth to Funerals:
> The pale companion is not for our pompe,
> *Hippolita,* I woo'd thee with my sword,
> And wonne thy loue, doing thee iniuries:
> But I will wed thee in another key,
> With pompe, with triumph, and with reuelling."

4. *Lingers.* For the transitive use cf. *Rich. II.* ii. 2. 72:

> "Who gently would dissolve the bands of life,
> Which false hope lingers in extremity."

Holinshed has "to linger his businesse." See Gr. 290.

5. *Like to a stepdame,* etc. Whalley cites Horace (not Ovid, as some eds. give it), *Epist.* i. 1. 21:

> "Ut piget annus
> Pupillis, quos dura premit custodia matrum,
> Sic mihi tarda fluunt ingrataque tempora."

Halliwell quotes Drant's translation (1567), which resembles Shake-speare's:

> "Slow seames the yeare vnto the warde
> Which houlden downe must be,
> In custodie of stepdame straite,—
> Slowe slydes the time to me."

Dowager, as K. remarks, is here used in the original sense of a widow receiving *dower* out of the revenue which has descended to the heir with

this customary charge. Slender (*M. W.* i. i. 284) alludes to this custom:
"I keep but three men and a boy yet, till my mother be dead."

6. *Withering out.* Steevens quotes Chapman's *Homer:* "there the
goodly plant lies withering out his grace."

Revenue. Accented by S. either on the penult or antepenult. Cf. line
158 below. See Gr. 490.

7. *Steep.* "A similar use of the verb *steep* occurs in *Cymb.*, *Oth.*, and
in several other plays" (Halliwell). See *Cymb.* v. 4. 131; *Oth.* iv. 2. 50;
T. N. iv. 1. 66; *A. and C.* ii. 7. 113, etc.

8. *Four nights.* The 2d quarto has "daies."

10. *New-bent.* Rowe's emendation for the "Now bent" of the early eds.

13. *Pert.* Lively. Used by S. only here and in *L. L. L.* v. 2. 272. Cf.
pertly = promptly, in *Temp.* iv. 1. 58: "appear, and pertly."

15. *Companion.* Often used contemptuously, as *fellow* is now. Cf.
M. W. iii. 1. 123: "this same scall, scurvy, cogging companion ;" *J. C.* iv.
3. 138: "Companion, hence !" *2 Hen. IV.* ii. 4. 132: "scurvy companion," etc. Smollett uses it in the same sense in *Roderick Random* (1748):
"Scurvy companion ! saucy tarpaulin ! Rude, impertinent fellow !"

Dr. Grey (quoted by Halliwell without comment) says that S. calls the
moon "the pale companion of the night" in *T. G. of V.* He was probably thinking of *T. G. of V.* iv. 2. 100: "by this pale *queen* of night."

16. *I woo'd thee with my sword.* See extracts from Chaucer and Plutarch above.

19. *Triumph.* "A public festivity or exhibition of any kind, particularly a tournament" (Schmidt). Cf. *T. G. of V.* iv. 4. 161: "With triumphs,
mirth, and rare solemnity;" *Rich. II.* v. 2. 52: "justs and triumphs" (see
note in our ed. p. 212); *3 Hen. VI.* v. 7. 43: "With stately triumphs,
mirthful comic shows," etc. Steevens quotes *The Duke of Anjou's Entertainement at Antwerp,* 1581: "Yet notwithstanding, their triumphes
[those of the Romans] have so borne the bell above all the rest, that the
word *triumphing*, which cometh thereof, hath been applied to all high,
great, and statelie dooings."

20. *Duke.* S. found the word in Chaucer and in North's *Plutarch;*
and it is also used in the *A. V.* (1 *Chron.* i. 51) in the same sense of
leader (Latin *dux*) or ruler. Steevens cites Lydgate's *Fall of Princes*,
xii. 21: "Duke Theseus had the victorye ;" and Skelton :

> "Not like Duke Hamilcar,
> Not like Duke Hasdrubal."

Stanyhurst, in his trans. of Virgil, calls Æneas "Duke Æneas." So in
Heywood's *Iron Age*, we find "Duke Ajax," "Duke Palamedes," "Duke
Nestor," etc.

21. *Egeus.* S. took the name from Plutarch, who gives it as that of
the father of Theseus.

24. *Stand forth, Demetrius.* These words, like "Stand forth, Lysander," two lines below, are given as a stage-direction in all the early eds.
The measure shows that they belong in the text, to which Rowe restored
them.

27. *This man hath bewitch'd.* The reading of the quartos and 1st folio. The later folios omit "man."

31. *Feigning love.* Walker suggests "feigned love."

32. *Stolen*, etc. "Stealthily obtained influence over her fancy" (J. H.). Schmidt explains *the impression of her fantasy* as "the form, the image dwelling in her imagination."

33. *Gawds.* Baubles, toys. Cf. iv. 1. 164 below. See also *T. of S.* ii. 1. 3, and *T. and C.* iii. 3. 176.

34. *Knacks.* Knick-knacks. Cf. *T. of S.* iv. 3. 167 : "A knack, a toy, a trick, a baby's cap;" *W. T.* iv. 4. 360 : "To load my she with knacks," etc.

35. *Unharden'd.* Susceptible, impressible. Used nowhere else by S.

39. *Be it so.* See Gr. 133.

44. *Our law.* By a law of Solon's, parents had power of life and death over their children. The poet anticipates that statute here, though he may have known nothing about it.

45. *Immediately.* Expressly, specially.

46. *Be advis'd.* Take heed, be considerate. Often used by S. in this sense. Cf. *V. and A.* 615; *L. L. L.* iv. 3. 368; *M. of V.* ii. 1. 42; *Hen. VIII.* i. 1. 139, 145, etc.

50, 51. "The sense is, you owe to your father a being which he may at pleasure continue or destroy" (Johnson).

54. *In this kind.* Cf. v. 1. 88 and 208 below. See also *T. G. of V.* iii. 2. 56 ; *M. W.* iii. 3. 232, etc.

65. *To die the death.* Cf. *M. for M.* ii. 4. 165 ; *A. and C.* iv. 14. 26 ; *Cymb.* iv. 2. 96, etc. See also *Matt.* xv. 4.

68. *Know of your youth.* "Bring your youth to the question ; consider your youth" (Johnson). For *know of*=ask, cf. *T. N.* iii. 4. 278 ; *Lear*, v. 1. 1; *Oth.* v. 1. 117, etc.

69. *Whether.* Metrically a monosyllable. Gr. 466.

70. *Nun.* For the anachronism, cf. *V. and A.* 752 : "Love-lacking vestals and self-loving nuns."

71. *Mew'd.* Shut up. Cf. *Rich. III.* i. 1. 132 :

> "More pity that the eagle should be mew'd,
> While kites and buzzards prey at liberty."

Mew up is more common ; as in *T. of S.* i. 1. 87, 188 ; *K. John*, iv. 2. 57 ; *Rich. III.* i. 1. 38, i. 3. 139, etc. *Emmew* occurs in *M. for M.* iii. 1. 91.

Mew seems originally to have meant to moult, or shed the feathers ; and as a noun, "the place, whether it be abroad or in the house, in which the hawk is put during the time she casts, or doth change her feathers" (R. Holmes's *Academy of Armory*, etc.). Spenser has both verb and noun ; as in *F. Q.* i. 5. 20 :

> "forth comming from her darksome mew,
> Where she all day did hide her hated hew ;"

Id. ii. 3. 34 :

> "Unto the bush her eye did suddein glaunce,
> In which vain Braggadocchio was mewd."

Milton uses the verb in the magnificent description of Liberty in *Of Unlicensed Printing:* "Methinks I see her as an eagle mewing her

mighty youth, and kindling her undazzled eyes at the full midday beam."
In England the noun is still used in the plural to denote a stable for
horses. According to Pennant (*London*, p. 151), the royal stables in
London were called *mews* from the original use of the buildings for
keeping the king's falcons.

73. *Faint.* Without feeling or fervour. Cf. *T. of A.* iii. 1. 57 : "Has
friendship such a faint and milky heart," etc.

75. *To undergo.* For the omission of *as*, see Gr. 281.

76. *Earthlier happy.* Halliwell remarks : "*Earthlier* is merely the
comparative adjective, in the sense of more earthly, more corporeally.
Milton uses the word *amplier*, more amply ; and *wiselier* occurs in *Temp.*
ii. 1. 21." Pope proposed "earlier happy ;" and Capell "earthly hap-
pier," which some modern eds. adopt. *Earthlier-happy*, as Walker remarks, is="more earthly-happy." He also cites in illustration of the
passage Erasmus, *Colloquies :* "Ego rosam existimo feliciorem, quæ
marcescit in hominis manu, delectans interim et oculos et nares, quam
quae senescit in frutice." Steevens quotes Lyly's *Midas* (1592) : "You
bee all young and faire, endeavour to bee wise and vertuous ; that when,
like roses, you shall fall from the stalke, you may be gathered, and put
to the still." Malone refers to *Sonn.* 5. 13 and 54. 3-12.

81. *Unto his lordship, whose unwished yoke.* So in quartos and 1st
folio ; the later folios read "to whose." For the omission of the preposition, see Gr. 201. On *lordship*, cf. *A. W.* v. 3. 156 : "Swear them
lordship." In these passages Schmidt is doubtful whether the word
means "conjugal right and duty" or simply "sway, sovereignty."

92. *Crazed.* "Invalid" (Schmidt). J. H. explains it as "weak, fee-
ble," and quotes Spenser, *F. Q.* iii. 9. 26 : "Her crased helth."

98. *Estate.* Used by S. as a verb elsewhere only in *Temp.* iv. 1. 85
(followed by *on*) and in *A. Y. L.* v. 2. 13 (followed by *upon*). Hanmer
reads "upon" here.

100. *As well possess'd.* As rich. For the use of the passive, see Gr.
295.

102. *If not with vantage.* If not superior to his. Cf. *R. of L.* 249 :
"Urging the worser sense for vantage still" (that is, "placing it in a
more advantageous light," as Schmidt explains it).

103. *Which.* See Gr. 271 ; and for *of* in next line, Gr. 170.

110. *Spotted.* "As *spotless* is innocent, so *spotted* is wicked" (Johnson). Cf. Cavendish, *Metrical Visions :* "the spotted queen, causer of
all this strife."

111. *So much.* See Gr. 275.

113. *Self-affairs.* My own business. On the use of *self* as an adjective in S., see Gr. 20.

116. *Schooling.* Reprimand (Schmidt). Cf. 1 *Hen. IV.* iii. 1. 190 :
"Well, I am school'd."

117. *For you.* As regards you. Gr. 149.

120. *Extenuate.* Relax, mitigate.

123. *Go along.* Abbott (Gr. 30) remarks that here (as in *T. of S.* iv.
5. 9 ; 2 *Hen. IV.* ii. 1. 191, etc.) *go* is used where we should say *come*.

125. *Nuptial.* S. regularly uses the singular, though the plural is

found in *Per.* v. 3. 80. In *Oth.* ii. 2. 8 the quartos have *nuptials,* the folios *nuptial ;* and in *Temp.* v. 1. 308, *nuptials* is found in the later folios, as it is in the present passage and in v. 1. 75 below.

126. *Nearly that concerns.* That nearly concerns. Gr. 421.

129. *How chance.* How does it chance that? Cf. v. 1. 318 below: "How chance Moonshine," etc. See also *M. W.* v. 5. 230; *C. of E.* i. 2. 42; *Lear*, ii. 4. 64, etc.

130. *Belike.* "As it seems, I suppose" (Schmidt). It is followed by *that* in *T. G. of V.* ii. 4. 90: "Belike that now she hath enfranchis'd them," etc.

131. *Beteem.* Grant, allow. Used by S. only here and in *Ham.* i. 2. 141. Cf. Spenser, *F. Q.* ii. 8. 19 :

> "So would I (said th' enchaunter) glad and faine
> Beteeme to you this sword, you to defend."

Golding uses it (=endure or deign, translating *dignatur*) in Ovid's *Met.*:

> "Yet could he not beteeme
> The shape of any other bird than eagle for to seeme."

132. *Ay me!* The quartos have "Eigh me ;" the 1st folio omits the words, and also reads "ever I could ;" the later folios read, "Hermia for ought that ever I could," etc. Here, as elsewhere, many eds. print "Ah me !" a phrase which is found in the early eds. only in *R. and J.* v. i. 10. "Ay me !" occurs frequently in the plays; as it does in Milton (*Lyc.* 56, 154; *Comus*, 511 ; *P. L.* iv. 86, etc.).

Halliwell remarks that a similar passage occurs in *V. and A.* 1135–1146.

134. *The course of true love*, etc. This passage appears to have been imitated by Milton in *P. L.* x. 896–908.

136. *Too high*, etc. That one of too high rank should be enslaved by love for one of low degree. "Lysander's speech would be improved by the omission of the interpositions of Hermia" (Halliwell). The early eds. have "loue" (love) for *low,* which Theo. corrected.

137. *Misgraffed.* Misgrafted. Used by S. nowhere else.

139. *Of friends.* The quarto reading; the folios have "of merit," which W. retains, on the ground that it could not have been accidentally substituted for "friends." He adds : "The sense of the line is also made subtler and less commonplace by the introduction of the new word, while its relation to the next is not changed; for 'the choice of *merit*' is, plainly enough, not the spontaneous, and at first unconscious, preference of the lover."

140. *Eyes.* So in the quartos. The folios have "eie" or "eye."

143. *Momentany.* The quarto reading; the folios have "momentary," which S. elsewhere uses. *Momentany* is from the Latin *momentaneus,* as *momentary* is from *momentarius.* It is used by Bacon, Hooker, and other writers of the time, and was not wholly obsolete in Dryden's day. Coll. notes that Philip Stubbes, in 1593, preferred it to *momentary*, since in the list of errors of the press in his *Motive to Good Works* he mentions the latter as misprinted for *momentany* in this passage on p. 188 : "this life is but momentary, short and transitory," etc.

144. *Swift as a shadow*, etc. As Halliwell suggests, these images are probably taken from the Bible. Cf. *Job*, viii. 9, xx. 8. See also Chaucer, *C. T.* 9189:

> "giftes of fortune,
> That passen as a schadow on a wal."

145. *Collied.* Blackened, darkened; literally, smutted with *coal*. Cf. *collier* and *colliery*. Steevens quotes Ben Jonson, *Poetaster:* "Thou hast not collied thy face enough." S. uses the word only here and in *Oth.* ii. 3. 206, where the quartos have "coold."

146. *Spleen.* "A sudden motion, a fit" (Schmidt). S. often uses it to express any sudden impulse; as of laughter (*M. for M.* ii. 2. 122; *L. L. L.* iii. 1. 77, etc.), of passion (1 *Hen. IV.* v. 2. 19; *J. C.* iv. 3. 47, etc.), of caprice (*V. and A.* 907; *T. of S.* iii. 2. 10, etc.), and the like.

147. *Ere a man*, etc. Cf. *R. and J.* ii. 2. 119:

> "Too like the lightning that doth cease to be
> Ere one can say 'It lightens.'"

149. *Confusion.* Ruin, destruction; as in *Macb.* ii. 3. 71, iii. 5. 29, etc. The word is here a quadrisyllable. Gr. 479. Cf. *patience*, three lines below.

151. *Edict.* Accented on the last syllable, as in 2 *Hen. VI.* iii. 2. 258; *L. L. L.* i. 1. 11, etc. Elsewhere (as in *Rich. III.* i. 4. 203; 1 *Hen. IV.* iv. 3. 79, etc.) it has the modern accent.

154. *Due.* Naturally pertaining, belonging. Cf. *Macb.* iv. 3. 197: "a fee-grief, due to some single breast," etc.

155. *Fancy's.* Love's. Cf. iv. 1. 160 below; also *M. of V.* iii. 2. 63, 68, 70, etc. So *fancy-free* (ii. 1. 161)=free from the power of love, and *fancy-sick* (iii. 2. 96)=love-sick. In the extract from North's *Plutarch*, p. 121 above, "fallen in fancy"=fallen in love.

156. On the measure, see Gr. 469.

157. *Dowager.* See on 5 above; and for the accent of *revenue* in next line, on 6 above.

159. *Remote.* So in quartos; the folios have "remov'd."

160. *Respects.* Considers, regards. Cf. 1 *Hen. IV.* v. 4. 20: "I do respect thee as my soul," etc. So we have *respecting* where we should use *considering*, in 2 *Hen. VI.* iii. 1. 24: "Respecting what a rancorous mind he bears," etc.

164. *Forth.* From. Cf. 2 *Hen. VI.* iii. 2. 89: "loos'd them forth their brazen caves," etc. Gr. 156.

167. *To.* So in quartos; the folios have "for." For the line, cf. Chaucer, *Troilus and Creseide*, ii. 112: "And let us done to May some observaunce;" also Turbervile's *Poems*, 1570:

> "You that in May have bathde in blis,
> And founde a salve to ease your sore,
> Doe May observaunce, reason is
> That May should honorde be therfore."

170. *His best arrow*, etc. An allusion to the two arrows mentioned in Ovid, *Met.* i. 466; the one that causes love being, to quote Golding's translation, "all of gold, with point full sharp and bright." Cf. *The*

I

King's Quair: "And with the first that headed is of gold, he smites soft, and that has easy cure;" and Sidney's *Arcadia:* "But arrowes two, and tipt with gold or lead."

171. *Simplicity.* Artlessness, innocence. Cf. v. i. 104 below.

173. *The Carthage queen.* We need not comment upon such obvious anachronisms as the introduction of Dido and English May-day customs. On the use of *Carthage*, cf. *J. C.* v. 5. 19 : "Philippi fields ;" *Id.* i. 1. 63 : "Tiber banks," etc. See Gr. 22 and 430.

174. *Troyan.* The reading of the early eds., changed in most modern ones to *Trojan.*

175, 176. On *broke* and *spoke*, see Gr. 343.

180. *Whither away?* Where are you going? Cf. *T. G. of V.* iii. 1. 51 ; *L. L. L.* iv. 3. 186 ; *Hen. VIII.* ii. 1. 1, etc.

182. *Your fair.* The quarto reading; the folios have "you fair," which W. adopts, printing it "you, fair." S. often uses *fair* as a noun=beauty. See *V. and A.* 1083, 1086 ; *Sonn.* 16. 11 ; *C. of E.* ii. 1. 98 ; *A. Y. L.* iii. 2. 99, etc. Steevens quotes Greene, *Never too Late:* "Though she were false to Menelaus, yet her fair made him brook her follies ;" and again :

> "Flora in tawny hid up all her flowers,
> And would not diaper the meads with fair."

183. *Lode-stars.* The preferable orthography. See Wb. Cf. *R. of L.* 179 : "Which must be lode-star to his lustful eye." Johnson quotes Milton, *L'All.* 80 :

> "Where perhaps some beauty lies,
> The cynosure of neighbouring eyes ;"

and Steevens adds *The Spanish Tragedy:* "Led by the loadstar of her heavenly looks ;" and *The Battle of Alcazar* (1594) : "The loadstar and the honour of our line." Many other instances of the figure might be added.

186. *Favour.* Features, outward appearance; as often in S. Cf. *Macb.* i. 5. 73 ; *M. for M.* iv. 2. 34, 185, etc.

187. *Yours would I.* Hanmer's emendation (generally adopted) for the "Your words I" of the quartos and 1st folio. The later folios have "Your words Ide."

188. *My.* On the use of *my* and *mine* in S., see Gr. 237.

190. *Bated.* Excepted. Cf. *Ham.* v. 2. 23 : "no leisure bated," etc.

191. *I'd.* The early eds. have here "Ile" or "I'le ;" the correction is due to Hanmer.

Translated. Transformed, changed. Cf. *Sonn.* 96. 8 :

> "So are those errors that in thee are seen
> To truths translated and for true things deem'd.
> How many lambs might the stern wolf betray,
> If like a lamb he could his looks translate !"

See also iii. 1. 108 and iii. 2. 32 below.

200. *No fault of mine.* The reading of 1st quarto (Fisher's) ;* the other quarto and the folios have "none of mine."

---

* Throughout these notes Fisher's quarto is referred to as "1st quarto," and Roberts's as "2d quarto;" though it is possible, as Halliwell suggests, that the former was a revised edition of the latter.

205. *Like.* The reading of 2d quarto (Roberts's) and folios; the 1st quarto has "as."

207. *Into.* So in the early eds. except 1st quarto, which has "unto."

209. *Phœbe.* Cf. *L. L. L.* iv. 2. 39 : "A title to Phœbe, to Luna, to the moon." See also *T. A.* i. 1. 316.

211. *Decking,* etc. Cf. ii. 1. 14 :

> "I must go seek some dewdrops here,
> And hang a pearl in every cowslip's ear."

See also iv. 1. 51.

212. *Still.* Constantly. See Gr. 69.

215. *Faint.* "Whether the epithet *faint* has reference to the colour or smell of primroses, let the reader determine" (Steevens).

216. *Sweet.* All the early eds. have "sweld," and in 219 "strange companions." Theo. substituted *sweet* and *stranger companies* for the sake of the rhyme, and has been generally followed. Halliwell, however, prefers the old reading. He says: "If Shakespeare had written *sweet* and *stranger companies*, it is very improbable that these words could have been changed either by the actors or printers. Moreover, the antithesis in the first of these instances is a strong argument in favour of the old reading :

> '*Emptying* our bosoms of their counsel *swell'd.*' "

Heath thinks that S. had in mind *Psalms*, lv. 14.

223. *Midnight.* As Blackstone has pointed out, this is inconsistent with 209, 210 above. It appears from lines 2, 3 that "to-morrow night would be within three nights of the new moon, when there is no moonshine at all, much less at deep midnight." Cf. the extract from Halliwell, p. 122 above.

225. *Dote.* For the construction, see Gr. 365. The folios have "dotes."

226. *Other some.* See Gr. 21 and p. 6. Cf. *Acts*, xvii. 18. It was sometimes printed as one word; as in *Gaulfrido and Barnardo*, 1570 : "To othersome as kinde." *Happy*=fortunate.

231. *Of.* See Gr. 178.

232. *Holding no quantity.* "Bearing no proportion to what they are estimated at by love" (Schmidt). Cf. *Ham.* iii. 2. 177 : "For women's fear and love holds quantity" (that is, have the same proportion).

235. *Cupid painted blind.* This is a modern idea, no trace of it being found in the old Greek or Latin poets. Douce says that the earliest English writer who gives it is Chaucer, in his translation of the *Roman de la Rose :* "The god of love, blind as stone ;" but the line is not in the French original.

237. *Unheedy.* Unheeding. Gr. 450. It is used by S. nowhere else. *Unheedful* occurs in *T. G. of V.* ii. 6. 11 and 1 *Hen. VI.* iv. 4. 7.

239. *He is so oft.* The reading of 1st quarto ; the 2d has "he is oft ;" the 1st folio, "he is often ;" the later folios, "he often is."

242. *Eyne.* Sometimes written *eyen ;* a plural analogous to *oxen, children, brethren, shoon,* etc. Cf. ii. 2. 99, iii. 2. 138, and v. 1. 174 below ; also *V. and A.* 633, *R. of L.* 643, *L. L. L.* v. 2. 206, etc. It is used *without rhyme* in *R. of L.* 1229 and *Per.* iii. prol. 5.

245. *So.* See Gr. 66. Capell substituted *"Lo."*

249. *A dear expense.* A costly sacrifice on my part. Steevens explains it : "It will cost him much (be a severe constraint on his feelings)
to make even so slight a return for my communication." The Coll. MS.
has "dear recompense."

250. *But herein*, etc. But I seek to repay myself for my pains by
having the sight of Demetrius, etc. On the use of *to have*, see Gr.
356.

SCENE II.—Halliwell remarks that there is a connection between the
name of *Bottom* and his trade, a ball of thread wound upon any cylindri-
cal body being called "a bottom of thread." He quotes *Nomenclator*,
1585 : "*Glomus*, a bottome of yarne, or a clew of threed ;" Grange's
Garden, 1577 :

> "A bottome for your silke it seemes,
>   My letters are become,
> Whiche, with oft winding off and on,
>   Are wasted whole and some ;"

and Howell's *Letters*, 1650 : "I could not wind it up closer, nor on a
lesser bottom."

It is passing strange that Halliwell should have overlooked the fact
that S. uses the word in this sense in *T. of S.* iv. 3. 138 : "beat me to
death with a bottom of brown thread."

2. *You were best.* It were best for you. See Gr. 230. By *generally*
Bottom of course means individually.

3. *Scrip.* Written list. In the only other instance in which S. uses
the word (*A. Y. L.* iii. 2. 171) it means a bag or wallet.

8. *Grow to a point.* "Come to a conclusion" (Halliwell) ; or "come
to an exact arrangement" (J. H.). Cf. *The Arraignment of Paris*, 1584 :

> "Our reasons will be infinite, I trow,
> Unless unto some other point we grow."

The Coll. MS. has "go on to appoint."

9. *Marry.* Probably a corruption of *Mary*, and originally a mode
of swearing by the Virgin.

The most lamentable comedy, etc. Steevens says that this is very probably a burlesque on the title-page of Thomas Preston's *Cambyses* : "A
lamentable Tragedie, mixed full of pleasant Mirth, containing, The Life
of Cambises King of Percia," etc.

11. *A very good piece of work.* Cf. *T. of S.* i. 1. 258 : "'Tis a very excellent piece of work." Verplanck remarks : "Bottom and Sly both
speak of the play as they would of a piece of cloth or a pair of shoes."

18. *Gallant.* The quarto reading ; the folios have "gallantly." See
Gr. 1.

19. *Ask.* Require. Cf. *T. of S.* ii. 1. 115 : "my business asketh
haste ;" *Rich. II.* ii. 1. 159 : "these great affairs do ask some charge,"
etc. See also Milton, *S. A.* 66 : "Would ask a life to wail."

21. *Condole.* Lament, bewail (Halliwell). Used by S. only in this
speech, and in that of Pistol in *Hen. V.* ii. 1. 133 : "Let us condole the
knight." Steevens quotes an old ballad, *A Pennyworth of good Counsell* :

> "Thus to the wall
> I may condole ;"

and another, *Three Merry Coblers:*

> "Poor weather beaten soles,
> Whose case the body condoles."

22. *Ercles.* Hercules. This may perhaps be an allusion to Martin Slaughter's play of *Hercules*, now lost, but written about 1594 ; or it may refer to a "mask of Greek Worthyes" of the time of Edward VI., in a list of properties for which we find the following entry : "a great clobb for one of them representing Hercules, iiij. *s.*" It is difficult to say whether the verses which Bottom uses are an actual quotation or a burlesque, but probably the latter. In 1581, a translation of one of Seneca's plays, entitled *Hercules*, was published, which may have suggested them. Cf. the opening lines :

> "O Lorde of ghostes! whose fyrye flashe
> That forth thy hande doth shake,
> Doth cause the trembling lodges twayne,
> Of Phœbus' carre to shake.
> Raygne reachlesse nowe: in every place
> Thy peace procurde I have,
> Aloffe where Nereus lookes up lande,
> Empalde in winding wave.'

And again,

> "The roring rocks have quaking sturd,
> And none thereat hath pusht ;
> Hell gloummy gates I have brast oape,
> Where grisly ghosts all husht
> Have stood." . . .

The following line occurs in *A Posie of Gilloflowers*, by Humphrey Gifford, published in 1580 : "The raged [ragged] rocks with rumbling noyse doe rore." See also G. Whitney, *Emblemes*, 1586 : "And shakes the shore, and ragged rockes doth rente" (that is, rend, as in iii. 2. 215 below).

23. *A part to tear a cat in.* Probably a burlesque of Hercules's killing a lion. Steevens cites the old comedy of *The Roaring Girl*, 1611, in which there is a character called *Tear-cat*, who says : "I am called, by those who have seen my valour, *Tear-cat;*" also *Histriomastix*, 1610 : "Sirrah, this is you that would rend and tear a cat upon a stage ;" and *The Isle of Gulls*, 1606 : "I had rather hear two such jests, than a whole play of such Tear-cat thunderclaps."

To make all split, as Halliwell remarks, was a common phrase, perhaps originally a naval one. Cf. B. and F., *Wild-Goose Chase:* "I love a sea-voyage, and a blustring tempest, and let all split ;" Taylor, the Water-Poet, *Workes:* "Some ships beare so great a sayle, that they beare their masts by the boord and make all split againe ;" Greene, *Never too Late:* "as the Marriners say, a man would have thought al would have split againe," etc. Farmer quotes *The Scornful Lady:* "two roaring boys of Rome, that made all split."

30. *Make and mar.* Apparently a common phrase in that day. Cf. Turbervile, *To the Countess of Warwick*, 1570 : "Should make or marre as she saw cause." Halliwell cites many other instances.

34. *Bellows-mender.*   One who repaired the bellows of organs, etc.

39. *Let me not play a woman,* etc.   "This passage shows how the want of women on the old stage was supplied.   If they had not a young man who could perform the part with a face that might pass for fem-mine, the character was acted in a mask, which was at that time a part of a lady's dress in use that it did not give any unusual appear-ance to the scene; and he that could modulate his voice in a female tone might play the woman very successfully" (Johnson).

Coryat, in his *Crudities* (1611), speaking of Venice, says: "here I ob-served certaine things that I never saw before, for I saw women acte, a thing that I never saw before, though I have heard that it hath beene sometimes used in London; and they performed it with as good a grace, action, gesture, and whatsoever convenient for a player, as ever I saw any masculine actor."

The appearance of female actors was certainly rare on the English stage before the accession of Charles II.   Halliwell quotes the *Key to the Rehearsal* (1704), in which "the reviving the stage and bringing women on't" is mentioned among the bad results of "this sudden revo-lution, which is best known by the name of the Restauration."

42. *As small as you will.*   Cf. *M. W.* i. 1. 49 : "She has brown hair, and speaks small like a woman;" Chaucer, *The Floure and the Leafe*:

> "With voice sweet entuned, and so small
>   That me thought it the sweetest melody;"

Fairfax, *Godfrey of Bulloigne*: "She warbled forth a treble small," etc. See also *T. N.* i. 4. 32, and *Cor.* iii. 2. 114.

43. *An I may.*   On *an* or *and*=if, see Gr. 101.

44. *Thisne, Thisne.*   The Camb. editors think "it may be questioned whether the true reading is not 'thisne, thisne;' that is, 'in this manner,' a meaning which 'thissen' has in several dialects."   The word is more probably Bottom's blunder for *Thisbe,* as Schmidt and others explain it. No one, however, has attempted to explain why he should make the blunder only here, and there may be some corruption of the text.

52. *Thisby's mother.*   See above, p. 122.

56, 57. *A play fitted.*   Cf. v. 1. 65 : "There is not one word apt, one player fitted;" *T. of S.* ind. i. 87 :

> "but sure, that part
> Was aptly fitted and naturally perform'd."

62. *I will roar, that.*   For the omission of *so,* see Gr. 283.

68. *Every mother's son.*   As Halliwell shows, a phrase of great an-tiquity.   He cites the *Thornton MS.* in Lincoln Cathedral (15th century) : "And he and his oste umbylapped alle thaire enemys, and daunge thame doune, and slewe thame ilke a moder sone;" also *MS. Cantab.* v. 48 :

> "Thryes thorow at them he ran,
>   Then forsothe as I yow sey,
> And woundyt many a modur sone,
>   And xij. he slew that day."

72, 73. *An 't were.*   Cf. *T. and C.* i. 2. 189 : "He will weep you, an 't were a man born in April."   See Gr. 104.

75. *Sweet-faced.* Cf. *C. of E.* v. i. 418 : "a sweet-faced youth." Halliwell quotes Copley's *Wits, Fits, and Fancies*, 1614: "many a scurvy fellow and many an ill faced woman, have I cal'd honest gentleman and swete-fac'd gentlewoman," etc.

See in a summer's day. A common phrase. Cf. Sidney, *Arcadia :* "a tricke and bonny lasse, as in a sommer day a man might see ;" Lyly, *Mother Bombie :* "as goodly a youth as one shall see in a summer's day ;" *Gratiæ Ludentes*, 1638 : "One walking abroad in a cleare mooneshining night, said it was as fine a night as any is in England. Another swore it was as fine a night as a man shall see in a summer's day," etc.

78. *What beard*, etc. It was the custom at that time to dye the beard. Steevens quotes the old comedy of *Ram-Alley*, 1611 :

> "What colour'd beard comes next by the window? . . .
> I think, a red : for that is most in fashion ;"

also B. J., *The Alchemist :* "he had dyed his beard and all ;" and B. and F., *The Silent Woman :* "I have fitted my divine and canonist, dyed their beards and all."

81. *Discharge.* Perform. Cf. *Temp.* iii. 1. 22, etc.

82. *Orange-tawny.* Cf. iii. 1. 115 below.

91. *Properties.* Stage requisites ; still used in the same sense. Cf. *M. W.* iv. 4. 78 :

> "Go get us properties
> And tricking for our fairies."

We have a curious list of ancient properties in *The Antipodes*, a comedy by R. Brome, 1640 :

> "He has got into our tyring-house amongst us,
> And tane a strict survey of all our properties ;
> Our statues and our images of gods,
> Our planets and our constellations,
> Our giants, monsters, furies, beasts, and bugbeares,
> Our helmets, shields and vizors, haires and beards,
> Our pastbord marchpaines, and our wooden pies."

94. *Obscenely.* Used for *obscurely* (Halliwell). If Bottom, like Mrs. Malaprop, "reprehends anything in this world, it is the use of his oracular tongue, and a nice derangement of epitaphs."

Take pains ; be perfect : adieu. The Coll. MS. and Sr. give these words to Quince, who is evidently the "manager" of the play.

96. *Hold or cut bow-strings.* That is, whatever may happen. The origin of the phrase is uncertain, but it seems to belong to archery. Cf. *Much Ado*, iii. 2. 11 : "he hath twice or thrice cut Cupid's bow-string, and the little hangman dare not shoot at him." Steevens quotes *The Country Girl*, 1647 :

> "fiddler, strike ;
> I'll strike you else, and cut your begging bowstrings ;"

and *The Ball*, 1639 :

> "have you devices to jeer the rest?
> *Luc.* All the regiment of them, or I'll break my bowstrings."

In these instances the strings of a fiddle-bow may be meant.

HEAD OF EROS (CUPID), FROM THE ANTIQUE.

ACT II.

SCENE I.—1. As Abbott remarks (Gr. 504), the "verse with four accents" is rarely used by S., except when fairies, witches, and other ex-
traordinary beings are speaking. See *Temp., M. W., Macb.,* etc. The
metre employed is generally trochaic, with iambic and other variations;
as in the opening lines of this scene.

3. *Thorough.* The reading of 1st quarto; the other early eds. have
"Through." The words are the same, and S. uses either as suits the
measure; and so with the derivatives, *thoroughly* and *throughly, thorough-
fares* and *throughfares* (see *Mer.* p. 144), etc. Cf. Gr. 478.

This passage is imitated in "The Pranks of Puck"—if, as is probable,
that poem was written after the play:

> "If any wanderers I meet
>   That from their night-sport do trudge home,
> With counterfeited voice I greet,
>   And call them on with me to roam:
>   Through woods, through lakes,
>   Through bogs, through brakes,
>   O'er bush and brier with them I go;
>   I call upon
>   Them to come on,
>   And slide out laughing, ho, ho, ho!"

also in Drayton's *Nymphidia:*

> "Quoth Puck,—My liege, I'll never lin,
> But I will thorough thick and thin,
> Until at length I bring her in;
>   My dearest lord, ne'er doubt it.
> Thorough brake, thorough brier,
> Thorough muck, thorough mier,
> Thorough water, thorough fier !—
>   And thus goes Puck about it."

7. *Moon's sphere.* Steevens prints "moones," and compares Spenser, *F. Q.* iii. 1. 15: "And eke, through feare, as white as *whales* bone." He might have added *L. L. L.* v. 2. 332 : "To show his teeth as white as whales bone." W. adopts "moony," also suggested by Steevens. "Moony sphere" is found in Sidney's *Arcadia.* But *moon's* may be metrically a dissyllable, as Abbott makes it (Gr. 484).

9. *To dew.* For the infinitive, see Gr. 356. *Dew* is used as a verb in *V. and A.* 66, *Macb.* v. 2. 30, *R. and J.* v. 3. 14, etc. The *orbs* are the "fairy-rings" so called, which were supposed to be formed by the fairies dancing in a circle. Cf. also 86 below, and see note on that passage.

10. *Tall.* The Coll. MS. substitutes "all ;" but the cowslips would be tall to beings so diminutive that they could "creep into acorn cups and hide them there."

Pensioners. S. uses the word only here and in *M. W.* ii. 2. 79. In both places there is an allusion to Queen Elizabeth's band of military courtiers called *pensioners.* They were the handsomest and tallest young men of good family that could be found. For the use of *be*, see Gr. 300.

11. *In their gold coats*, etc. The Coll. MS. substitutes "cups." Cf. *Cymb.* ii. 2. 38 :

> "A mole cinque-spotted, like the crimson drops
> I' the bottom of a cowslip."

There is an allusion to the splendid dresses of the pensioners, their coats adorned with gold and jewels ; as in Milton, *Il Penseroso*, 6 :

> "And fancies fond with gaudy shapes possess,
>   As thick and numberless
> As the gay motes that people the sun-beams;
>   Or likest hovering dreams,
> The fickle pensioners of Morpheus' train."

13. *Freckles.* Used by S. nowhere else. He has *freckled* in *Temp.* i. 2. 283 and *Hen. V.* v. 2. 49, in the latter place applied to the cowslip.

14. *I must go seek.* For the omission of *to*, see Gr. 349.

15. *And hang a pearl*, etc. Steevens quotes the old comedy of *The Wisdome of Doctor Dodypoll*, known to have been written as early as 1596 :

> "'Twas I that led you through the painted meades,
>   Where the light fairies daunst upon the flowers,
>   Hanging on every leaf an orient pearle."

Cf. iv. 1. 51 below.

16. *Lob.*   Lubber.   Cf. Milton's description of Robin Goodfellow *L'Allegro*, 110: "Then lies him down the lubbar fiend."   Steevens quotes the interlude of *Jacob and Esau*, 1568: "Should find Esau such a lout or a lob;" and Arthur Hall's translation of Homer, 1581: "yet fewe he led, because he was a lobbe."

17. *Her elves.*   The Globe ed. misprints "our elves."

20. *Passing fell and wrath.*   Exceedingly fierce and wrathful.   Cf. *T. and C.* iv. 5. 269: "fell as death," etc.   S. does not elsewhere use *wrath* as an adjective; nor does he use *wroth*=wrathful (*wroth*=ruth, misery, occurs in *M. of V.* ii. 9. 78).

21. *Because that.*   See Gr. 287.

22. *Stolen from an Indian king.*   Halliwell remarks that this is not very easily reconcilable with Titania's own account of the boy's mother in lines 123-134 below.

23. *Changeling.*   It was a common superstition that fairies stole beautiful children, leaving elves in their place.   Cf. Spenser, *F. Q.* i. 10. 65:

> "From thence a Faery thee unweeting reft,
> There as thou slepst in tender swading band;
> And her base Elfin brood there for thee left:
> Such, men do Chaungelings call, so chaung'd by Faeries theft."

See also "The Pranks of Puck," quoted on 3 above:

> "When larks gin sing
> Away we fling,
> And babes new-born steal as we go;
> An elf instead
> Leave we in bed,
> And wind out laughing, ho, ho, ho!'

and Drayton, *Nymphidia:*

> "These when a child haps to be got,
> Which after proves an idiot,
> When folk perceive it thriveth not,
> The fault therein to smother,
> Some silly doting brainless calf,
> That understands things by the half,
> Says that the Fairy left this aulf,
> And took away the other."

Changeling is here a trisyllable.   Gr. 487.

24. *Would.*   See Gr. 329.

25. *Trace.*   Pace; as in *Much Ado*, iii. 1. 16: "As we do trace this alley up and down."

26. *Perforce.*   By force; as in *C. of E.* iv. 3. 95, v. 1. 117, *Rich. II.* ii. 3. 121, etc.   It is=of necessity, in iii. 2. 90 below; as in 2 *Hen. IV.* i. 1. 165, iii. 1. 105, etc.

29. *Spangled starlight sheen.*   Cf. *T. of S.* iv. 5. 31: "What stars do spangle heaven with such beauty," etc.   *Sheen* is used by S. only here and in *Ham.* iii. 2. 167, where also it is a rhyming word.

30. *Square.*   Quarrel.   Cf. *T. A.* ii. 1. 100:

> "are you such fools
> To square for this?"

See also *A. and C.* ii. 1. 45, iii. 3. 41, etc. *Squarer*=quarreller, in *Much Ado*, i. 1. 82.

For the omission of *so* before *that*, see Gr. 283.

32. For the measure, see Gr. 466. Cf. i. 1. 69.

33. *Shrewd.* Mischievous. See *Hen. VIII.* p. 202, and *J. C.* p. 145.

34. *He.* Abbott (Gr. 224) notes that *he* and *she* are sometimes used for "man" and "woman;" and that this makes more natural the use of *he that* with the third person of the verb here. Cf. *A. Y. L.* iii. 2. 411 : "are you he that hangs the verses on the trees," etc. For the change of person in *skim*, see Gr. 415.

35. *Villagery.* Villages. Used by S. only here. Gr. 468.

36. *Sometimes.* Two lines below we have *sometime.* S. used either as suited his ear. See *Mer.* p. 130, or *Rich. II.* p. 158. Gr. 68a.

Quern. A hand-mill for grinding corn. Burton (*Anat. of Melancholy*, i. 2) says : "A bigger kind there is of them [fairies], called with us Hobgoblins and Robin Goodfellows, that would, in those superstitious times, grind corn for a mess of milk," etc. Cf. "The Pranks of Puck," quoted above :

> "Yet now and then, the maids to please,
>   I card, at midnight, up their wool ;
> And while they sleep, and take their ease,
>   With wheel to thread their flax I pull ;
>   I grind at mill
>   Their malt up still,
>   I dress their hemp, I spin their tow ;
>   If any wake,
>   And would me take,
>   I wend me laughing, ho, ho, ho !"

See also Milton, *L'All.* 105–109. Steevens quotes R. Scot, *Discoverie of Witchcraft*, 1584 : "Your grandames' maids were wont to set a bowl of milk for him, for his pains in grinding malt and mustard, and sweeping the house at midnight," etc.

37. *Bootless.* Bootlessly, to no purpose. Gr. 1.

38. *Barm.* Frothy head ; showing that the beer had "worked" or fermented properly. Harsenet, in his *Declaration of Popish Impostures* (1603), says : "And if that the bowle of curds and creame were not duly set out for Robin Good-fellow, the frier, and Sisse the dairy-maid, why then either the pottage was burnt to next day in the pot, or the cheeses would not curdle, or the butter would not come, or the ale in the fat [vat] never would have good head."

Halliwell quotes Withal's *Dictionarie*, 1608 : "Barme or yeast, flos ve, spuma cervisiæ ;" and Lyly's *Mother Bombie :* "It behoveth my wits to worke like barme, alias yeast, alias sizing, alias rising, alias godsgood." He adds : "This provincial term is still in use in Warwickshire, and in 1847 I observed a card advertising 'fresh barm' in Henley Street, at Stratford-on-Avon, within a few yards of the poet's birthplace"

39. *Mislead night-wanderers.* See quotation in note on 3 above. Cf. Drayton, *Nymphidia :*

> "This Puck seems but a dreaming dolt,
>   Still walking like a ragged colt,
> And oft out of a bush doth bolt,
>   Of purpose to deceive us ;

> And leading us makes us to stray
> Long winter's nights out of the way
> And when we stick in mire and clay,
> He doth with laughter leave us."

Milton seems to have had this line in mind in writing *P. L.* ix. 640. "Misleads the amaz'd night-wanderer from his way," etc.

40. *Hobgoblin.* Halliwell quotes the following from *MS. Harl.* 6482 :

"Of spirits called Hobgoblins, or Robin Goodfellowes.

"These kinde of spirits are more familiar and domestical then the others, and for some causes to us unknown, abode in one place more then in another, so that some never almost depart from some particular houses, as though they were their proper mansions, making in them sundry noises, rumours, mockeries, gawds, and jests, without doing any harme at all, and some have heard them play at gitterns and Jews' harps, and ring bells, and make answer to those that call them, and speake with certain signes, laughters, and merry gestures, so that those of the house come at last to be so familiar and well acquainted with them that they fear them not at all.   But in truth, if they had free power to put in execution their mallicious desire, we should finde these pranks of theirs not to be jests, but earnest indeed, tending to the destruction both of our body and soul, but their power is so restrained and tyed that they can passe no further then to jests and gawds, and if they do any harm at all, it is certainly very little, as by experience hath been founde."

Sweet Puck. Tyrwhitt remarks that the epithet is by no means superfluous, as *Puck* signified nothing better than *fiend* or *devil*.   The author of *Piers Ploughman* puts "the pouk" for the devil. Cf. *Richard Coer de Lion :* "He is no man, he is a pouke, that out of helle is i-stole."   See also Spenser, *Epithalamion,* 341 :

> "Ne let the Pouke, nor other evill sprights,
> Ne let mischivous witches with theyr charmes,
> Ne let hob Goblins, names whose sence we see not,
> Fray us with things that be not ;"

and Golding's *Ovid, Met.* ed. 1587, p. 126 :

> "and the country where Chymæra, that same pouke,
> Hath goatish bodie," etc.

42. The Coll. MS. completes the measure by reading "Fairy, thou speak'st aright ;" but, as Abbott remarks (Gr. 506), "lines with four accents, where there is an interruption in the line, are not uncommon."

46. *Filly.* So in 1st quarto ; all the other early eds. have "silly," which Halliwell retains.

48. *Crab.* A crab-apple ; as in *Temp.* ii. 2. 171, *L. L. L.* iv. 2. 6, v. 2. 935, etc. Steevens quotes the anonymous play of *King Henry V.* (1598):

> "Yet we will have in store a crab in the fire,
> With nut-brown ale, that is full stale ;"

and *Damon and Pythias* (1582) :

> "And sit down in my chaire by my wife fair Alison,
> And turne a crabbe in the fire," etc.

In Sumner's *Last Will and Testament* (1600), Christmas is described as

> "sitting in a corner, turning crabs,
> Or coughing o'er a warmed pot of ale.''

Halliwell adds *Gammer Gurton's Needle* (1575):

> "I love no rost but a nut-brown toste,
> And a crab layde in the fyre.''

54. *Tailor cries.* Johnson says: "The custom of crying *tailor* at a sudden fall backwards, I think I remember to have observed. He that slips beside his chair falls as a tailor squats upon his board." Capell gives "rails or" for "tailor," and mentions "tail-sore" as an anonymous conjecture.

Halliwell thinks that the expression is "probably one of contempt, equivalent to *thief;*" and he cites *Pasquil's Night-Cap* (1612):

> "Thieving is now an occupation made,
> Though men the name of *tailor* doe it give.''

55. Steevens quotes Milton, *L'All.* 32: "And Laughter holding both his sides."

All the early eds. have "coffe" and "loffe." Halliwell refers to the old nursery ballad of Mother Hubbard, who, after she had bought her dog a *coffin*, came home and found him *loffing*. He adds that there appears to have been some difference of opinion as to the pronunciation of the word. Marston (*Parasitaster*, 1606) mentions a critic who vowed "to leve to posteritie the true orthography and pronunciation of laughing."

56. *Waxen.* Wax, increase. Gr. 332. S. has the participle *waxen* in *R. of L.* 1663: "lips new-waxen pale;" and 2 *Hen. VI.* iii. 2. 76: "waxen deaf." Sr. adopts Farmer's conjecture of *yexen*, an old word meaning to hiccough.

Neeze. The old form of *sneeze* (A. S. *niesan*). It is found in the *A. V.* in *Job*, xli. 18, and originally occurred in 2 *Kings*, iv. 35. In the former passage Wiclif has the form "fnesynge" (A. S. *fneósung*).

57. *Wasted.* Spent; as in *V. and A.* 24, *M. of V.* iii. 4. 12, etc. Cf. Milton, *Sonnet to Mr. Lawrence*:

> "Where shall we sometimes meet, and by the fire
> Help waste a sullen day?"

58. *Room* may be here a dissyllable, as Abbott makes it (Gr. 484). Cf. *moon's*, ii. 1. 7. Pope has "make room;" Johnson remarks that *Fairy* or *Faëry* is sometimes a trisyllable, as in Spenser.

60. Pope (followed by some of the modern editors) begins a new scene here; but there is no change of place, though new characters enter.

61. *Fairies, skip hence.* All the early eds. have "Fairy." Theo. changed it to "Fairies," which is also in the Coll. MS. Harness suggests "Fairies, keep hence;" and Dyce, "Fairies, trip hence." J. H. retains "Fairy," which he thinks is used in a plural sense. He quotes Chaucer, *C. T.:* "All was this land fulfilled of faerie."

67. *Pipes of corn.* Cf. *L. L. L.* v. 2. 913: "pipe on oaten straws." Ritson quotes Chaucer's "pipes made of grene corne."

Versing. Used nowhere else by S. as a verb. Gr. 290.

69. *Steep.* The reading of 2d quarto and the folios; the 1st quarto has "steppe," which S. does not use elsewhere. *Steep* as a noun is found only here.

71. *Buskined.* Neither this word nor *buskin* is found elsewhere in S.

72. *Must be.* "Sometimes used by S. to mean no more than definite futurity, like our *is to be*" (Gr. 314).

75. *Glance.* Hint (Schmidt); as in *J. C.* i. 2. 324. It is sometimes transitive=hint at; as in *C. of E.* v. 1. 66: "I often glanced it."

77. *Glimmering.* Cf. iii. 2. 61 and v. 1. 380 below. Warb. conjectured "glimmering through the night."

78. *Perigenia.* See extract from North's *Plutarch*, p. 121 above. W. takes thence the spelling "Perigouna."

79. *Ægle.* All the early eds. have "Eagles."

80. *Antiopa.* It is "Atiopa" in the 1st folio.

82. *The middle summer's spring.* "Probably the beginning of midsummer" (Halliwell). In Churchyard's *Charitie*, 1595, we have "a summer spring"=beginning of summer. Cf. *2 Hen. IV.* iv. 4. 35: "the spring of day;" an expression also used by Holinshed.

84. *Paved.* Probably=pebbly; not, as Johnson explains it, "laid round the edge with stone."

85. *Margent.* Cf. *L. C.* 39:

> "Which one by one she in a river threw,
> Upon whose weeping margent she was set."

Elsewhere S. uses the word for the margin of a book (*L. L. L.* v. 2. 8); for a gloss or comment written on such margin (*Ham.* v. 2. 162); and for the eyes, "as interpreters of the mind, compared to the margin of books" (Schmidt). See *R. of L.* 102; *L. L. L.* ii. 1. 246; and *R. and J.* i. 3. 86. Pope changed *in* to "on."

86. *Ringlets.* Fairy rings. See on *orbs*, line 9 above. S. uses the word only here and in *Temp.* v. i. 37:

> "you demi-puppets that
> By moonshine do the green sour ringlets make
> Whereof the ewe not bites."

See *Temp.* p. 139.

87. *Hast disturbed.* For the use of this tense after *met* above, see Gr. 347.

88. For the possible allusion to the weather of 1594, see p. 10.

90. *Contagious.* Poisonous, pestilential. Cf. *K. John,* v. 4. 33: "night, whose black, contagious breath;" *Hen. V.* iii. 3. 31: "filthy and contagious clouds," etc.

91. *Hath.* For the singular verb with a plural relative, see Gr. 247.

Pelting. Paltry, petty. Cf. *Rich. II.* ii. 1. 60: "pelting farm;" *Lear*, ii. 3. 18: "Poor pelting villages;" *M. for M.* ii. 2. 112: "every pelting petty officer," etc. The folios have "petty" here.

92. *Their continents.* The banks that *contain* or restrain them. Cf. *Lear*, iii. 2. 58:

> "close pent-up guilts,
> Rive your concealing continents," etc.

95. *Ere his youth*, etc. *His*=its. Gr. 228. For the figure, cf. *Sonn.* 12. 7 :

> "And summer's green all girded up in sheaves
> Borne on the bier with white and bristly beard."

97. *Murrain.* The early eds. have "murrion," which is retained by the Camb. editors. It is not found as an adjective anywhere else in S. The noun occurs three times (*Temp.* iii. 2. 88 ; *T. and C.* ii. 1. 20 ; *Cor.* i. 5. 3), but only as an imprecation.

98. *The nine men's morris.* A game played on three squares cut in the turf, one within another, each party having nine "men," which were moved somewhat as in draughts, or "checkers." Cotgrave, in his *Dict.*, under "Merelles," has the following : "Le jeu des Merelles. The boyish game called Merils, or fivepenny morris ; played here most commonly with stones, but in France with pawns, or men made on purpose, and termed *merelles*." Douce says that it was also a table-game ; and that a representation of two monkeys playing it may be seen in a German edition of *Petrarch de Remedio Utriusque Fortunæ*, the cuts in which were done in 1520.

99. *Mazes.* "This alludes to a sport still followed by boys ; that is, what is now called *running the figure of eight*" (Steevens).

Wanton. Luxuriant (Schmidt). Cf. *Rich. II.* i. 3. 214 : "wanton springs ;" 1 *Hen. IV.* iii. 1. 214: "the wanton rushes," etc. J. H. explains *the wanton green* as a metonymy for "the green where sports were carried on."

100. *Undistinguishable.* Used by S. only here and in iv. 1. 184 below.

101. *The human mortals.* "S. might have employed this epithet, which at first sight appears redundant, to mark the difference between *men* and *fairies*. *Fairies* were not *human*, but they were yet *subject to mortality*. It appears from the romance of *Sir Huon of Bordeaux* that Oberon himself was mortal" (Steevens).

Their winter here. If this is what S. wrote, it may mean "have no distinct winter season here." Cf. 106–113 just below. Capell explains the words, "their accustomed winter ;" namely, as the next line shows, "a winter enlivened with mirth," etc. Theo. proposed "their winter cheer," which Halliwell, Coll., D., and some others adopt. It is plausible, as it adds but a single letter to the "heere" of the early eds. K., following the suggestion of an anonymous critic, reads :

> "The human mortals want ;* their winter here,
> No night is now with hymn or carol blest ;"

which is adopted by Verplanck and H. W. thinks "it is barely possible that *want* is a misprint for *chant*, and that Titania, wishing to contrast the gloom of the spurious with the merriment of the real winter, says, 'when their winter is here, the human mortals chant ; but *now* no night

---

* We wonder that those who give this meaning to *want* do not point the passage thus :

> "The human mortals want, their winter here ;
> No night is now," etc.

is blessed with hymn or carol.'" He adds, however, that Theobald's emendation "most nearly conforms to the sense of the passage and the style of the author;" but "as even that is unsatisfactory," he retains the original reading.

102. *No night,* etc. "Hymns and carols, in the time of S., during the season of Christmas, were sung every night about the streets" (Steevens).

103. *The moon,* etc. Cf. *W. T.* i. 2. 427:

> "you may as well
> Forbid the sea for to obey the moon;"

1 *Hen. IV.* i. 2. 35: "governed, as the sea is, by the moon," etc. In Walter Gray's *Almanacke* for the year 1591, the moon is called "the chiefe governesse of fluddes and streames."

104. *Washes.* Wets, moistens.

105. *Rheumatic diseases.* "Not here used in its modern acceptation. Colds, coughs, etc., were included under this class of complaints, and their prevalence agrees with Forman's statement [see p. 10], 'ther was moch sicknes but lyttle deth'" (Halliwell).

For the accent of *rheumatic,* cf. *V. and A.* 135: "O'erworn, despised, rheumatic, and cold." Gr. 492.

106. For *thorough,* see on line 3 above. *Distemperature=*disorder. Cf. 1 *Hen. IV.* iii. 1. 34:

> "Our grandam earth, having this distemperature,
> In passion shook;"

Id. v. 1. 3:

> "How bloodily the sun begins to peer
> Above yon busky hill! the day looks pale
> At his distemperature."

109. *Hiems' thin and icy crown.* The early eds. have "chinne" or "chin." *Thin* was Tyrwhitt's emendation, and has been generally adopted. Coll. retains "chin." *Hiems* is mentioned by S. only here and in *L. L. L.* v. 2. 901: "This side is Hiems, Winter."

112. *Childing.* Fruitful. Used nowhere else by S. W. suggests "chiding" as more in keeping with "angry winter" and the spirit of the whole passage.

113. *Mazed.* Amazed, bewildered. Used by S. only here and in 1 *Hen. VI.* iv. 2. 47 and *Hen. VIII.* ii. 4. 185.

114. *By their increase.* By their produce. Cf. *Sonn.* 97. 6: "The teeming autumn, big with rich increase," etc. See also *Psalms,* lxvii. 6, lxxxv. 12, etc.

116. *Dissension.* See on i. 1. 149. Gr. 479.

117. *Original.* Used by S. as a noun here and in 2 *Hen. IV.* i. 2. 131; nowhere as an adjective.

121. *Henchman.* Page of honour. The word originally meant "a horseman attendant on a knight or person of high degree" (Halliwell). Cf. Chaucer, *The Floure and the Leafe:* "Every knight had after him riding three henshmen, on him awaiting." Meres, in his *Palladis Tamia* (1598), says: "As the visible light is the henchman of the sun's brightnes, so are the benefits of God heralds of the divine bounty."

123. *Votaress.* Used by S. only here and in 160 below; unless we add *Per.* iv. prol. 4. *Votary* is used as feminine in *Sonn.* 154. 5; and *votarist* in *M. for M.* i. 4. 5 and *Oth.* iv. 2. 190.

124. *The spiced Indian air.* Halliwell cites *Bartholomæus de Glanvilla* (1582), fol. 252: "As the rivers there are very many, so are they very great, through whose watery overflowing it commeth to passe that in the moyst grounde, the force of the sunne approaching, ingendreth or bringeth forth all things in great quantitie, and seemeth almost to fill the whole world *with spice* and precious stones, of which it aboundeth more than all other countries of the world."

126. *Neptune's yellow sands.* Cf. *Temp.* i. 2. 376: "Come unto these yellow sands."

131. *Voyage.* A dissyllable here. Gr. 484.

135. *Intend you stay.* For the omission of *to*, see Gr. 349.

137. *Round.* Cf. *Macb.* iv. 1. 130: "While you perform your antic round." See on 9 and 86 above.

142. *Chide.* Scold, quarrel. Cf. iii. 2. 45 below. We have it used transitively, as now, in iii. 2. 200, 218, and in a slightly different sense in 312. In iv. 1. 112 it is applied to the noise of dogs.

143. *Thou shalt not.* See Gr. 405.

146. *Since.* For the peculiar use of the word, see Gr. 132.

147. *Mermaid.* Siren; as often in S. Cf. *V. and A.* 429, 777; *R. of L.* 1411; *C. of E.* iii. 2. 45, 169; *3 Hen. VI.* iii. 2. 186, etc.

Warb. tries to make out that, as the *vestal* (155) is Queen Elizabeth, the *mermaid* must be "some eminent personage of her time," which can be no other than Mary, Queen of Scots. She is called a mermaid, he thinks, "to denote her reign over a kingdom situate in the sea," and also her beauty and unchastity. The phrase *on a dolphin's back* "evidently marks out that distinguishing circumstance of Mary's fortune, her marriage with the Dauphin of France!" *Dulcet and harmonious breath* "alludes to her great abilities of genius and learning." *The rude sea* is "Scotland encircled with the ocean, which rose up in arms against the regent while she was in France; but her return home presently quieted those disorders," etc. The *stars* that *shot madly from their spheres* were "the Earls of Northumberland and Westmoreland, who fell in her quarrel," and "the great Duke of Norfolk, whose projected marriage with her was attended with such fatal consequences." "On the whole," says the imaginative author of this elaborate explanation, which Steevens and Ritson have wasted much ink in refuting, "it is the noblest and justest allegory that was ever written."

On a dolphin's back. The description is doubtless derived from the ancient pageantry, and Boaden suggested that there was an allusion to the celebrated festivities at Kenilworth in 1575, at which it is not only possible but probable the poet was a spectator, for, although he was then in his boyhood, the distance of Kenilworth from Stratford (13 miles) was comparatively short even for those days of inconvenient modes of travel. Laneham and other writers of the time mention as features of the display Arion on a dolphin's back (singing, of course), "Triton in the likenesse of a mermaide," and the like. The mermaid, moreover, commanded the waves to be calm ; and there were shooting-stars in the shape of "fire-works shewed upon the water," etc.

148. *Dulcet and harmonious breath.* Cf. *T. N.* ii. 3. 21 : "So sweet a breath to sing." See also iv. 2. 38 below.

150. *Stars shot madly,* etc. Cf. *R. of L.* 1525 : "And little stars shot from their fixed places ;" *Ham.* i. 5. 17 : "Make thy two eyes, like stars, start from their spheres ;" *A. and C.* iii. 13. 145 :

> "When my good stars, that were my former guides,
> Have empty left their orbs, and shot their fires
> Into the abysm of hell."

155. *A fair vestal,* etc. There is no doubt about the allusion to Queen Elizabeth here, whatever we may think of Warburton's "mermaid." She received many compliments of the kind, but never one so graceful. They were generally of the type of those quoted by Steevens from *Soliman and Perseda* (1599), in which Death vows he will spare

> "none but sacred Cynthia's friend,
> Whom Death did fear before her life began ;
> For holy fates have graven it in their tables,
> That Death shall die, if he attempt her end
> Whose life is heaven's delight, and Cynthia's friend ;"

and from *Tancred and Gismund* (1592) :

> "There lives a virgin, one without compare,
> Who of all graces hath her heavenly share ;
> In whose renowne, and for whose happie days,
> Let us record this Pæan of her praise," etc.

As Steevens adds, "if incense was thrown in cart-loads on the altar, this propitious deity was not disgusted with the smoke of it."

On the use of *by,* see Gr. 145.

156. *Smartly.* Vigorously. Used by S. only here.

157. *As it should pierce.* "The *if* is implied in the subjunctive." See Gr. 102, 107.

158. *Might see.* See Gr. 312.

159. *The chaste beams of the watery moon.* Cf. i. i. 73 : "the cold fruitless moon ;" iii. 1. 185 : "The moon methinks looks with a watery eye ;" *Rich. III.* ii. 2. 69 : "the watery moon ;" *R. and J.* i. 4. 62 : "the moonshine's watery beams."

161. *Fancy-free.* See on i. 1. 155. In *Queen Elizabeth's Entertainement in Suffolke and Norfolke,* written by Churchyard, Chastity deprives Cupid of his bow and presents it to the queen : "and bycause that the Queene had chosen the best life, she gave the Queene Cupid's bow, to learne to shoote at whome she pleased : since none could wound her highnesse hart, it was meete (said Chastitie) that she should do with Cupid's bowe and arrowes what she pleased."

165. *Love-in-idleness.* Halliwell quotes *MS. Sloan.* 797, fol. 61 : "Viola tricolor, hart's ease ; herba Trinitatis, herba clavellata, paunsies, love-in-idlenes." Cf. *Ham.* iv. 5. 176 : "and there is pansies, that's for thoughts." Taylor, the Water-Poet, quibbling on the names of plants, says :

> "When passions are let loose without a bridle,
> Then precious *time* is turn'd to *love-in-idle.*"

168. *Or man or woman.* See Gr. 136.

169. *It sees.* As Coll. remarks, "this is not strictly grammatical, since *it* can only apply to *man* or *woman* in the previous line; nevertheless it is probably what S. wrote;" so he does not adopt the "is seen" of the Coll. MS.

171. *The leviathan.* Elsewhere mentioned in *T. G. of V.* iii. 2. 80 and *Hen. V.* iii. 3. 26.

172. *I 'll.* The Coll. MS. has "I 'd." The 2d quarto and the folios omit *round*.

176. For the omission of the relative, see Gr. 244; and for the redundant *it* in 179, Gr. 242.

180. *From off.* The 1st quarto has "from of;" the other early eds. "off from."

187. *The one I 'll slay,* etc. All the early eds. have "stay" and "stayeth," which Verplanck, Halliwell, K., and H. retain, making the line = "The one I 'll stop, the other hindereth me." *Slay* and *slayeth*, first suggested by Thirlby and adopted by Theo., are accepted by most of the modern editors. It has been objected to *slay* that it makes Demetrius bloodthirsty, but W. compares what Lysander says, ii. 2. 106 below:

> "Where is Demetrius? O, how fit a word
> Is that vile name to perish on my sword!"

and the words of Demetrius himself, iii. 2. 64: "I had rather give his carcass to my hounds." He also calls attention to the fact that as *sl* and *st* in the old fonts of type were single characters (like *fi* and *fl* now), they were very liable to be confounded by a compositor.

188. *Enter Demetrius, Helena following him.* "However forward and indecorous the conduct of Helena in pursuing Demetrius may appear to modern readers, such examples are very frequent in old romances of chivalry, wherein S. was undoubtedly well read. The beautiful ballad of *The Nut-Brown Maid* might have been more immediately in his recollection, many parts of this scene having a very strong resemblance to it" (Douce).

189. *Wode within this wood.* The 1st quarto has "wodde . . . wood;" the other early eds. "wood . . . wood." *Wode* or *wood*=mad, frantic. Cf. *V. and A.* 740: "frenzies wood;" 1 *Hen VI.* iv. 7. 35:" raging-wood." The same quibble occurs in the *Countess of Pembroke's Yuychurch:*

> "Daphne goes to the *woods,* and vows herself to Diana;
> Phœbus goes stark *wood* for love and fancie to Daphne."

See also Spenser, *F. Q.* i. 4. 34: "Through unadvized rashnes woxen wood;" *Id.* ii. 4. 11: "And calme the tempest of his passion wood," etc. "The name *Woden*," says Verstegan in his *Restitution of Decayed Intelligence*, 1605, "signifies fierce or furious; and in like sense we still retain it, saying when one is in a great rage, that he is *wood*, or taketh on as if he were *wood*." The word is said to be still in use in the north of England.

191. *Get thee gone.* See Gr. 296.

192. *Adamant.* Used here for the magnet; as in *T. and C.* iii. 2. 186:
"As iron to adamant." In 1 *Hen. VI.* i. 4. 52 (the only other passage in
which S. uses the word) it has its modern meaning:

> "I could rend bars of steel
> And spurn in pieces posts of adamant."

Steevens quotes Edward Fenton, *Certaine Secrete Wonders of Nature,*
1569: "there is now a dayes a kind of adamant which draweth unto it
fleshe, and the same so strongly, that it hath power to knit and tie together two mouthes of contrary persons, and drawe the heart of a man
out of his bodie without offendyng any parte of him." Halliwell cites
Chaucer, *Romaunt of the Rose:*

> "Right as an adamant i-wis
> Can drawin to him subtilly
> The iron, that is laied therby,
> So draweth folkis hertes i-wis
> Silver and golde that yevin is;"

and Mandeville, *Travels:* "the ademand, that is the schipmannes ston,
that drawethe the nedle to him." Cf. Bacon, *Essay* 18: "which is a
great Adamant of Acquaintance" (in the Latin, "*magnes* est attrahendi
familiaritates et consuetudines hominum complurium"). Magnetic re-
pulsion is referred to in the old play of *The White Devil:*

> "We'll be as differing as two adamants;
> The one shall shun the other."

196. *Speak you fair.* Speak kindly or gently to you. Cf. *C. of E.* iv.
2. 15: "Didst speak him fair?" *Id.* iv. 4. 157: "you saw they speak us
fair;" *M. of V.* iv. 1. 275: "speak me fair in death" (that is, speak well
of me), etc.

198. *Nor I cannot.* See Gr. 406.

205. *Worser.* Often used by S. It occurs as an adverb in *A. and C.*
ii. 5. 90; *Oth.* i. 1. 95 and iv. 1. 105.

207. *As you use.* So in quartos; the folios read "as you do."

211. *Impeach.* Bring into question, expose to reproach or scandal.
Cf. *M. of V.* iii. 3. 29: "impeach the justice of his state;" *Rich. II.* i. 1.
189: "impeach my height" (see note in our ed. p. 155).

215. *The ill counsel.* The evil suggestions. On the passage, cf. Milton, *Comus,* 398–407.

217. All the early eds. point the line thus: "Your virtue is my privilege: for that;" which is retained by the Camb. editors. *That* is then
"a conjunctional affix" (Gr. 287). The pointing in the text was suggested by Tyrwhitt and adopted by Malone, and is followed by K., Coll.,
D., W., and others.

218. *It is not night,* etc. Johnson thought this a paraphrase of Tibul-
lus:

> "Tu nocte vel atra
> Lumen, et in solis tu mihi turba locis."

Steevens suggests that the poet had in mind *Psalms,* cxxxix. 11.

220. Malone compares 2 *Hen. VI.* iii. 2. 360:

> "A wilderness is populous enough,
> So Suffolk had thy heavenly company."

221. *In my respect.*   In my eyes, in my view.   Cf. *Cymb.* ii. 3. 140 :

> "His meanest garment,
> That ever hath but clipp'd his body, is dearer
> In my respect than all the hairs above thee,
> Were they all made such men."

Cf. the use of the verb in i. 1. 160 above.

228. *Daphne.*   The same myth is alluded to in *T. of S.* ind. 2. 59, and *T. and C.* i. 1. 101.

229. *Griffin.*   Mentioned by S. only here and in 1 *Hen. IV.* iii. 1. 152 : "A clip-wing'd griffin."

230. *Makes speed.*   Makes haste ; as in *Sonn.* 50. 8, *T. G. of V.* iii. 1. 169, 3 *Hen. VI.* ii. 5. 135, etc.

232. *Stay.*   Stay or wait *for ;* as in v. 1. 248 below.   Cf. *M. of V.* ii. 8. 40 ; *Rich. II.* i. 3. 4, etc.

234. *But.*   See Gr. 122.

235. *The field.*   So in 1st quarto ; the other early eds. have "and field."

241. *To die.*   For the use of the infinitive, see Gr. 356.

242. *Fare thee well.*   For *thee* probably = *thou,* see Gr. 212.

246. *Where.*   Metrically a dissyllable.   Gr. 480.   Pope changed it to "whereon."

247. *Oxlips.*   "The greater cowslip, *Primula elatior*" (Schmidt).   Cf. *W. T.* iv. 4. 125 : "bold oxlips."   Steevens quotes Drayton, *Polyolbion,* xv. :

> "To sort these flowers of showe, with other that were sweet,
> The cowslip then they couch, and th' oxlip for her meet."

248. *Over-canopied with luscious woodbine.*   The early eds. have "over-canopi'd," "overcanoped," or "over - cannoped."   For *luscious* Theo. suggested "lush," which is also in the Coll. MS.   *Luscious* is used by S. nowhere else except in *Oth.* i. 3. 354.   *Lush* occurs only in *Temp.* ii. 1. 52.   *Luscious* may be metrically a monosyllable.   Cf. Gr. 470, 471.

249. *Musk-roses.*   Mentioned also in ii. 2. 3 and iv. 1. 3 below ; nowhere else in S.   The only other reference to the *eglantine* is in *Cymb.* iv. 2. 223.

250. *Sometime of.*   "Sometimes during" (Gr. 176).

251. *Flowers.*   The Coll. MS. has "bowers," which W. adopts, though Coll. does not.

253. *Weed.*   Robe, garment.   Cf. ii. 2. 71 below : "Weeds of Athens." See also *Cor.* ii. 3. 229 ; *Lear,* iv. 7. 7, etc.

263. *Fond on her.*   Cf. *J. C.* i. 2. 71 : "jealous on me."   Gr. 180.

264. *Look thou meet.*   For the subjunctive after verbs of command, see Gr. 369.   Cf. ii. 1. 19 above.

265. *Shall.*   See Gr. 315.

SCENE II.—1. *Roundel.*   The word here probably means a dance in a circle ; like *round* in ii. 1. 137 above.   S. uses the word nowhere else. Ben Jonson has it in *A Tale of a Tub,* ii. 1 :

> "you'd have your daughters and maids
> Dance o'er the fields like faies to church, this frost.
> I'll have no rondels, I, in the queen's paths."

The usual meaning of *roundel* is "a kind of rhyming sonnet."

2. *The third part of a minute.* Warb. wanted to read "of the mid-night;" but, as Halliwell remarks, "the quaint subdivision of time exactly suits the character of the fairy speaker and her diminutive world."

3. *Cankers.* Canker-worms; as in *V. and A.* 656, *Sonn.* 35. 4, 95. 2, *Temp.* i. 2. 415, etc. It means the wild rose in *Much Ado* i. 3. 28, and 1 *Hen. IV.* i. 3. 176. Cf. Milton, *Lycidas*, 45: "As killing as the canker to the rose."

The *musk-rose* is not the flower now known by that name in England, which is of more recent introduction. Titania's rose is described by Gerard in his *Herbal*, 1597, the Latin name being given as *Rosa Moscha-ta:* "The single muske-rose hath divers long shootes of a greenish colour, and woodie substance, armed with very sharpe prickles, dividing it selfe into divers branches: whereon do growe long leaves, smooth and shining, made of divers leaves set upon a middle rib, like the other roses. The flowers growe on the tops of the branches of a white colour, and pleasant sweete smell, like that of muske, whereof it took his name; having certaine yellow seedes in the middle, as the rest of the roses have," etc.

4. *Rere-mice.* Bats. Also spelled *rear-mice.* Cf. Golding's *Ovid, Met.* iv.: "And we in English language bats or reremice call the same;" Ben Jonson, *New Inn*, iii. 4:

> "Once a bat and ever a bat,—a rere-mouse,
>   And bird of twilight;"

Holland's *Pliny*, x. 61: "The rere-mouse, or bat, alone of all creatures that fly, bringeth forth young alive, and none but she hath wings made of pannicles or thin skins," etc.

6. *Clamorous.* Perhaps, as Walker suggests, here = wailing. He compares Virgil, *Æn.* iv. 462:

> "Solaque culminibus ferali carmine bubo
>   Saepe queri, et longas in fletum ducere voces."

It may have the same sense in *Rich. II.* v. 5. 56: "Clamorous groans." The noun *clamour* is evidently often used by S. in the sense of wailing; as in *R. of L.* 681, 1804, *Lear*, iv. 3. 33, v. 3. 208, etc. So the verb in *Macb.* ii. 3. 65:

> "the obscure bird
> Clamour'd the livelong night."

Chapman translates κωκυτῷ in *Iliad*, χ. 408, by *clamour:*

> "About both, the people prostrate lay,
> Held down with clamour; all the town veil'd with a cloud of tears;"

and again κωκυτοῦ δ' ἤκουσε καὶ οἰμωγῆς ἀπὸ πύργου (χ. 447) is rendered.

> "But now the clamour flew
> Up to her turret."

7. *Quaint spirits. Quaint* = "fine, neat, pretty, pleasant" (Schmidt). Cf. *Temp.* i. 2. 317: "My quaint Ariel;" *Much Ado*, iii. 4. 22: "a fine, quaint, graceful, and excellent fashion," etc.

For *spirits* Warb. substituted "sports;" and, according to Farmer, *spirit* was sometimes used for *sports.* He quotes Dekker's *If it be no*

Good, etc. : "Now Shalcan, some new spirit?" where the connection shows that it refers to a game of leap-frog. But in the present passage *spirits* probably means fairies.

8. *Offices.* Duties, employments ; as often. Cf. *R. of L.* 1000 ; *Temp.* i. 1. 40, i. 2. 312, v. 1. 156 ; *M. of V.* ii. 6. 43, ii. 9. 61, etc.

9. *Double tongue.* Forked tongue. Cf. iii. 2. 72 :

> "An adder did it ; for with doubler tongue
> Than thine, thou serpent, never adder stung ;"

and *Temp.* ii. 2. 13 : "All wound with adders, who with cloven tongues," etc.

11. *Newts and blind-worms.* The *newt* was supposed to be poisonous. Topsell, in his *Historie of Serpents*, 1608, says that when it is "mooved to anger," its whole body becomes white, "through a kind of white humour or poyson," etc. The *blind-worm* is the slow-worm, of which the same writer says that "it is harmlesse except being provoked," when "the poyson thereof is very strong." "Eye of newt" and "blind-worm's sting" are ingredients of the Witches' cauldron, *Macb.* iv. 1. See note in our ed. p. 228.

13. *Philomel.* The nightingale. Cf. *R. of L.* 1079 :

> "By this, lamenting Philomel had ended
> The well-tun'd warble of her nightly sorrow."

See also *Id.* 1128 ; *Sonn.* 102. 7 ; etc. We have the full name *Philomela* in *P. P.* 197 ; *T. A.* ii. 4. 38, and iv. 1. 53.

14. *Our.* The quarto reading ; the folios have "your."

15. A similar burden is found in several old songs. One, printed in 1530, begins "By, by, lullaby, rockyd I my chyld" (Halliwell).

20. *Spiders.* Topsell says : "Our spyders in England are not so venomous as in other parts of the world, and I have seene a madde man eate many of them without eyther death or death's harme, or any other manifest accident or alteration to ensue," etc. Cowdray, *Treasurie of Similies*, 1600, remarks : "the spider gathereth poyson to the same flowers, that the bee gathereth honie ; so in the Word of God," etc.

25. *Hence, away*, etc. In the old eds. this is made part of the song ; but, as Steevens has noted, it appears to be spoken after the song is over.

30. *Ounce.* The *Felis uncia* (Schmidt) ; mentioned by S. only here.

31. *Pard.* Leopard. Cf. *Temp.* iv. 1. 262 :

> "more pinch-spotted make them
> Than pard or cat o' mountain."

35. *With.* See Gr. 193.

36. *Troth.* Truth. Cf. *Cor.* iv. 5. 198 : "to say the troth on't ;" *Cymb.* v. 5. 274 : "I 'll speak troth," etc. On *forgot*, see Gr. 343 ; and on the reflexive use of *us* in next line, Gr. 223.

45. *O, take the sense*, etc. "Understand *the meaning of my innocence*, or *my innocent meaning*. Let no suspicion of ill enter thy mind" (Johnson).

46. *Love takes the meaning*, etc. "In the conversation of those who are assured of each other's kindness, not *suspicion* but *love takes the*

meaning. No malevolent interpretation is to be made, but all is to be received in the sense which *love* can find, and which *love* can dictate" (Johnson). Henley says : " The idea is exactly similar to that of St. Paul : ' Love thinketh no evil.' " The Coll. MS. has " confidence" for *conference.*

48. *We can.* So in the quartos ; the folios read " can you."

49. *Interchained.* The quarto reading, which, as Halliwell remarks, is "far more forcible and pertinent" than the " interchanged " of the folios.

54. *Beshrew.* " Originally a mild, indeed very mild, form of imprecation = woe to ; sometimes so far from implying a curse, as to be uttered coaxingly, nay even with some tenderness " (Schmidt). In phrases like the present it is " a form of simple asseveration." Cf. v. 1. 295 below : " Beshrew my heart, but I pity the man ;" *M. of V.* ii. 6. 52 : " Beshrew me, but I love her heartily," etc. *Beshrew* is used by S. only in the 1st person of the present, except in *R. and J.* v. 2. 26 : " She will beshrew me much ;" and the pronoun *I* is expressed only in *L. L. L.* v. 2. 46 : " I beshrew all shrews."

61. *Thy love ne'er alter,* etc. For "the subjunctive used optatively or imperatively," as here and in 63, 64, and 65 below, see Gr. 364, 365.

67. *Found.* So in 1st quarto ; " find " in the other early eds. There is little to choose between the two.

68. *Approve.* Prove. Cf. *M. of V.* iii. 2. 79 : " approve it with a text," etc.

71. *Weeds.* See on ii. 1. 253 above.

72. *Despised.* On the omission of the relative, see Gr. 244 ; and for the measure of this and the following lines, Gr. 504.

77. The metre of this line has sorely troubled the critics. Pope changed it to " Near to this lack-love, this kill-curtesie ;" Theo. to " Near to this kill-courtesie ;" Warb. to " Near to this lack-love kill-curtesie ;" Steevens and the Coll. MS. to " Near this lack - love, kill-courtesy." Walker suggested "Nearer this lack-love, this kill-courtesy." Abbott (Gr. 504) says : " It is of course possible that *kill-curt'sy* may have the accent on the first ; but thus we shall have to accent the first *this* and *love* with undue emphasis." On the whole, however, this seems better than the scanning which Abbott prefers : " (Near this) láck-love, thís kill-cóurtesý."

79. *Owe.* Own, possess ; as very often. Cf. *A. W.* v. 3. 297 : " The jeweller that owes the ring is sent for," etc. For the other meaning of *owe,* see iii. 2. 85 below.

80, 81. Cf. *Macb.* i. 3. 19 :

> " Sleep shall neither night nor day
> Hang upon his pent-house lid."

86. *Darkling.* In the dark. Cf. *Lear,* i. 4. 237 : " So out went the candle, and we were left darkling ;" *A. and C.* iv. 15. 10 :

> " O sun,
> Burn the great sphere thou movest in ! darkling stand
> The varying shore o' the world !"

Palsgrave (1530) translates " I went darkeling " by "*je alloye sans chandelle.*" Milton uses the word once, in *P. L.* iii. 39 :

> "as the wakeful bird
> Sings darkling," etc.

See also Johnson, *Vanity of Human Wishes*, 346:

> "Must helpless man, in ignorance sedate,
> Roll darkling down the torrent of his fate?"

and again, in one of his hymns: "On darkling man in pure effulgence shine," etc.

87. *I alone*, etc.   I will go alone.   Gr. 420, 421.

89. *The lesser is my grace.*   S. often uses *lesser* both as adjective and as adverb.   For an example of the latter, see *Macb* v. 2. 13.   *Grace* here either = favour, as Johnson explains it (the less ravour I gain), or good fortune, happiness (Schmidt), as in *M. for M.* i. 4. 69:

> "Unless you have the grace by your fair prayer
> To soften Angelo," etc.

99. *Compare.*   Think myself equal (Schmidt); attempt rivalry (J. H.). Cf. *T. N.* i. 3. 126: "I will not compare with an old man;" 2 *Hen. IV.* ii. 4. 180: "Shall pack-horses . . . Compare with Cæsars," etc.

Sphery = starlike, heavenly.   For *eyne*, see on i. 1. 242.

104. *Nature shows art.*   The quarto reading.   The 1st folio has "Nature her shewes;" and the later folios, 'Nature here shews." Halliwell and some other editors follow Malone's "Nature shows her art." Steevens, who retains "here," explains the passage thus: "On this occasion, says Lysander, the work of nature resembles that of art, namely (as our author expresses it in *L. C.* 286) an object 'glaz'd with crystal.'"

108, 109. Lines like these, and 125, 126 below, certainly give support to the theory that parts at least of this play were written even earlier than 1594.   As W. suggests, "this Dream may have been one of the very first conceptions of the young poet," and was perhaps partly written before he went to London, where, after being laid aside for some years, it was resumed and finished in its present form.

113. *Helena I love.*   So in 1st quarto; the other early eds. have "Helena now I love."

118. *Ripe not.*   "Not ripe;" which Rowe substituted.   For transpositions of *not* in S., see Gr. 305, 420.   Schmidt strangely makes *ripe* here a verb.

119. *Touching now the point*, etc.   Cf. *Hen. VIII.* iii. 2. 223: "I have touch'd the highest point of all my greatness."

120. *Reason becomes the marshal*, etc.   "Reason is now the director of my will" (Halliwell).   Cf. *Macb.* ii. 1. 42: "Thou marshall'st me the way that I was going."

121. *O'erlook.*   Look over, peruse.   Cf. *T. G. of V.* i. 2. 50: "And yet I would I had o'erlooked the letter;" *Lear*, v. 1. 50: "I will o'erlook thy paper," etc.

122. *Love's stories.*   Walker suggested "love-stories."

129. *Good troth.*   Cf. *Hen. VIII.* ii. 3. 33: "Nay, good troth," etc.   It is a contraction of *in good troth* (*T. and C.* iii. 1. 124).   The commonest form of the asseveration is *by my troth* (*M. W.* i. 1. 199, etc.).   *In good sooth* and *good sooth* are both common; so *in sooth* and *sooth* (iii. 2. 265 below).   *Sooth*, like *troth*, originally = truth.   See *Mer.* p. 127.

132. *True gentleness.* "What, in modern language, we should call the *spirit of a gentleman*" (Percy).

133. *Of.* By; as in *Macb.* iii. 6. 27: "Received of the most pious Edward," etc. So in 134, 140, and 142 just below. Gr. 170. Cf. *Acts,* xxiii. 10, 27.

147. *Ay me.* See on i. 1. 132.

149. *Eat.* Ate; which is substituted by many editors, though never found in the early eds. For the participle S. uses both *eat* and *eoten.* See *Macb.* p. 204.

150. *You.* The folios have "yet."

153. *An if.* See Gr. 105.

154. *Of all loves.* For all the love between us; for love's sake. Cf. *M. W.* ii. 2. 119: "Mistress Page would desire you to send her your little page, of all loves." In *Oth.* iii. 1. 13, the quarto of 1622 has "of all loves;" the folio, "for love's sake." Halliwell remarks that the literal signification of the phrase is perhaps seen in the words addressed by Queen Katherine on her trial to Henry VIII.: "Sir, I beseech you for all the loves that hath been between us, and for the love of God, let me have justice and right" (Cavendish's *Life of Wolsey*). Cf. also *A Woman Killed with Kindness* (1617): "Of all the loves betwixt thee and me, tell me what thou thinkest of this?" The phrase occurs in *Gammer Gurton's Needle* in the form, "for al the loves on earth."

For *of* in adjurations, see Gr. 169.

I swoon almost. I almost swoon. The transposition is a common one. See Gr. 29.

156. *Either.* Metrically a monosyllable, as in ii. 1. 32, etc. Gr. 466.

A SEA-NYMPH (ii. 1. 147).

"Up and down, up and down,
I will lead them up and down" (iii. 2. 396, 397).

ACT III.

SCENE I.—2. *Pat, pat.* Exactly. Cf. v. 1. 183 below; also *Hen. VIII.* ii. 3. 84, *Lear*, i. 2. 146, etc.

4. *Tiring-house.* Dressing-room. See quotation in note on i. 2. 91. S. uses the word only here.

7. *Bully Bottom.* Cf. *M. W.* i. 3. 6 : "bully Hercules ;" *Id.* ii. 3. 18 : "bully doctor ;" *Id.* iv. 5. 17 : "Bully knight ! Bully Sir John !" etc.

12. *By 'r lakin.* A colloquial contraction of *By our ladykin*, referring to the Virgin Mary. S. uses it only here and in *Temp.* iii. 3. 1. *By 'r lady* occurs frequently ; as in *M. W.* i. 1. 28, etc.

Parlous. A popular corruption of *perilous.* It came to be used as a mere intensive=*excessive*, or sometimes *wonderful* (Halliwell). Cf. *A. Y. L.* iii. 2. 45 : "a parlous state ;" *Rich. III.* ii. 4. 35 : "a parlous boy." See Gr. 461.

18. *More better.* See Gr. 11.

22. *Eight and six.* That is, in alternate verses of eight and six syllables.

25. *Afeard.* Not a vulgarism, but used by S. interchangeably with
afraid. Cf. *Macb.* i. 7. 39 :

> "Art thou afeard
> To be the same in thine own act and valour
> As thou art in desire?"

and see note in our ed., p. 163.

30. *Your lion.* A common colloquial use of *your.* See Gr. 221.
Howell, in his *Instructions for Forraine Travel* (1642), says : "There is
an odd kind of Anglicism, wherein some do frequently express themselves, as to say—Your Boores of Holland, sir ; Your Jesuits of Spain,
sir ; Your Courtesans of Venice, sir ; whereunto one answered (not im-
pertinently) *My* Courtesans, sir ? Pox on them all for me ! they are
none of *my* Courtesans."

39. *Pity of my life.* For the *of*, see Gr. 174.

41. *Tell them plainly*, etc. As Malone remarks, it is not improbable
that this was suggested by an incident related in a collection of jests in
MS. Harl. 6395 : "There was a spectacle presented to Queen Elizabeth
on the water, and among others Harry Goldingham was to represent
Arion upon the dolphin's backe ; but finding his voice to be very hoarse
and unpleasant, when he came to performe it, he teares off his disguise,
and sweares he was none of Arion, not he, but eene honest Harry Goldingham ; which blunt discoverie pleas'd the Queene better than if it
had gone through in the right way ; yet he could order his voice to an
instrument exceeding well." Scott has made good use of the incident
in *Kenilworth.*

42. *There is two*, etc. See Gr. 335.

48. *It doth shine.* On the anachronism, see above, p. 122.

50. *The great chamber.* "The state-room" (Halliwell).

52. *A bush of thorns.* An old superstition identified the man in the
moon with the man that gathered sticks on the Sabbath day (*Numb.* xv.
32). Cf. *The Testament of Creseide* :

> "Next after him come lady Cynthia,
>
> . . . .
>
> And on her brest a chorle painted ful even
> Bering a bushe of thornis on his bake,
> Which for his theft might clime no ner the heven."

54. *Present.* Represent ; not a vulgarism. Cf. *Temp.* iv. 1. 167 :
"when I presented Ceres ;" *Hen. VIII.* prol. 5 :

> "Such noble scenes as draw the eye to flow
> We now present ;"

Milton, *Il Pens.* 99 : "Presenting Thebes, or Pelops' line," etc.

67. *Cue.* Still used as a stage term for the ending of a speech, as the
catch-word given to the actor who is to speak next. Cf. *M. W.* iii. 3.
39 : "remember you your cue," etc. It is used figuratively in *Hen. V.*
iii. 6. 130, *Oth.* i. 2. 83, etc.

70. *A play toward.* That is, "in preparation, near at hand" (Schmidt).
Cf. *T. of S.* i. 1. 68 : "here's some good pastime toward ;" *Ham.* i. 1. 77 :

"What might be toward?" *Lear*, iii. 3. 21 : " There is some strange thing toward," etc. Halliwell cites many instances from other writers of the time.

73. *Savours.* Abbott (Gr. 333) makes this a verb, Schmidt a noun. The Coll. MS. changes *of* to "have." In the next line Pope substituted "doth" for *hath ;* but, as Halliwell remarks, "it is scarcely requisite to correct the sense of a speech which is probably intended to be ignorantly formed."

77. *A while.* Theo. suggested "a whit," for the sake of the rhyme.

79. *A stranger Pyramus,* etc. The quartos assign this speech to *Quince ;* the folios, to *Puck*, to whom it evidently belongs. *Here,* as Steevens suggests, probably means in the theatre where the play is being acted.

85. *Brisky* is of course burlesque for *brisk. Juvenal* (=youth) is used only here, and by Armado (*L. L. L.* i. 2. 8, iii. 1. 67) and Falstaff in jesting (2 *Hen. IV.* i. 2. 22). *Eke,* then obsolescent, S. puts into the mouth of no other character except Pistol and the Host (*M. W.* i. 3. 105, ii. 3. 77).

92. *Bottom with an ass's head.* Scot, in his *Discoverie of Witchcraft,* 1584, gives the following recipe for such a transformation : "Cut off the head of a horsse or an ass (before they be dead), otherwise the vertue or strength thereof will be the lesse effectuall, and make an earthen vessell of fit capacitie to conteine the same, and let it be filled with the oile and fat thereof ; cover it close, and dawbe it over with lome : let it boile over a soft fier three daies continuallie, that the flesh boiled may run into oile, so as the bare bones may be seen : beate the haire into powder, and mingle the same with the oile ; and annoint the heads of the standers by, and they shall seeme to have horsses or asses heads."

93. *If I were fair,* etc. "Perhaps we ought to point thus : If I were, [that is, as true, etc.] fair Thisby, I were only thine " (Malone).

97. *Through bog,* etc. As two syllables are wanting, Johnson suggested " Through bog, through mire ;" and Ritson (to preserve the alliteration) "Through bog, through burn," etc.

98. *Sometime a horse,* etc. Cf. the old ballad, quoted above (on ii. 1. 3) :

> "Sometimes I meete them like a man,
>   Sometimes an ox, sometimes an hound ;
> And to a horse I turn me can,
>   And trip and trot them round and round," etc.

See also the ballad of *The Merry Pranks of Robin Good-fellow :*

> "Sometimes a neighing horse was he,
>   sometimes a gruntling hog,
> Sometimes a bird, sometimes a crow,
>   sometimes a snarling dog.
>
> . . . .
>
> Sometimes a cripple he would seeme,
>   sometimes a souldier brave :
> Sometimes a fox, sometimes a hare ;
>   brave pastimes would he have.
> Sometimes an owle he'd seeme to be,
>   sometimes a skipping frog ;

> Sometimes a kirne, in Irish shape,
>   to leape ore mire or bog:
> Sometime he'd counterfeit a voyce,
>   and travellers call astray,
> Sometimes a walking fire he'd be,
>   and lead them from their way."

The *fire*, both here and in the play, is of course the *ignis fatuus*, or Will-of-the-wisp.

100, 101. *And neigh, and bark*, etc. Cf. *Ham.* iii. i. 151 : " The courtier's, scholar's, soldier's, eye, tongue, sword ;" *Macb.* i. 3. 60 :

> " Speak then to me, who neither beg nor fear
> Your favours nor your hate ;"

and *W. T.* iii. 2. 164 :

> " though I with death and with
> Reward did threaten and encourage him."

106. *An ass-head of your own.* Johnson inferred from this that Snout had mentioned an ass's head, and therefore wanted to read : " *Snout.* O Bottom, thou art changed ! what do I see on thee ? an ass's head ?" But this is unnecessary, "the phrase being a vernacular one of the day" (Halliwell). The fact that Bottom is unconscious of his transformation makes its introduction here very comical. So with "this is to make an ass of me," just below.

108. *Translated.* Transformed. See on i. 1. 191.

114. *The ousel cock.* The *ousel, oosel*, or *woosel* (as it is spelled in the early eds.) was the blackbird. Halliwell quotes Barnefield, *The Affectionate Shepherd* (1594) :

> " House-doves are white, and oozels blackebirdes bee,
> Yet what a difference in the taste we see ;"

Castell of Health (1595) : " Blacke-birds or ousyls among wild-foule have the chief praise for lightnes of digestion," etc. The name is now applied to a species which is larger than the ordinary English blackbird, and has a white crescent on the breast.

116. *The throstle.* The thrush, *Turdus musicus* (Schmidt) ; also mentioned in *M. of V.* i. 2. 65. Cf. Gower, *Conf. Am.* (1554) : " The throstel with the nightingale ;" Drayton, *Shepherd's Garland* (1593) :

> "The throstlecock, by breaking of the day,
> Chants to his swete full many a lovely lay," etc.

117. *Quill.* Probably = pipe ; not wing-feather, as Schmidt explains it. Cf. Milton, *Lycidas*, 188 : " He touch'd the tender stops of various quills."

118. *What angel*, etc. Malone says : " Perhaps a parody on a line in *The Spanish Tragedy*, often ridiculed by the poets of our author's time : ' What outcry calls me from my naked bed ?' "*

120. *Plain-song.* A musical term, meaning "the simple melody without any variations." Cf. Chaucer, *The Cuckow and the Nightingale*, 118,

---

* It could hardly have been the "naked bed" that was ridiculed, for that was a common phrase. Cf. *V. and A.* 397 : " in her naked bed ;" and see other examples in Nares.

where the cuckoo says : " For my song is both true and plaine ;" Skel-ton, *Phyllyp Sparrowe :*

> "To kepe just playne songe
> Our chanters shall be your cuckoue," etc.

123. *Set his wit.* Oppose his wit. Cf. *T. and C.* ii. 1. 94 : " Will you set your wit to a fool's ?" *K. John,* iii. 1. 264 :

> "And like a civil war set'st oath to oath,
> Thy tongue against thy tongue," etc.

124. *Cry 'cuckoo.'* Cf. *L. L. L.* v. 2. 908 :

> "The cuckoo then, on every tree,
> Mocks married men," etc.

Never so = ever so much.

128. *Enthralled.* Cf. i. 1. 136 above.

129. *Perforce.* See on ii. 1. 26 above.

130. In the 2d quarto and the folios this line precedes 128.

135. *Gleek.* Jest. Cf. *Hen. V.* v. 1. 78 : I have seen you gleeking and galling at this gentleman," etc. We have the noun in 1 *Hen. VI.* iii. 2. 123 and *R. and J.* iv. 5. 115.

141. *Whether.* See on i. 1. 69.

142. *Rate.* Cf. *Temp.* i. 2. 92 : " o'erpriz'd all popular rate," etc. Some eds. put a comma after *spirit.*

146. *Jewels from the deep.* Cf. *Rich. III.* i. 4. 32 :

> "reflecting gems
> Which woo'd the shiny bottom of the deep."

150. In the 1st folio this line appears as a stage direction : " *Enter Pease-blossome, Cobweb, Moth, Mustard-seede, and foure Fairies.*"

151. The reading of the early eds. is : "*Fai.* Ready ; and I, and I, and I. Where shall we go ?"

154. *Apricocks.* Apricots (*Prunus Armeniaca*). The word is used by S. only here and in *Rich. II.* iii. 4. 29. *Dewberries* (*Rubus cæsius*) he mentions nowhere else. For the derivation of *apricock,* see Wb.

158. *Eyes.* Johnson says : " I know not how Shakespeare, who commonly derived his knowledge of nature from his own observation, happened to place the glow-worm's light in his eyes, which is only in his tail." But, as M. Mason and Halliwell suggest, the poet may have intended to designate the lights of the insect as *eyes* without any reference to their situation. For other allusions to the glow-worm, see *V. and A.* 621 ; *M. W.* v. 5. 82 ; *Ham.* i. 5. 89 ; and *Per.* ii. 3. 43.

159. *To have my love to bed.* Cf. *T. of S.* ind. 2. 39 : " Or wilt thou sleep ? we 'll have thee to a couch," etc.

162. *Do him courtesies.* Cf. *T. of S.* iv. 2. 91 : " to do you courtesy," etc. So we have " do respect " (*Lear,* ii. 2. 137), " do salutation " (*Rich. III.* v. 3. 210 ; *J. C.* iv. 2. 5), " do obsequious sorrow " (*Ham.* i. 2. 92), etc.

167. *Cry your worships mercy.* That is, I beg your pardon. Cf. *M. W.* iii. 5. 27 ; *Much Ado,* i. 2. 26 ; *T. G. of V.* v. 4. 94, etc. In *Oth.* v. 1. 93, we have, " I cry you gentle pardon." Some eds. print " worship's."

170. *Desire you of more acquaintance.* Needlessly altered by Rowe to "of you." Steevens quotes *An Humorous Day's Mirth*, 1599 : "I do desire you of more acquaintance;" Greene, *Groatsworth of Wit*, 1621 : "craving you of more acquaintance," etc. See also Spenser, *F. Q.* ii. 9. 42 : "If it be I, of pardon I you pray." Gr. 174. In line 176 below, the folios have "of you," the quartos "you of."

171. *If I cut my finger*, etc. Alluding to the household use of cobweb for stopping the effusion of blood.

174. *Squash.* An immature peascod. Cf. *T. N.* i. 5. 166 : "as a squash is before it is a peascod;" *W. T.* i. 2. 160 : "this kernel, this squash, this gentleman." Our Yankee word *squash* is of wholly different origin. See Wb.

179. *Your patience.* Perhaps, as Halliwell suggests, an ironical reference to the proverb, "as hot as mustard." Hanmer suggested "parentage;" Farmer, "passions;" and M. Mason, "you passing well."

181. *I promise you.* I assure you. Cf. *M. W.* iii. 2. 72 ; *Much Ado*, iv. 2. 47, etc.

182. *I desire you of more.* The reading of the Coll. MS. The quartos and first two folios have "desire you more;" the other folios, "your more."

185. *The moon*, etc. Cf. ii. 1. 159. Walker considers it an allusion to the supposed origin of dew in the moon, and compares *Macb.* iii. 5. 23 ; also Fletcher, *Faithful Shepherdess*, iv. 4 :

> "Showers of more price, more orient, and more round,
> Than those that hang upon the moon's pale brow."

187. *Enforced.* Violated ; as in *T. A.* v. 3. 38, *Cymb.* iv. 1. 18, etc.

188. *Love's.* Pope's emendation for the "lovers" of the early eds. The Coll. MS. has "lover's tongue and." Halliwell (who reads "lover's") remarks that "to tie up one's tongue" was a common phrase=to be silent. Cf. *Cynthia's Revels :* "Tye up your tongue, mungril;" *Women Pleased :* "First, there's to tye your tongue up ;" B. and F., *Elder Brother :* "You may tie his tongue up, as you would doe your purse-strings," etc.

SCENE II.—3. *In extremity.* To the utmost, in the extreme. Cf. *Ham.* iii. 2. 178 : "In neither aught, or in extremity," etc. For *must*, see Gr. 314.

5. *Night-rule.* According to some authorities, a corruption of *night-revel* (from the old spelling "night-reuel "), and Wb. gives no other derivation. Nares suggests that it means "such conduct as generally *rules* in the night." Halliwell remarks that there was a common use of the word *rule*, which may be intended here. He cites the old statutes of London, as given by Stowe : "No man shall, after the houre of nine at the night, keep any rule whereby any such sudden outcry be made in the still of the night, as making any affray," etc. See also Middleton, *Tom Tyler and his Wife :* "Here is good rule !— . . . here is pretty rule !"

9. *Patches.* Clowns. Cf. *M. of V.* ii. 5. 46 : "The patch is kind enough ;" *Temp.* iii. 2. 71 : "Thou scurvy patch !" *Macb.* v. 3. 15 : "What soldiers, patch ?" etc.

Mechanicals. Mechanics. Used as a noun again in 2 *Hen. VI.* i. 3. 196 ; as an adjective in the same sense, in *J. C.* i. 1. 3, *M. W.* ii. 2. 90, and 2 *Hen. IV.* v. 5. 38.

13. *Barren sort.* Dull company. Cf. *T. N.* i. 5. 90 : "such a barren rascal ;" *Ham.* iii. 2. 46 : "barren spectators," etc. For *sort* cf. 21 below : "many in sort" (that is, many in a flock, many together) ; *Rich. II.* iv. 1. 245 : "a sort of traitors ;" 2 *Hen. VI.* ii. 1. 167 : "a sort of naughty persons," etc. See also *Psalm* lxii. 3 (Prayer-Book version) : "Ye shall be slain, all the sort of you." Halliwell gives many examples of the word from writers of the time.

Thick-skin (which Hanmer changed to "thick-skull") was a common term of contempt for a country clown. S. uses it again in *M. W.* iv. 5. 2. Cf. *Albion's England*, 1602 : "That he, so foul a thick-skin, should so fair a lady catch," etc. The idea is an old one. See Holland's *Pliny*, i. 346 : "Some measure not the finenesse of spirit and wit by the puritie of bloud, but suppose that creatures are brutish, more or lesse, according as their skin is thicker or thinner."

14. *Presented.* See on iii. 1. 54.

15. *In.* Into. See Gr. 159.

17. *Nole.* Also spelled *nowl.* It means properly the top of the head, but is also used for the head itself. Cf. Spenser, *F. Q.* vii. 7. 39 : "For yet his noule was totty of the must ;" *Mirror for Magistrates :* "All kinds of causes in their craftie noles," etc.

18. *Answered.* See Gr. 474.

21. *Choughs.* The *Corvus monedula* (Schmidt). Cf. *Macb.* iii. 4. 125 ; *Temp.* ii. 1. 266 ; *Lear,* iv. 6. 13, etc.

25. *At our stamp.* Johnson wished to change this to "at a stump," since fairies are not represented as stamping, or as big enough to stamp with much force. Steevens quotes what Oberon says, iv. 1. 82 below :

> "Sound, music ! Come, my queen, take hands with me,
> And rock the ground whereon these sleepers be."

Scot, in his *Discoverie of Witchcraft,* 1584, represents Robin Goodfellow, when offended, as crying "What have we here ? Hemton, hamten, here will I never more tread nor stampen."

26. *He.* This one. See Gr. 217. On *murther,* see *Rich. II.* p. 158.

30. *Yielders.* Cf. 1 *Hen. IV.* v. 3. 11 : "I was not born a yielder."

36. *Latch'd.* Caught, infected. Some explain it as=anointed, smeared ; but, as Schmidt remarks, no other instance of that meaning has been pointed out. S. uses it (=catch) in *Macb.* iv. 3. 195, *Lear,* ii. 1. 54 (folio reading), and *Sonn.* 113. 6. Cf. Spenser, *Shep. Kal.,* March :

> "From bough to bough he lepped light,
> And oft the pumies latched."

40. *Of force.* Of necessity ; used only in connection with *must.* Cf. *L. L. L.* i. 1. 148 ; *M. of V.* iv. 1. 56 ; *J. C.* iv. 3. 203, etc. *Perforce* is used in the same sense ; as in 90 below.

44. *Breath.* Language. See on ii. 2. 148. Cf. *M. for M.* v. 1. 122 :

> "Shall we thus permit
> A blasting and a scandalous breath to fall
> On him so near us?"

L

45. *Chide.* See on ii. 2. 141. On *should*, see Gr. 323.
48. *Being o'er shoes*, etc. Cf. *Macb.* iii. 4. 136 :

> "I am in blood
> "Stepp'd in so far that, should I wade no more,
> Returning were as tedious as go o'er."

Walker (who approves Coleridge's conjecture, "knee-deep") quotes Heywood, *Woman Killed with Kindness :*

> "Come, come, let's in;
> Once o'er shoes, we are straight o'er head in sin."

55. *With the Antipodes.* Warb. suggested "i' th' Antipodes;" but Steevens shows that "with the Antipodes" was a common expression. Cf. *Rich. II.* iii. 2. 49 : "While we were wandering with the Antipodes." See also *Much Ado*, ii. 1. 273 and *M. of V.* v. 1. 127.

56. *Murther'd.* The folio has "murdred" here, and "murderer" in 58 and 60 ; but "mutrherer" in 57 and "murther" in 26.

57. *Dead.* Pope substituted "dread;" but *dead* is sometimes=deadly (Schmidt). Cf. *W. T.* iv. 4. 445 : "From the dead blow of it ;" *K. John*, v. 7. 65 : "these dead news ;" *Rich. II.* iv. 1. 10 : "that dead time when Gloster's death was plotted."

61. *Venus.* The planet is again alluded to in 107 below; also in 2 *Hen. IV.* ii. 4. 286, 1 *Hen. VI.* i. 2. 144, and *T. A.* ii. 3. 30.

70. *Brave touch.* Schmidt explains this "test or proof of bravery," and cites *Cor.* iv. 1. 49 : "of noble touch" (=of tried nobleness). Steevens makes it="a cunning feat or trick." Cf. Palsgrave : "Touche, a crafty dede, *tour*." Johnson says : "*Touch* in Shakespeare's time was the same with our *exploit*, or rather *stroke*;" and quotes Ascham : "Mason was very merry, pleasantly playing both with the shrewd touches of many curst boys, and the small discretion of many lewd schoolmasters."

71. *Worm.* Serpent. Cf. *Macb.* iii. 4. 29 ; *A. and C.* v. 3. 243, 256, 261, 268, 282, etc. Schmidt remarks that "it is in this sense undoubtedly that Venus calls Death 'earth's worm,' *V. and A.* 933."

72. *Doubler tongue.* See on ii. 2. 9.

74. *On a mispris'd mood.* On a mistaken fancy. Steevens explains it "in a mistaken manner." For *on*=in, see Gr. 180. The Coll. MS. has "in a misprised flood." S. uses *misprised* nowhere else. Cf. *misprision* in 90 below.

80. *So.* Inserted by Pope. All the early eds. read :

> "And from thy hated presence part I: see me no more
> Whether he be dead or no."

81. *Whether.* See on i. 1. 69. Gr. 466.

87. *If for his tender*, etc. If I wait a little for the offer it will make me.

90. *Misprision.* Mistake. Cf. *Sonn.* 87. 11 ; *Much Ado*, iv. 1. 187 ; *L. L. L.* iv. 3. 98, etc.

92. *Holding troth.* Keeping faith. See on ii. 2. 36.

93. *Confounding.* Breaking. It is often=destroying, ruining, etc. See *M. of V.* iii. 2. 278 ; *Rich. II.* iii. 4. 60, etc. Cf. the use of *confusion* in 2 *L.* 1. 149.

96. *Fancy-sick.* Lovesick. See on i. 1. 155. *Cheer* = face; as in *M. of V.* iii. 2. 314, etc. Cf. Spenser, *F. Q.* i. 1. 2 : "But of his cheere did seeme too solemne sad ;" Dryden, *Hind and Panther,* iii. 437 : "Till frowning skies began to change their cheer," etc.

97. *That costs the fresh blood dear.* Alluding to the old superstition that every sigh was indulged at the expense of a drop of blood. Cf. 2 *Hen. VI.* iii. 2. 61, 63 ; 3 *Hen. VI.* iv. 4. 22 ; *Ham.* iv. 7. 123 ; *Much Ado,* iii. 1. 78. On *costs*, see Gr. 247.

99. *Against she do appear.* See Gr. 142.

101. *Swifter than arrow,* etc. Cf. *R. and J.* i. 4. 5 : "a Tartar's painted bow of lath." Douce quotes Golding's *Ovid* :

> "and though that she
> Did fly as swift as arrow from a Turkye bowe."

For *Tartar,* cf. 263 below.

103. *Hit with Cupid's archery.* See ii. 1. 163 above.

112. *Mistook.* See Gr. 343.

113. *A lover's fee.* This may mean a lover's reward or recompense, in a general sense ; but, according to Halliwell, the phrase had the specific meaning of "three kisses." He quotes an old MS. ballad (of about 1650) : "How many, saies Batt ; why, three, saies Matt, for that's a mayden's fee ;" and Warner, *Albion's England :* "Or Mercurie had apted me to plead for lovers fees."

114. *Fond pageant.* Silly show. On *fond,* cf. 317 below ; also *V. and A.* 1021 ; *Sonn.* 3. 7 ; *M. of V.* ii. 9. 27, iii. 3. 9 ; *J. C.* iii. 1. 39, etc. Here the meanings of *silly* and *doting* seem to be blended, as in ii. 2. 88. *Pageant,* as Schmidt notes, means usually a theatrical exhibition, literal or figurative. Cf. *Temp.* iv. 1. 155 : "this insubstantial pageant ;" *L. L. L.* v. 1. 118 : "show, or pageant, or antique, or firework ;" *A. Y. L.* iii. 4. 55 : "a pageant truly played," etc. S. uses *pageant* once as a verb (= play, mimic) in *T. and C.* i. 3. 151 : "He pageants us."

119. *Needs.* Of necessity. Gr. 125. For *alone* = "above all things," see Gr. 18. Halliwell quotes Withals' *Dict.,* ed. 1608 : "This is sport alone for the cat. He meaneth, the beast, the fool, is delighted with it ;" and *Englishman for my Money,* 1616 : "Why this were sport alone for me to doe."

121. *Preposterously.* Perversely. Cf. *Hen. V.* ii. 2. 112 ; *Oth.* i. 3. 62, etc.

122. *Should woo.* See Gr. 328.

123. *Comes.* For the singular form, see Gr. 336.

124. *Vows so born.* That is, being so born. Gr. 376, 377.

127. *The badge of faith.* Alluding to the badges (that is, family crests) anciently worn on the sleeves of servants and retainers (Steevens). Cf. *Temp.* v. 1. 267 :

> "Mark but the badges of these men, my lords,
> Then say if they be true ;"

R. of L. 1054 : "A badge of fame to slander's livery," etc. In *Sonn.* 44. 14, tears are called "badges of either's love."

128. *Advance.* Show. Cf. *Much Ado,* iii. 1. 10 ; "princes, that advance their pride," etc.

140. *Cherries.* Cf. v. 1. 187 : "cherry lips;" *Rich. III.* i. 1. 94: "A cherry lip."

141, 142. *High Taurus' snow*, etc.   Makes the snow of Mount Taurus look black as a crow.

144. *Princess.*   Changed by Hanmer to "pureness," and by the Coll. MS. to "impress."   Steevens refers to Sir W. Raleigh's *Discovery of Guiana*, where the pine-apple is called "the princess of fruits;" and to Wyatt's *Poems:* "Of beauty princesse chief."   Dyce remarks : "When Mr. Collier offered the very unnecessary conjecture *impress* on account of the context (*seal*), he did not perceive that these two rapturous enco- miums on the hand of Helena have no connection with each other.   De- metrius terms it *princess of pure white* because its whiteness exceeded all other whiteness, and *seal of bliss* because it was to confirm the happiness of her accepted lover."

On *seal of bliss*, cf. *A. and C.* iii. 13. 125 :

> "My playfellow, your hand ; this kingly seal
> And plighter of high hearts."

See also *K. John,* ii. 1. 20, and *M. for M.* iv. 1. 6.

150. *Join in souls.*   "That is, join heartily, unite in the same mind" (Steevens).   Hanmer changed it to "join in flouts;" Warb. to "join in- solents ;" M. Mason conjectured "join in soul ;" and Tyrwhitt, "join, ill souls."

151. *Were men.*   The quarto reading ; the folios have "are men."

153. *Superpraise.*   Used by S. nowhere else.   *Parts*=gifts, endow- ments, qualities.   Cf. *Sonn.* 17. 4 ; *L. L. L.* iv. 2. 118, etc.   The singular is used in the same sense in *L. L. L.* iv. 1. 32 ; *Ham.* iv. 7. 77, etc.

156. *Rivals to mock.*   Rivals in mocking.

157. *Trim.*   Fine, nice ; usually, as here, ironical.   Cf. *T. and C.* iv. 5. 33 ; *T. A.* v. 1. 96, etc.

158. *Conjure.*   Accented by S. on either syllable, without regard to the meaning.   Thus we have *conjúre*, in the magical sense, in *R. and J.* ii. 1. 26, *Oth.* i. 3. 105, etc. ; and *cónjure*=solemnly appeal to, in *M. for M.* v. 1. 48, *Macb.* iv. 1. 50, etc.

159. *Of noble sort.*   Of noble nature.   Cf. 2 *Hen. IV.* v. 2. 18: "of vile sort," etc.   Malone explains *sort* here as=quality or rank ; a mean- ing which it sometimes has in S.   Cf. *M. for M.* iv. 4. 19 ; *Much Ado*, i. 1. 7, 33 ; *Hen. V.* iv. 7. 142 and iv. 8. 80.

160. *Extort.*   Take away (make impatient).

169. *I will none.*   I will none of her, will have nothing to do with her.   Cf. *T. N.* i. 3. 113: "She will none of me," etc.   Gr. 53.

171. *With her.*   Johnson's emendation for the "to her" of the early eds.   Halliwell quotes Phaer's translation of Virgil, 1573 : "And after service don, do him in gestwise entertaine ;" Warner's *Albion's England,* vi. 31 : "I entring guest-wise on a time the frolicke Thebane court," etc.

172. *Home return'd.*   Cf. *Sonn.* 109. 5 :

> "That is my home of love; if I have rang'd,
> Like him that travels I return again."

Johnson quotes Prior :

"No matter what beauties I saw in my way,
They were but my visits; but thou art my home."

175. *Aby.* The reading of 1st quarto; the other early eds. have "abide." *Aby it dear*, though not found elsewhere in S., was a common phrase with the writers of the time. Halliwell quotes many examples of it; as Holinshed, *Hist. of Scotland:* "they should deere abye it;" *Tragedie of Gorboduc*, 1565: "Thou, Porrex, thou shalt dearely abye the same;" *Pinner of Wakefield*, 1599: "Thou shalt dear aby this blow," etc.

177. *His function.* Its office. *Function* is elsewhere used of bodily organs; as in *Sonn.* 113. 3, *L. L. L.* iv. 3. 332, *Hen. VIII.* iii. 2. 187, etc.

188. *Oes.* Orbs. S. elsewhere uses *O* for anything round. See *L. L. L.* v. 2. 45, *Hen. V.* prol. 13, and *A. and C.* v. 2. 81. Steevens quotes John Davies of Hereford's *Microcosmos*, 1605: "Which silver oes and spangles over-ran;" and *The Partheneia Sacra*, 1633: "the purple canopy of the earth, powdered over and beset with silver oes," etc. Cf. Bacon, *Essay* 37: "And *Oes*, or *Spangs*, as they are of no great Cost, so they are of most Glory." Halliwell notes that the eyes were sometimes called *oes;* as in *MS. Bodl.* 160: "Frome your oes the teres wald starte."

194. *In spite of.* In derision of. Cf. *R. and J.* i. 1. 85 and 1 *Hen. VI.* ii. 4. 106.

195. *Injurious Hermia.* Cf. 3 *Hen. VI.* iii. 3. 78: "injurious Margaret;" *Cor.* iii. 3. 69: "thou injurious tribune," etc.

197. *Derision.* A quadrisyllable, like *partition* in 210 below. See also i. 1. 149, 152, etc. Gr. 479.

200. *Chid.* S. uses both *chid* and *chidden* as the participle; the latter always before a noun. Cf. *J. C.* i. 2. 184. See line 312 below.

Hasty-footed time. Cf. *Sonn.* 19. 6: "swift-footed Time."

201. *O, is all.* The reading of quartos and 1st folio; the later folios have "O, and is all." Gibbon observes that in a poem of Gregory Nazianzen on his own life there are some beautiful lines which speak the pangs of injured and lost friendship, resembling these. He adds: "Shakespeare had never read the poems of Gregory Nazianzen: he was ignorant of the Greek language; but his mother tongue, the language of nature, is the same in Cappadocia and in Britain."

202. *Childhood innocence.* Often printed with a hyphen. See Gr. 430.

203. *Like two artificial gods.* Like two creators in art; or, as Walker Latinizes it, "deabus artificibus similes." *Artificial*=artful (a word not used by S.) in *Per.* v. 1. 72: "thy prosperous and artificial feat."

204. *Needles.* Metrically a monosyllable. Gr. 465. Many eds. follow Steevens in printing "neelds," an old way of spelling the word. Cf. Stanyhurst's *Virgil*, 1582: "on neeld-wrought carpets;" Gorges's *Lucan*, 1614: "Like pricking neelds," etc.

205. *Sampler.* Used by S. only here and in *T. A.* ii. 4. 39.

206. *Of.* For the use of the preposition, see Gr. 178.

208. *Incorporate.* Cf. *C. of E.* ii. 2. 124: "undividable, incorporate;" *Hen. V.* v. 2. 494: "their incorporate league," etc. For the form of the word, see Gr. 342.

211. *Lovely.* The Coll. MS. substitutes "loving."

213. *Two of the first, like*, etc. The early eds. all have "first life." Theo. made the correction. The allusion is to "the double coats in heraldry that belong to man and wife as *one person*, but which have but *one crest*" (Douce). Cf. *2 Hen. VI.* iv. 10. 75: "a herald's coat."

214. *Due.* Belonging. See on i. 1. 154.

215. *Rent.* The reading of all the early eds. Rowe changed it to "rend." S. uses the word six times; as in *Macb.* iv. 3. 168, *T. A.* iii. 1. 261, etc. It is found in *Jer.* iv. 30, and in older eds. of the *A. V.* in many other passages; as in *Exod.* xxxix. 23, *Isa.* lxiv. 1, *Matt.* vii. 6, etc. See on i. 2. 22 above.

220. *Passionate.* The folio reading; omitted in the quartos.

225. *Even but now.* See Gr. 38.

230. *Affection.* See on 197 above.

232. *Grace.* Good fortune (Schmidt). See on ii. 2. 89 above.

233. *Hung upon.* Clung to. Cf. 260 below.

237. *Persever.* The regular spelling and accent in S. We have it rhyming with *ever* in *A. W.* iv. 2. 36, 37:

> "Say thou art mine, and ever
> My love, as it begins, so shall persever."

So *perseverance* is accented on the second syllable. See *T. and C.* iii. 3. 150 and *Macb.* iv. 3. 93. Gr. 492.

In the present passage the 2d quarto and folios read "I, do, persever;" the 1st quarto, "I doe. Persever." In the old eds. *ay* is always printed "I."

239. *Each at other.* Cf. *Macb.* i. 3. 155: "each to other" (so also in *A. and C.* ii. 2. 138), etc. Gr. 12.

240. *Well carried.* Well managed, or executed. Cf. *Much Ado*, iv. 1. 212; *Hen. VIII.* i. 1. 100, etc.

242. *Argument.* "Subject of light merriment" (Johnson). Cf. *1 Henry IV.* ii. 2. 100: "it would be argument for a week," etc.

248. *She.* That is, Hermia.

250. *Prayers.* The early eds. all have "praise." The correction is due to Theo.

257. *Ethiope.* Cf. *R. and J.* i. 5. 48: "Like a rich jewel in an Ethiope's ear," etc. The word is used adjectively in *A. Y. L.* iv. 3. 35: "Such Ethiope words, blacker in their effect."

257, 258. *No, no, sir*, etc. The 1st quarto reads "No, no; heele Seeme to breake loose;" the 2d quarto, "No, no, hee 'l seeme to breake loose" (as one line); the 1st folio, "No, no, Sir, seeme to breake loose" (one line), which is followed by the other folios. Malone combined the two readings: "No, no, he 'll—Sir, Seem to break loose," etc., and explained the passage thus: "Demetrius, I suppose, would say,— 'No, no: he 'll not have the resolution to disengage himself from Hermia.' But turning abruptly to Lysander, he addresses him ironically: 'Sir, seem to break loose,' etc." The meaning is essentially the same if we adopt the folio reading, except that the whole is addressed to Lysander: "No, no, sir, you are not really trying to get free; keep up the pretence of doing so, you coward !" On the whole this seems preferable to the quarto reading, though there is not much to choose between them.

The Camb. editors think that a line or more may have been lost from the text at this point.

260. *Cat.* Cf. *Temp.* ii. 2. 86: "here is that which will give language to you, cat." On *burr*, cf. *M. for M.* iv. 3. 189: "Nay, friar; I am a kind of burr; I shall stick."

263. *Tartar.* See on 101 above. Cf. *Macb.* iv. 1. 29.

264. *Potion.* The reading of 1st quarto; the other early eds. have "poison."

265. *Sooth.* See on ii. 2. 129. Cf. *J. C.* ii. 4. 20: "Sooth, madam, I hear nothing," etc.

267. *Bond.* For other instances of play upon the word, see *C. of E.* iv. 4. 128 and *Cymb.* v. 4. 28.

272. *Wherefore.* For the accent, see Gr. 490.

What news, my love! The reading of all the early eds. "In other words, what novelty is this?" (Halliwell). The Coll. MS. has "What means my love?"—but no change seems called for.

275. *Since night you loved me.* For the tense after *since*, see Gr. 132, 347. Cf. ii. 1. 146.

279. For the measure, see Gr. 456.

282. *Juggler.* Metrically a trisyllable. Gr. 477.

Canker-blossom. Steevens and Halliwell understand this to mean the canker-worm, like *cankers* in ii. 2. 3; but Schmidt explains it as the blossom of the canker (see *Much Ado*, i. 3. 28) or wild rose. S. does not use the compound elsewhere, but he has *canker-bloom* in *Sonn.* 54. 5, where the scentless flower is contrasted with "sweet roses."

286. *Touch.* Sense, feeling. Cf. *Temp.* v. 1. 21 ; *Macb.* iv. 2. 9; *Rich. III.* i. 2. 71, etc.

290. *Compare.* Cf. *V. and A.* 8: "sweet above compare ;" *Sonn.* 130. 14: "with false compare," etc. Gr. 451.

291. *Urg'd.* Cf. *M. of V.* i. 1. 144: "I urge this childhood proof;" *Rich. II.* iii. 1. 4: "With too much urging your pernicious lives," etc.

292. *Personage.* Cf. *T. N.* i. 5. 164: "Of what personage and years is he?" See also quotation from *Roister Doister* in note on v. 1. 109 below. For the measure, see Gr. 476.

296. *Painted maypole.* Steevens quotes Stubbes's *Anatomie of Abuses*, 1583, in which the "Maie pole" is said to be "some tyme painted with variable colours," etc.

300. *Curst.* Shrewish; as the next line shows. Cf. 341, 439 below. The word is often used in this sense in *T. of S.;* as in i. 1. 185, i. 2. 70, 128, ii. 1. 187, 294, 307, etc. We have the comparative *curster* in *T. of S.* iii. 2. 156, and the superlative in ii. 1. 315.

302. *Right.* Like our *downright.* Gr. 19.

304. *Something.* For the adverbial use, see Gr. 68.

307. *Evermore.* Always; as often in S. Cf. *M. of V.* i. 1. 52; *Rich. II.* ii. 3. 65, etc.

310. *Stealth.* Stealing (going secretly). Cf. iv. 1. 157 below. See also *Sonn.* 77. 7 ; *T. N.* i. 5. 316, etc.

312. *Chid.* See on 200 above.

314. *So.* Cf. "be it so" in i. 1. 39. Gr. 133.

317. *Fond.* Foolish. See on iii. 2. 114.

321. For the measure, see Gr. 469.

323. *Shrewd.* Shrewish. Cf. *Much Ado*, ii. 1. 20 : "so shrewd of thy tongue ;" *T. of S.* i. 1. 185 : "curst and shrewd," etc. See *J. C.* p. 145.

329. *Minimus.* The Latin for *minim.* Used by S. only here. Theo. wished to change it to "minim, you." Cf. Milton, *P. L.* vii. 482 : "Minims of nature."

Knot-grass. The *Polygonum aviculare* (Schmidt), which was anciently supposed to hinder the growth of an animal or child. Steevens quotes B. and F., *Knight of the Burning Pestle :* "Should they put him into a straight pair of gaskins, 't were worse than knot-grass, he would never grow after it ;" Id., *The Coxcomb :* "a boy . . . kept under for a year with milk and knot-grass."

331. *That.* For the relative after *her,* see Gr. 218.

334. *Never so.* See Gr. 52.

335. *Aby.* The quarto reading (spelled "abie" in 2d quarto) ; the folios have "abide." See on 175 above.

337. *Of thine or mine.* Theo. would read "Or thine or mine ;" but cf. *Temp.* ii. 1. 27 : "Which, of he or Adrian, for a good wager, first begins to crow ?" On *most,* see Gr. 409.

338. *Cheek by jole.* A common phrase then as since, but not elsewhere used by S.

339. *Coil.* Turmoil. Cf. *Temp.* i. 2. 207 ; *C. of E.* iii. 1. 48 ; *R. and J.* ii. 5. 67, etc.

Long. Equivalent to *along,* but not a contraction of that word. See Wb. or Schmidt. For *of,* see Gr. 168.

344. This line is not in the folios.

349. *Garments.* The Globe ed. misprints "garment." See also on ii. 1. 17 and on iv. 1. 147.

351. *'Nointed.* For the contraction, see Gr. 460.

352. *Sort.* Fall out, happen. Cf. *Much Ado*, iv. 1. 242 : "And if it sort not well, you may conceal her ;" *Id.* v. 4. 7 : "Well, I am glad that all things sort so well," etc. Steevens quotes *Monsieur d'Olive,* 1606 : "never look to have any action sort to your honour."

353. *Jangling.* Cf. *L. L. L.* ii. 1. 225 : "Good wits will be jangling," etc.

356. *Welkin.* Cf. *Temp.* i. 2. 4 : "the sea, mounting to the welkin's cheek ;" *M. W.* i. 3. 101 : "By welkin and her star," etc. It is an adjective in *W. T.* i. 2. 136 : "your welkin eye."

357. *Acheron.* Hell. Cf. *T. A.* iv. 3. 44 :

> "I 'll dive into the burning lake below,
> And pull her out of Acheron by the heels."

See also *Macb.* iii. 5. 15.

359. *As.* See Gr. 275. *Another* = the other ; as often in S. Cf. *T. of S.* iii. 2. 46 : "a pair of boots, . . . one buckled, another laced ;" *W. T.* v. 2. 82 : "one eye declined for the loss of her husband, another elevated," etc.

360. *Sometime.* S. uses *sometime* and *sometimes* interchangeably. We have the latter in 435 below. See on ii. 1. 36.

365. *Leaden legs.* Cf. *Rich. III.* v. 3. 105 (also *R. of L.* 124): "leaden slumber;" *J. C.* iv. 3. 268:

> "O murderous slumber,
> Lay'st thou thy leaden mace upon my boy?" etc.

Batty (Gr. 450) is used by S. only here.

367. *Liquor.* Juice; as in ii. 1. 175. *Virtuous*=powerful. Cf. *2 Hen. IV.* iv. 5. 76:

> "like the bee, culling from every flower
> The virtuous sweets."

See also Milton, *Comus,* 621: "every virtuous plant and healing herb;" *Il Pens.* 113: "the virtuous ring and glass;" Spenser, *F. Q.* ii. 12. 26: "his virtuous staffe," etc.

368. *His might.* Its power. Gr. 228.

370. *Derision.* A quadrisyllable. See on i. 1. 149.

373. *Date.* Duration; as often. Cf. *Sonn.* 18. 4: "And summer's lease hath all too short a date;" *K. John,* iv. 3. 106: "My date of life," etc.

374. *Whiles.* Cf. *Temp.* ii. 1. 217, 284, 310; *J. C.* i. 2. 209, etc.

379. *Night's swift dragons.* The chariot of Night was fabled to be drawn by dragons. Steevens quotes Golding's *Ovid:* "the dragon fell, whose eyes were never shet." Cf. *T. and C.* v. 8. 17: "The dragon wing of Night;" *Cymb.* ii. 2. 48: "Swift, swift, you dragons of the night," etc. See also Milton, *Il Pens.* 59: "While Cynthia checks her dragon yoke."

380. *Aurora's harbinger.* The morning star. S. mentions Aurora only here and in *R. and J.* i. 1. 142. For the original meaning of *harbinger,* see *Macb.* p. 168. Cf. Milton, *Song on May Morning,* 1: "Now the bright morning star, day's harbinger."

381. *At whose approach,* etc. Cf. Milton, *Hymn on the Nativity,* 232:

> "The flocking shadows pale
> Troop to the infernal jail;
> Each fettered ghost slips to his several grave;
> And the yellow-skirted fayes
> Fly after the night-steeds, leaving their moon-lov'd maze."

383. *That in cross-ways,* etc. "The ghosts of self-murderers, who are buried in cross-roads; and of those who, being drowned, were condemned (according to the opinion of the ancients) to wander for a hundred years, as the rites of sepulture had never been regularly bestowed on their bodies" (Steevens). See quotation in note on iv. 2. 14 below.

384. *Wormy beds.* Cf. Milton, *On the Death of a Fair Infant,* 31: "thy beauties lie in wormy bed."

385. *Upon.* For the transposition, see Gr. 203.

386. *Exile.* For the accent, see Gr. 490.

387. *Black-brow'd night.* Cf. *R. and J.* iii. 2. 20: "come, loving, black-brow'd night." See also *K. John,* v. 6. 17: "in the black brow of night."

389. *The morning's love.* Steevens takes this to refer to Tithonus, the aged husband of Aurora. Holt White and others make it refer to

Cephalus (the "Shafalus" of v. 1. 195), the lover of the goddess. Cf. Milton, *Il Pens.* 122 :

> "Till civil-suited Morn appear,
> Not tricked and frounced as she was wont
> With the Attic boy to hunt," etc.

Halliwell says : "Oberon merely means to say metaphorically that he has sported with Aurora, the morning's love, the first blush of morning ; and that he is not, like a ghost, compelled to vanish at the dawn of day." The 2d and later folios have "morning love," which Rowe adopted ("morning-love") in his 1st ed., changing it to "morning-light" in the 2d.

391. *Eastern gate.* Cf. Milton, *L'All.* 59 :

> "Right against the eastern gate,
> Where the great sun begins his state."

392. *Neptune.* Cf. ii. 1. 126. Hanmer, following Warb., changed *fair blessed* to "far-blessing." Halliwell prints "fair-blessed." So Walker, who points the passage thus :

> "Opening on Neptune, with fair-blessed beams
> Turns into yellow gold," etc.

Cf. the description of the sun in *Sonn.* 33. 3 :

> "Kissing with golden face the meadows green,
> Gilding pale streams with heavenly alchemy ;"

and *K. John*, iii. 1. 77 :

> "To solemnize this day the glorious sun
> Stays in his course and plays the alchemist,
> Turning with splendour of his precious eye
> The meagre cloddy earth to glittering gold."

402. *Drawn.* With drawn sword. Cf. *Temp.* ii. 1. 308 : "Why are you drawn?" Gr. 374.

412. *We'll try no manhood here.* That is, we'll not fight here. Cf. *Much Ado*, v. 1. 66 : "Do challenge thee to trial of a man."

417. *That.* So that. Gr. 283.

418. *Me.* For the reflexive use, see Gr. 223.

421. *Ho, ho, ho!* The traditional shout of Robin Goodfellow. See the old ballad quoted on ii. 1. 3 and 36 above. So in Drayton's *Nymphidia* : "Ho, ho, quoth Hob, God save thy grace," etc. The devil, however, as Ritson and others have pointed out, had an earlier title to it. Thus in *Histriomastix* a "roaring devil" enters, with the *Vice* on his back, *Iniquity* in one hand, and *Juventus* in the other, crying : "Ho, ho, ho! these babes mine are all." So in *Gammer Gurton's Needle :* "But Diccon, Diccon, did not the devil cry *ho, ho, ho?*" and again :

> "By the masse, ich saw him of late cal up a great blacke devill.
> O, the knave cryed *ho, ho*, he roared and he thundered."

Cf. also the epitaph attributed to Shakespeare : "Ho! quoth the Devil, 'tis my John a Combe;" and Goulart's *Histories*, 1607 : "The fellow . . . sawe the Diuills in horrible formes, some sitting, some standing, others walking, some ramping against the walles, but al of them assoone as they beheld him ran unto him, crying *Hoh, Hoh,* what makest thou here?"

422. *Abide me.* Await me, meet me in combat. See on *aby,* 335 above.

Wot. Know. Used only in the present tense and the participle *wotting* (Schmidt). The former occurs often in S. (cf. iv. 1. 161 below), the latter only in *W. T.* iii. 2. 77.

426. *Buy.* Coll. and others change this to "'by" (as if a contraction of *aby* in 175 and 335 above)—"a blundering correction," as Schmidt calls it. Cf. *C. of E.* iv. 1. 81 ; 1 *Hen. IV.* v. 3. 7, etc.

429. *To measure out my length.* Cf. *Lear,* i. 4. 100 ; *Cymb.* i. 2. 25 ; *A. Y. L.* ii. 6. 2, etc.

434. *Detest.* The word probably has its ordinary meaning, as Schmidt explains it ; but Walker believes that it is used in the sense of the original *detestari,* to cry out against. He cites other passages which he considers parallel ; as *Cymb.* ii. 5. 33, *A. and C.* iv. 14. 57, etc.

435. *And sleep,* etc. And now may sleep, etc. Gr. 364, 365. Malone quotes *Cleopatra,* 1594 :

> "Therefore come thou oi wonders wonder chief,
>   That open can'st with such an easy key
>   The dore of life, come, gentle cunning thief,
>   That from ourselves so steal'st ourselves away."

437. *Three.* Metrically a dissyllable. Gr. 484. For *comes,* two lines below, see Gr. 486.

438. *Makes.* For the form, see Gr. 433.

439. *Curst.* See on 300 above.

441. *Females.* We do not find in S. the modern vulgarism of *female* for *woman.* He uses the word only in its strict sense, as opposed to *male,* except when he puts it into the mouth of clowns. Cf. *L. L. L.* i. 1. 267 : "with a child of our grandmother Eve, a female ; or, for thy more sweet understanding, a woman ;" *A. Y. L.* v. 1. 54 : "Therefore, you clown, abandon,—which is in the vulgar leave,—the society,—which in the boorish is company,—of this female,—which in the common is woman," etc.

442. *Never so.* See Gr. 52.

443. *Bedabbled with the dew.* Cf. *V. and A.* 703 : "the dew-bedabbled wretch."

451. *To your eye.* The *to* is not in the early eds., but was added by Rowe. Halliwell omits it.

461. *Jack shall have Jill.* These nicknames, as generic titles for a man and a woman, are of great antiquity (Halliwell). "All shall be well, Jack shall have Jill," occurs in Heywood's *Epigrammes upon Proverbes,* 1567. So *The Scourge of Folly,* 1611 : "All shall bee well, and Jack shall have Jill." Cf. *L. L. L.* v. 2. 885 : "Jack hath not Jill."

463. *The man shall have his mare again.* Halliwell quotes Ray's *English Proverbs:* "All is well, and the man hath his mare again ;" and Fletcher's *Chances:* "Why, the man has his mare again, and all's well." Steevens wanted to change *well* to "still," to improve the rhyme.

MOUNT TAYGETUS FROM THE SITE OF SPARTA.

ACT IV.

Scene I.—1. *Come, sit thee down*, etc. Halliwell quotes *The Shoe-maker's Holiday*, 1600 :

> "Here sit thou downe upon this flowry banke,
> And make a garland for thy Lacies head,—
> These pinkes, these roses, and these violets,
> These blushing gille-flowers, these marigoldes."

2. *Coy.* Stroke, caress. S. uses the verb only here and in *Cor.* v. 1. 6, where it means to disdain. Steevens quotes *The Arraignment of Paris*, 1584 : "Plays with Amyntas' lusty boy, and coys him in the dales ;" and Golding's *Ovid* :

> "and with her hand had coid
> The dragons' reined neckes," etc.

7. *Mounsieur.* The spelling of all the early eds. It may be retained here (like *Cavalery* below) as in keeping with the character. So "Mounseur" in *M. W.* ii. 3. 59. It should be noted, however, that "Monsieur," "Mounsieur," "Mounsier," etc., are forms quite promiscuously used by the printers of that time.

15. *Overflown.* Overflowed. So in *A. W.* ii. 1. 142 we have *flown* = flowed.

18. *Neaf.* Fist, or hand ; also spelled *neif.* Used by S. nowhere else except in *2 Hen. IV.* ii. 4. 200 (Pistol's speech). Cf. Ben Jonson, *Poetaster :* "reach me thy neaf."

19. *Leave your courtesy.* Cf. *L. L. L.* iv. 2. 147 : "Stay not thy compliment ; I forgive thy duty : adieu."

20. *Cavalery.* Cavalero; as printed in the 2d and later folios. Cf. *M. W.* ii. 3. 77 : "Cavalero Slender ;" 2 *Hen. IV.* v. 3. 62 : "all the cav-aleros about London." As Grey points out, we ought to have "Cava-lero Peaseblossom" here, Cobweb having been sent after a honey-bag.

26. *A reasonable good ear,* etc. Schmidt remarks that weavers were supposed to be good singers, and particularly given to singing psalms, being most of them Calvinists and refugees from the Netherlands. Cf. *T. N.* ii. 3. 61 : "a catch that will draw three souls out of one weaver ;" I *Hen. IV.* ii. 4. 147 : "I would I were a weaver ; I could sing psalms or anything."

27. *The tongs and the bones.* According to J. R. Planché, the *tongs* were a rural instrument of music, struck by a "key." The *bones,* or *knockers,* were made of bone or hard wood, and were played between the fingers, as by boys and Ethiopian minstrels in our day. The folio has here the stage-direction, "*Musicke Tongs, Rurall Musicke.*"

30. *Bottle of hay.* A truss of hay. S. has the phrase nowhere else. It is still used in England in the old proverb, " to look for a needle in a bottle of hay." In a court-book dated 1551, the halfpenny bottle of hay is said to weigh two pounds and a half, and the penny bottle five pounds. Halliwell quotes Copley, *Wits, Fits, and Fancies,* 1614 : "A country-man passing along the street, met with a car, and the horse spying his bouns-ing beard, snap'd at it instead of a bottle of hay ; then the country-man said : The dev'll take thee, who made thee a barber ?" See another ex-ample of the word on p. 13 above.

Bottle, in this sense, must not be confounded with *pottle* (*M. W.* ii. 1. 223, iii. 5. 30, *Oth.* ii. 3. 87, etc.), which means in S. a large tankard (orig-inally a measure of two quarts), and is still used in England to denote "a long tapering basket, holding about a quart."

33. For the measure, see Gr. 484.

38. *All ways.* In all directions ; Theo.'s emendation for the "alwaies" of the early eds. Hanmer substituted "a while," which W. adopts.

39. *So doth the woodbine,* etc. This passage has been the subject of much dispute. The question is whether the *woodbine* and the *honeysuckle* are the same plant or different ones. If the former, we must adopt Stee-vens's explanation : "So the woodbine, that is, the sweet honeysuckle, doth gently entwist the barky fingers of the elm, and so does the female ivy enring the same fingers." But it is certain that the woodbine and the honeysuckle were sometimes considered as different plants. Farmer quotes one of Taylor's poems : "The woodbine, primrose, and the cow-slip fine, the honisuckle, and the daffadill." In a passage in Ben Jonson, the blue bindweed is mentioned as twining with the honeysuckle, and Gifford thinks the former synonymous with the woodbine. In Lynacre's *Herball,* the woodbine is made synonymous with the withwind, another name for the bindweed. Halliwell thinks that S. "either intended to re-fer to the plant (woodbine) entwining the flower (honeysuckle), or to the circumstance of the smaller tendrils of this plant twining around the stronger branch : the woodbine thus entwists the honeysuckle, because it twines round itself."

W. remarks that the woodbine and the honeysuckle are often seen twining together in this country, and that the commentators have blundered "because they went not to Shakespeare's teacher—Nature—but to books," etc.   He appears to forget that the popular names of plants are not always the same in England as with us.   They vary, indeed, in different localities here.   In some parts of New England, for instance, the "woodbine" is the Virginia creeper (*Vitis quinquefolia*); and the name "honeysuckle" is given to many species of *Lonicera* besides the scarlet-flowered one he mentions.

According to Schmidt, the *honeysuckle* of S. is *Lonicera caprifolium*. The *woodbine* he gives as "bindweed, convolvulus," from which we infer that he is in doubt as to the botanical species.

The *ivy* is called *female* "because it always requires some support, which is poetically called its husband" (Steevens).   Cf. *C. of E.* ii. 2. 176:

> "Thou art an elm, my husband, I a vine,
> Whose weakness married to thy stronger state
> Makes me with thy strength to communicate."

See also Milton, *P. L.* v. 215.   Spenser (*F. Q.* i. i. 8) speaks of "The vine-propp Elme."   The figure is a common one in the Latin poets.

Enrings and *barky* are used by S. only here.

44. *Dotage.*   Doting affection.   Cf. *Much Ado*, ii. 3. 175 : "I would she had bestowed this dotage on me ;" *A. and C.* i. 1. 1 : "this dotage of our general's," etc.

46. *Favours.*   Presents, love-tokens (Schmidt).   Cf. *L. L. L.* v. 2. 30, 125, 130, 292, 468, etc.

51. *Like round and orient pearls.*   See on ii. 1. 15 above.

55. *Patience.*   A trisyllable, as in i. 1. 152.   Gr. 479.

63. *Other.*   See Gr. 12.

64. *May all.*   All may ; or *they* may be implied.   Gr. 399.

66. *But.*   Except.   Gr. 127.   *Fierce*=wild, disordered ; as in *Cymb.* v. 5. 382, *Ham.* i. 1. 121, etc.

68. *Be as.*   So in the quartos ; the folios have "Be thou as."

70. *O'er.*   The early eds. have "or ;" Theo. made the correction. *Cupid's flower* is the one referred to in ii. 1. 163 ; and *Dian's bud* is the other "herb" of ii. 1. 181, which was to "take the charm from off her sight."   Steevens takes the latter to be the bud of the *Agnus castus.*   Cf. Lynacre's *Herball* : "The vertue of this herbe is, that he wyll kepe man and woman chaste ;" Gerard's *Herbal*, 1597 : "*Agnus castus* is a singular medicine and remedie for such as would willingly live chaste," etc.

76. *His.*   So the 1st quarto ; the other early eds. have "this."   In the next line, both quartos have "this," and the folios "his."

79. *Sleep of all these five.*   The quartos and 1st and 2d folios have "sleepe : of all these fine ;" the 3d and 4th folios, "sleep : of all these find," etc.   Thirlby suggested the emendation to Theo., and it has been generally adopted.   The *five* are of course the two pairs of lovers and Bottom.

80. The folio has here the stage-direction "*Musick still*," which probably means "music, softly," or "soft music"—"such as charmeth sleep."

85. *Solemnly.*   Ceremoniously (Schmidt).   Cf. *Rich. II.* iv. 1. 319 ; *Rich. III* i. 2. 214 ; *Hen. VIII.* i. 2. 165, etc.

87. *Posterity.* The reading of the 2d quarto and the folios, which, on the whole, we prefer to the "prosperity" of the 1st quarto. The latter is perhaps favoured by ii. 1. 73, and the former by v. 1. 396 fol.

92. *Sad.* Serious, grave. Cf. *M. of V.* ii. 2. 205 : "sad ostent ;" *Much Ado*, i. 1. 185 : "But speak you this with a sad brow ?" *Id.* i. 3. 62 : "in sad conference," etc.

93. *Trip we*, etc. See on iii. 2. 381 above. Cf. v. 1. 375 : "Following darkness like a dream." *Trip* is often used of fairies, nymphs, and the like. Cf. *V. and A.* 146 : "Or, like a fairy, trip upon the green ;" *Sonn.* 154. 4 : "many nymphs . . . Came tripping by ;" *Temp.* iv. 1. 46 : "Each one tripping on his toe." See also *M. W.* v. 4. 1, v. 5. 96, and 1 *Hen. IV.* i. 1. 87. In v. 1. 408 below, we have "Trip away ;" and in v. 1. 385 "dance it trippingly."

101. *Observation.* Cf. i. 1. 167, and also 129 below.

102. *Vaward.* Forepart, beginning ; as in 2 *Hen. IV.* i. 2. 199 : "the vaward of our youth." Elsewhere it is=vanguard ; as in *Hen. V.* iv. 3. 130, *Cor.* i. 6. 53, etc. *Vanguard* is not found in S., and *van* occurs only in *A. and C.* iv. 6. 9.

103. "The fondness of Theseus for hunting—'and namely the grete hert *in May*'—is particularly noted in the *Knightes Tale*" (Halliwell).

104. *Uncouple.* Loose the hounds from their couples, set them loose. Cf. *V. and A.* 674 : "Uncouple at the timorous flying hare ;" *T. A.* ii. 2. 3 : "Uncouple here, and let us make a bay." S. uses the word only three times.

107, 108. For *confusion* and *conjunction*, see on i. 1. 149.

109. *Cadmus.* Not elsewhere mentioned by S.

110. *Crete.* Cf. *Hen. V.* ii. 1. 77 : "O hound of Crete," etc. The Cretan and Spartan hounds were much esteemed. Cf. the description of Actæon's dogs, *Met.* iii. 208 :

> "Gnosius Ichnobates, Spartana gente Melampus ;"

and again, 223 :

> "Et patre Dictaeo, sed matre Laconide nati,
> Labros et Agriodos."

The bear. So in all the early eds., but changed by Hanmer to "the boar." The hunting of the bear is, however, referred to more than once in the *Knightes Tale.* Malone reminds us that in the *W. T.* (iii. 3) Antigonus is destroyed by a *bear*, which is chased by hunters. Cf. *V. and A.* 884 :

> "For now she knows it is no gentle chase,
> But the blunt boar, rough bear, or lion proud."

112. *Chiding.* The word often means "to make an incessant noise." Cf. *A. Y. L.* ii. 1. 7 : "And churlish chiding of the winter's wind ;" *Hen. VIII.* iii. 2. 197 : "As doth a rock against the chiding flood," etc. See on ii. 1. 142 above.

114. *Seem'd.* The reading of 2d folio ; the earlier eds. have "Seeme."

117. *So flew'd, so sanded.* Having the same large hanging chaps and the same sandy colour. Cf. Golding's translation of the second quotation from Ovid in note on 110 above :

> "With other twaine, that had a syre of Crete,
> And dam of Sparta: tone * of them called Jollyboy, a great
> And large-flew'd hound."

118. *With ears*, etc. Steevens quotes Heywood, *Brazen Age*, **1613**:

> "the fierce Thessalian hounds,
> With their flag ears, ready to sweep the dew
> From their moist breasts."

120. *Like bells*, etc. That is, like a chime of bells.

121. *Tuneable.* Used by S. only here and in i. 1. 184 above.

122. *Holla'd.* Cf. *Lear*, iii. 1. 55:

> "That way, I'll this—he that first lights on him
> Holla the other."

Holla was the sportsman's call to the hounds, or the rider's to his horse, to stop. Cf. *A. Y. L.* iii. 2. 257: "Cry 'holla' to thy tongue, I prithee; it curvets very unseasonably;" *V. and A.* 284:

> "What recketh he his rider's angry stir,
> His flattering 'holla,' or his 'Stand, I say!'"

123. *Thessaly.* Mentioned by S. only here and in *A. and C.* iv. 13. 2.

124. *Soft.* "Hold, stop" (Schmidt). Cf. *M. of V.* i. 3. 59, iv. 1. 320: *Temp.* i. 2. 449, etc. So *soft you;* as in *Much Ado*, v. 1. 207, *Ham.* iii. 1. 88, etc.

128. *Of.* Needlessly changed by Pope to "at." See Gr. 174.

131. *In grace of.* In honour of. Cf. *Ham.* i. 2. 124: "in grace whereof," etc.

133. *That.* When. Cf. v. 1. 387: "That the graves," etc. See also *Gen.* ii. 17: "the day that thou eatest," etc. Gr. 284.

136. *Saint Valentine.* The anachronism is as obvious as it is amusing. Halliwell quotes Wither's *Epithalamia*, 1633: "Most men are of opinion that this day [St. Valentine's] every bird doth chuse her mate for that yeare."

137. *But.* Only. Gr. 129.

142. *To sleep.* As to sleep. Gr. 281.

144. *Sleep.* Some eds. print "'sleep," as if contracted from *asleep.* It seems better to explain it, as Schmidt does (p. 1419), as=sleeping; the inflection being often omitted in the first of a pair of words. Cf. *Temp.* i. 2. 249: "without or grudge or grumblings;" *T. and C.* iv. 4. 7: "a weak and colder palate;" *M. for M.* iv. 6. 13: "the generous and gravest citizens," etc.

147. *I do.* The Globe ed. misprints "do I." See on iii. 2. 349.

149. *Where we might.* The reading of the 1st quarto; the other early eds. have "might be." *Without* would then=beyond (Gr. 197).

150. We adopt Dyce's punctuation. The 1st quarto has a comma at the end of the line, which may indicate the interruption of the speech by Egeus.

157. *Stealth.* See on iii. 2. 310 above.

---

* The one. Cf. Sir P. Sidney, notes on Harington's *Ariosto*: "Tone doth enforce, the other doth entice," etc. It was sometimes used with the article, as in another passage of Golding's: "The tone for using crueltie, the tother for his trull."

160. *Following.* So in 1st quarto; "followed" in the other early eds. For *fancy*, see on i. 1. 155.

161. *Wot.* See on iii. 2. 422.

163. *Melted as*, etc. So in all the early eds. Gr. 486. Capell made it read "as doth the snow;" and Pope, "Is melted as."

164. *Gawd.* See on i. 1. 33.

170. *In sickness.* The early eds. have "a sickness." The emendation is Farmer's. Schmidt (p. 1422) would retain "a sickness," making it = one sick. He gives many similar instances of the use of the abstract for the concrete. Cf. *fear* = a dreaded object, in v. 1. 21 below.

171. *Come.* Having returned.

176. *Overbear.* Overrule; as in *K. John*, iv. 2. 37. See ii. 1. 92 for a slightly different meaning.

178. *Knit.* United. Cf. *K. John*, iii. 1. 226: "This royal hand and mine are newly knit." See also i. 1. 172 and ii. 2. 47 above.

179. *And for.* And because; introducing a subordinate, not a co-ordinate sentence (Schmidt). Cf. *Temp.* i. 2. 272: "And for thou wast a spirit too delicate;" *M. for M.* ii. 1. 28:

> "You may not so extenuate his offence
> For I have had such faults;"

that is, the fact that I have been guilty is no excuse for him. Here (as noted in *Mer.* p. 134) the modern meaning of *for* would be nonsensical.

181, 182. See reference to this passage, p. 118 above.

189. *Mine own, and not mine own.* "Helena, I think, means to say that, having *found* Demetrius *unexpectedly*, she considered her property in him as insecure as that which a person has in a jewel that he has *found* by *accident*; which he knows not whether he shall retain, and which therefore may properly enough be called *his own and not his own*" (Malone). Halliwell favours this explanation, but we prefer Heath's, which makes Helena simply say that she can hardly believe in her sudden good fortune in finding her lost "jewel" of a lover. Cf. *A. and C.* iv. 12. 8:

> "Antony
> Is valiant and dejected; and, by starts,
> His fretted fortunes give him hope, and fear,
> Of what he has, and has not."

See also *M. of V.* iii. 2. 20, 142–149, 183–185.

Warb. wished to read "gemell" = twin, for *jewel*, because "Hermia had observed that things appeared *double* to her!"

189, 190. *Are you sure That we are awake?* These words are in the quartos, but not in the folios. W. thinks they were intentionally omitted. D. follows Capell in reading:

> "But are you sure
> That we are well awake?"

200. *God 's my life.* Cf. *Much Ado*, iv. 2. 72: "God 's my life, where 's the sexton?"

203. *Go about.* Undertake, attempt. Cf. *Much Ado*, i. 3. 11: "I wonder that thou goest about . . . to apply a moral medicine to a mortifying mischief." See also *R. of L.* 412; *M. for M.* iii. 2. 215; *Hen. V.* iv. 1. 212, etc.

M

205. *Patched.* Probably referring to the motley dress of the professional fool. See *A. Y. L.* ii. 7. 13 : "a motley fool," etc. Schmidt prefers to make it=paltry. Cf. *patches,* iii. 2. 9 above.

206. *The eye of man,* etc. This kind of humour, as Halliwell remarks,
was so very common that it is by no means necessary to consider, as
some do, that S. intended here to parody Scripture. Boswell quotes
Selinus, 1594 : "keeping your hands from lying and slandering, and your
tongues from picking and stealing." Cf. the old comedy of *Wily Be-
guiled :*

> "I Pegg Pudding, promise thee William Cricket,
>   That I'le hold thee for mine own dear lilly,
>   While I have a head in mine own eye, and a face on my nose,
>   A mouth in my tongue, and all that a woman should have,
>   From the crown of my foot, to the soal of my head."

See also *T. N.* ii. 3. 58 : "To hear by the nose, it is dulcet in contagion."

210. *Ballad.* "Ballet" in the early eds. Cotgrave translates *balade*
by "a ballet."

212. *A play.* So in the early eds.; "the play" and "our play" have
been suggested as emendations.

213. *At her death.* That is, at Thisbe's. Theo. substituted "after
death;" that is, after his death in the play. The Coll. MS. has "Thisby's
death."

SCENE II.—4. *Transported.* Carried off; or, perhaps, killed, as Schmidt
explains it. Cf. *M. for M.* iv. 3. 72 :

> "And to transport him in the mind he is
>   Were damnable."

8. *Discharge.* Perform. See on i. 2. 81 above.

9. *The best wit of any.* For the "confusion of construction," see Gr.
409. See also on v. 1. 239 below.

14. *Naught.* The forms *naught* and *nought* were used interchangeably, but the former (as noted by Schmidt and others) seems to have been
preferred when the word meant *naughty,* that is, wicked or worthless
(see *Mer.* p. 152). *A thing of naught*=a wicked thing. There is a play
upon *nought* and *naught* in *Rich. III.* i. 1. 96–100. Halliwell quotes
Mill, *Night Search,* 1640 :

> "A crosse-way grave, according to the lawes,
>   Is made for her ; and thither she is brought
>   And tumbled in, just like a thing of naught."

16. *Is two or three.* For *is,* see Gr. 335.

17. *Made men.* Cf. *Temp.* ii. 2. 32 : "there would this monster make
a man," etc. Halliwell quotes *Terence in English,* 1614 : "I am well,
safe, in good case, a made man for ever, if this be true."

19. *Scaped.* Not "'scaped," as usually printed. Cf. Bacon, *Adv. of
L.* ii. 14. 9 : "such as had scaped shipwreck;" Palsgrave, *Fr. Dict.* 1530 :
"I scape or slyppe thorow a narowe place, *je me elapse.*" See Wb.

23. *Hearts.* Often used as a familiar address. Cf. *Temp.* i. 1. 6;
M. W. iii. 2. 88 ; *T. N.* ii. 3. 16, etc.

30. *Of me.* From me. Cf. Gr. 165, 166.

32. *Strings.* To tie on the false beards.

Pumps. Cf. *T. of S.* iv. 1. 136: "And Gabriel's pumps were all un-pink'd i' the heel." See also *R. and J.* ii. 4. 64, 66.

34. *Preferred.* Offered for approval. Needlessly changed by Theo. to "proferred." Cf. *T. of A.* iii. 4. 49; *J. C.* iii. 1. 28, etc.

38. *Sweet breath.* See on ii. 1. 148.

CENTAUR. (METOPE FROM THE PARTHENON.)

ACT V.

SCENE I.—2. *May.* Can. See Gr. 307.

3. *Antique.* The 1st folio has "anticke" here. *Antick* and *antique* (the accent always on the first syllable) are used promiscuously in the early eds. without regard to the meaning.

Toys. Trifles, nothings. Cf. *W. T.* iii. 3. 39; *Macb.* ii. 3. 99; *Cymb.* iv. 2. 193, etc.

4. *Seething brains.* Cf. *W. T.* iii. 3. 64: "these boiled brains of nine-teen and two-and-twenty;" *Temp.* v. 1. 59:

> "thy brains,
> Now useless, boil'd within thy skull."

Burton (*Anat. of Melancholy*) says that drunkards "drown their wits, and seeth their brains, in ale."

5. *That.* For *that* after *such*, see Gr. 279.

8. *All compact.* All composed, made up. Cf. *V. and A.* 149 : "Love is a spirit all compact of fire ;" *T. A.* v. 3. 88: "My heart is not compact of flint nor steel," etc. Halliwell quotes *Dido Queen of Carthage,* 1594 : "A man compact of craft and perjury ;" and Lyly, *Woman in the Moone,* 1597 : "compact of every heavenly excellence."

9, 10. The first folio, which is followed by some modern eds., points the passage thus :

> "One sees more diuels then vaste hell can hold ;
>   That is the mad man."

See Gervinus on this passage, p. 28 above.

11. *Helen's beauty.* The Grecian beauty is often alluded to by S. See *Sonn.* 53. 7 : "On Helen's cheek all art of beauty set ;" *A. Y. L.* iii. 2. 153 : "Helen's cheek, but not her heart," etc.

"By *a brow of Egypt* S. means no more than the *brow of a gypsey* " (Steevens).

12. *The poet's eye,* etc. Malone notes that this seems to have been imitated by Drayton in his description of Marlowe :

> "that fine madness still he did retain,
> Which rightly should possess a poet's brain."

21, 22. These lines are enclosed in brackets by W. as probably an interpolation. Halliwell quotes Quarles :

> "Is the road fair? we loyter ; clogg'd with mire?
>   We stick or else retire :
> A lamb appears a lion ; and we fear
>   Each bush we see 's a bear."

For the construction of *imagining,* see Gr. 378. For *fear*=object of fear, see on iv. 1. 170 above ; and cf. *Ham.* iii. 3. 25.

25. *More witnesseth,* etc. Shows something more than mere images of fancy.

26. *Constancy.* Consistency. There is no other clear instance of this sense of the word in S., but we have *constant*=consistent, in *T. N.* iv. 2. 53 : "my constant question ;" and Schmidt makes *constantly*=consistently, in ii. 3. 160 of the same play.

27. *But, howsoever,* etc. "But, anyhow, it is strange and wonderful " (J. H.). For *howsoever,* see Gr. 47.

30. *More than to us,* etc. May more joy than comes to us, etc.

34. *After-supper.* The time after supper (Schmidt). Cf. *Rich. III.* iv. 3. 31 : "at after-supper." Some make it="rere-supper," which seems to have been a late or second supper (Nares). Coles, in his *Dict.* (1677), has "a rear-supper, epidipnis."

38. *Philostrate.* The folios have "*Egeus ;*" but see i. 1. 11.

39. *Abridgment.* Pastime. Cf. *Ham.* ii. 2. 439, where the word means "that which is my pastime and makes me be brief " (Schmidt).

42. *Brief.* List. Cf. *A. and C.* v. 2. 138, etc. *Ripe*=ready. The 1st quarto has "ripe ;" the other early eds. have "rife."

43. *Of which.* See Gr. 179.

44. In the quartos, lines 44–60 are given to *Theseus,* as in the text ;

in the folios, Lysander reads the brief, and Theseus comments upon the successive items. K. remarks that "the division of so long a passage is clearly better, and is perfectly natural and proper;" and Halliwell adds that "the dignity of the monarch is better sustained by this arrangement." Verplanck makes the plausible suggestion that the change into dialogue was an after-thought to add to the theatrical effect.

The battle with the Centaurs. The battle of the Centaurs and the Lapithæ was a favourite subject with the classical sculptors and poets.

48. *The riot,* etc. The killing of Orpheus by the Thracian women while they were celebrating the orgies of Bacchus. Cf. Milton, *Lycidas,* 58:

> "What could the Muse herself that Orpheus bore,
> The Muse herself, for her enchanting son,
> When by the rout that made the hideous roar
> His gory visage down the stream was sent,
> Down the swift Hebrus to the Lesbian shore?"

52. *The thrice three Muses,* etc. See Introduction, p. 11.

54. *Critical.* "Censorious, snarling" (Schmidt). Used by S. only here and in *Oth.* ii. 1. 120: "nothing, if not critical."

56. *Young Pyramus,* etc. See p. 118 above.

58. *Merry and tragical.* "In ridicule of the absurd titles of some of our ancient dramas" (Halliwell). See on i. 2. 9. Lupton's *All for Money,* 1578, is called a "pitiful comedy" on the title-page, and a "pleasant tragedy" in the prologue.

59. *Strange snow.* The reading of all the early eds. Many emendations have been suggested; as "scorching snow" (Hanmer), "strange shew" (Warb.), "strange black snow" (Upton and Capell), "strong snow" (Mason), "seething snow" (Coll. MS.), "swarthy snow" (Staunton), etc. *Wondrous* is here a trisyllable. Gr. 477.

65. *One player fitted.* See on i. 2. 57.

74. *Toil'd.* Exerted, strained. Cf. *Ham.* i. 1. 72: "toils the subject;" and *Rich. II.* iv. 1. 96: "toil'd with works of war." *Unbreathed* (used by S. only here)=unpractised. Cf. *breathed*=in full vigour (like the French *mis en haleine*) in *A.Y.L.* i. 2. 230, and *T. of S.* ind. 2. 50. Halliwell quotes *Scots Philomythie,* 1616:

> "But being trencher-fed, the weather hot,
> Themselvs unbreath'd, to hunting used not."

75. *Nuptial.* See on i. 1. 125.

76. *And.* "Frequently found in answers in the sense of *you are right and* or *yes and,* the *yes* being implied" (Gr. 97).

79. *Intents.* "The design or scheme of the piece intended for representation; the conceit of which being far-fetched or improbable, it might be with propriety enough called *extremely stretched*" (Kenrick).

The line may be considered parenthetical, and *stretched* (=strained, affected, as Schmidt explains it) may refer to *it* (the play) in 78.

82, 83. *For never,* etc. Steevens notes that Ben Jonson has expressed a similar sentiment in *Cynthia's Revels,* when Cynthia is preparing to see a masque:

> "Nothing which duty and desire to please,
> Bears written in the forehead, comes amiss."

87. *Gentle sweet.*   Cf. *L. L. L.* v. 2. 373 : " Fair gentle sweet."

88, 89. There may be an intentional play on *kind* and *kinder ;* but Schmidt (p. 1421) considers it one of many instances of "involuntary obscurities caused by the confusion of different significations of the same word."

90. *To take what they mistake.*   That is, to take in good part even their blundering attempt.

91. *Noble respect,* etc.   A noble mind "accommodates its judgment to the abilities of the performers, not to the merit of the performance" (Schmidt).

93. *Where I have come,* etc.   Walker quotes Browne, *Britannia's Pastorals,* ii. 1 :

> "If e'er you saw a pedant gin prepare
> To speak some graceful speech to Master Mayor,
> And being bashful, with a quaking doubt,
> That in his eloquence he may be out ;
> He oft steps forth, as oft turns back again,
> And long 'tis ere he ope his learned vein :
> Think so Marina stood."

96. *Periods.*   Full stops.   Cf. *R. of L.* 565 :

> "She puts the period often from his place ;
> And midst the sentence so her accent breaks,
> That twice she doth begin ere once she speaks."

98. *Have broke.*   For the "ellipsis of nominative," see Gr. 399.

102. *Fearful.*   Full of fear, timorous.   Cf. 162 below, and see *J. C.* p. 175.

106. *To my capacity.*   "In my opinion" (Schmidt).

107. *Address'd.*   Ready.   Cf. *J. C.* iii. 1. 29 : "He is address'd ;" 2 *Hen. IV.* iv. 4. 5 : "Our navy is address'd," etc.

108. *Flourish of trumpets.*   Steevens remarks that the prologue was anciently ushered in by trumpets.   He quotes Dekker, *The Guls Hornbook,* 1609 : "Present not yourselfe on the stage (especially at a new play) until the quaking prologue hath (by rubbing) got cullor in his cheekes, and is ready to give the trumpets their cue that hee's upon point to enter."

The stage-direction that follows is, in the quartos, "*Enter the Prologue ;*" in the 1st folio, "*Enter the Prologue.   Quince.*"

109. *If we offend,* etc.   The prologue is carefully mispointed in the early eds.   As K. remarks, it was meant to be spoken thus :

> "If we offend, it is with our good will
> That you should think we come not to offend ;
> But with good will to show our simple skill :
> That is the true beginning of our end.
> Consider then.   We come : but in despite
> We do not come.   As minding to content you,
> Our true intent is all for your delight.
> We are not here that you should here repent you.
> The actors are at hand ; and by their show
> You shall know all that you are like to know."

For a similar piece of mispunctuation, see Udall's *Roister Doister* (1553), iii. 4, in Doister's letter to Dame Custance, which Merygreeke reads as follows :

> "Sweete mistresse whereas I love you nothing at all,
> Regarding your substance and richesse chiefe of all,
> For your personage, beautie, demeanour and wit,
> I commend me unto you never a whit,
> Sorie to heare report of your good welfare," etc.

In the first line, the comma should have been after "you," and the next one after "richesse;" and in the fourth line, after "you," not after "whit."

114. *Minding.* Intending. Cf. 3 *Hen. VI.* iv. 1. 8, 64, 106, 140. See also *Per.* ii. 4. 3.

122. *A recorder.* A kind of flageolet. Cf. *Ham.* iii. 2. 303, 360. See also Milton, *P. L.* i. 551:

> "the Dorian mood
> Of flutes and soft recorders."

Nares says the instrument was so called because birds were taught to *record* by it; one of the meanings of *record* being to warble. Cf. Browne, *Brit. Past.* ii. 4:

> "The nymph did earnestly contest
> Whether the birds or she recorded best;"

B. and F., *Valentinian*, ii. 1:

> "For you are fellows only know by rote,
> As birds record their lessons;"

Drayton, *Ecl.*:

> "Fair Philomel night-musicke of the spring,
> Sweetly records her tuneful harmony."

123. *Not in government.* "Not a regular tune" (Schmidt). Cf. what Hamlet says of the instrument (iii. 2. 372): "Govern these ventages with your finger and thumb."

125. *Who is next?* Here the 1st folio has the stage-direction, "*Tawyer with a Trumpet before them*," taken probably from the prompter's book, Tawyer being apparently a proper name. The Coll. MS. has the stage-direction, "*Enter Presenter*," and Coll. (followed by W. and D.) understands Tawyer to be the name of the actor who filled the part of Presenter and introduced the characters of the play. "The argument of the play," Coll. remarks, "was to be made intelligible, with a due observation of points, and could not properly be given to the same performer who had delivered the prologue, purposely made so blunderingly ridiculous." This is plausible, but we can conceive that the clown might find it easier to master a simple story like that of Pyramus and Thisbe than an artificial composition like the prologue, and that he might therefore tell the former straight enough though he got the latter "all disordered."

126. *Gentles.* Used as a familiar address (*M. W.* iii. 2. 92, etc.), especially to an audience, as here and in 416 below. See also *Hen. V.* prol. 8 and ii. chor. 25.

129. *Certain.* "A burlesque on the frequent recurrence of *certain* as a bungling rhyme in poetry more ancient than the age of S." (Steevens).

130. *Present.* Represent. See on iii. 1. 54.

134. *This man*, etc. See on iii. 1. 48.

138. *Grisly.* Grim, terrible. Cf. *R. of L.* 926: "grisly care;" 1 *Hen.*

VI. i. 4. 47 : "My grisly countenance." See also Gray, *Eton College*, 82 : "A grisly troop ;" *The Bard*, 44 : "a grisly band," etc. Not to be con- founded with *grizzly*. See Wb.

Lion hight by name. So in all the early eds. Theo. transposed it, for the sake of the rhyme, to "by name Lion hight." Steevens suggests that a line rhyming with *name* may have been lost. *Hight* (=is called) is used by S. as "a characteristic archaism" (Schmidt). See *L. L. L.* i. 1. 171, 258, and *Per.* iv. prol. 18.

141. *Did fall.* Changed by Pope to "let fall ;" but *fall* is often used transitively by S. Cf. *Temp.* ii. 1. 296, v. 1. 64 ; *J. C.* iv. 2. 26, etc. See *J. C.* p. 175. For the line, cf. the legend in Chaucer : "And, as she ran, her wimple she let fall ;" and Golding's *Ovid* (p. 119 above) : "And as she fled away for haste, she let her mantle fall."

144. *Trusty.* Omitted in 1st folio ; "gentle" in later folios.

145, 146. A burlesque of the excessive use of alliteration in many writers of the time. Cf. i. 2. 24, 25. Sidney ridicules the same affecta- tion in his *Astrophel and Stella*, 15 :

> "You that do Dictionaries' method bring
> Into your rimes running in rattling rows."

Halliwell quotes Puttenham, *Arte of English Poesie*, 1589 : "Ye have another manner of composing your metre nothing commendable, special- ly if it be too much used, and is when our maker takes too much delight to fill his verse with wordes beginning all with a letter, as an English rimer that said : 'The deadly droppes of darke disdaine, do daily drench my due desartes.' And as the monke we spake of before wrote a whole poeme to the honor of Carolus Calvus, every word in his verse beginning with C."

154. *Snout.* The folio reading ; the quartos have "Flute," an obvious error.

156. *Crannied.* Used by S. nowhere else. The whole passage was evidently suggested by Golding's version of the story (p. 119 above).

159. *Loam.* So in all the early eds. The Var. ed. (1821) incorrectly gives "lime" as the folio reading.

161. *Right and sinister.* Right and left. For the accent of *sinister*, see Gr. 490 ; and cf. *Hen. V.* ii. 4. 85.

164. *The wittiest partition*, etc. Farmer would read "*in* discourse," supposing it an allusion to "the many stupid *partitions* in the argument- ative writings of the time."

167. *Grim-look'd.* Grim-looking. See Gr. 374. Cf. our *well-spoken* =well-speaking.

177. *O wicked wall !* Cf. Chaucer :

> "Thus would thei saine, alas ! thou wicked wal,
> Thorough thine envie thou us lettist al."

179. *Sensible.* Possessed of sense, or perception. Cf. *Cor.* i. 3. 95 : "I would your cambric were sensible as your finger," etc.

183. *Pat.* See on iii. 1. 2. The pointing of the 1st folio is as follows :

> "You shall see it vvill fall.
>
> *Enter Thisbie.*
>
> Pat as I told you ; yonder she comes."

188. *Knit up in thee.* The folio reading; the quartos have "knit now againe."

189. *I see a voice.* See on iv. 1. 206. The 2d and later folios have "heare" for *see*, and in the next line "see" for *hear*.

193. *Limander.* For Leander, as *Helen* for Hero. *Shafalus* and *Procrus* are for Cephalus and Procris. A poem by Henry Chute, entitled *Procris and Cephalus*, was entered on the Stationers' Register by John Wolf in 1593, and probably published the same year. For a possible allusion to Cephalus, see on iii. 2. 389.

200. *Tide.* Betide, happen (A. S. *tídan*). Cf. Robert of Gloucester : "tyde wat so bytyde ;" Chaucer, *T. and C.* i. 908 : "Thee shulde never have tidde so faire a grace" (so fair a fortune should never have happened to thee).

203. *Mural down.* The quartos have "Moon used ;" the folios, "morall downe." *Mural* is Pope's emendation. Hanmer gave "mure all down." *Mure*=wall, is found in 2 *Hen. IV.* iv. 4. 119 ; *mural* does not occur elsewhere in S., and is properly an adjective. The Coll. MS. has "wall down," which may be what S. wrote.

206. *Hear.* Farmer says : "This alludes to the proverb, 'Walls have ears.' A *wall* between almost any *two neighbours* would soon be *down*, were it to exercise this faculty without previous *warning*." Hanmer adopted Warburton's conjecture of "rear ;" and Heath suggested "disappear." For the omission of *as*, see Gr. 281.

208. *The best*, etc. See Dowden's remarks on this passage, p. 35 above.

214. *Beasts in, a man*, etc. The early eds. put the comma after *beasts ;* Rowe made the change. Theo. changed *man* to "moon," and Farmer conjectured "mooncalf ;" but no change is called for.

220. *A lion fell, nor else*, etc. That is, neither a lion fell, nor a lioness. Johnson, in a note on *A. W.* i. 2. 36, remarks that "*nor* in the phraseology of our author's time often related to two members of a sentence, though only expressed in the latter ;" and Schmidt gives many examples of "*neither* omitted." Cf. *Oth.* iv. 1. 278 ; *Lear*, iv. 6. 124 ; *A. and C.* iii. 12. 21 ; *Cymb.* v. i. 28 ; *Sonn.* 141. 9, etc. D. adopts Barron Field's conjecture of "lion's fell" (skin), and W. follows Sr. in reading "lionfell." Perhaps S. wrote "No lion fell," as Rowe and St. read. Cf. iii. 1. 38 fol.

235. *No crescent.* Not a waxing moon, but "in the wane," as Theseus says just below.

237. *The horned moon.* Douce thinks there is here a burlesque reference to the materials of the lantern, in which horn was generally used instead of glass. He quotes the *History of the two Maids of Moreclacke*, 1609 : "Shine through the horne, as candles in the eve, to light out others." Grimm (*Deutsche Mythologie*, p. 412) informs us that there are three legends connected with the Man in the Moon ; the first, that this personage was Isaac carrying a bundle of sticks for his own sacrifice ; the second, that he was Cain ; and the third, taken from the history of the Sabbath-breaker in the Book of Numbers (see on iii. 1. 52). The Italians of the thirteenth century imagined the Man in the Moon to be Cain, who is going to sacrifice to the Lord thorns—the most wretched production

of the ground.   Dante refers to this in the twentieth canto of the In-
ferno:
> "chè già tiene 'l confine
> D'amenduo gli emisperi, e tocca l'onda
> Sotto Sibilia, Caino e le spine."

From Manningham's *Diary* (MS. Harl.) we learn that among the "de-
vises" at Whitehall, in 1601, was "the man in the moone with thornes
on his backe, looking downeward."   Middleton also refers to this mythological personage—"as soon as he comes down, and the bush left at his
back, Ralph is the dog behind him."

239. *Of all the rest.*   For this "confusion of construction," see Gr. 409.
J. H. takes the ground that the expression is good English, "as the
preposition does not mean *out of*, but *as compared with*."

243. *In snuff.*   A play upon words, *in snuff* being a common phrase
for *in anger*.   Cf. *L. L. L.* v. 2. 22 : "You 'll mar the light by taking it in
snuff ;" 1 *Hen. IV.* i. 3. 37 :
> "And 'twixt his finger and his thumb he held
> A pouncet-box, which ever and anon
> He gave his nose, and took 't away again;
> Who therewith angry, when it next came there,
> Took it in snuff."

244. *Aweary.*   So in 1st quarto; "weary" in the other early eds.
Gr. 24.   See also *Macb.* p. 252.

260. *Moused.*   Cf. *Macb.* ii. 4. 13 : "a mousing owl ;" *K. John,* ii. 1. 354 :
"mousing the flesh of men" (that is, tearing it, as a cat does a mouse).
Rowe unnecessarily substituted "mouth'd."

261, 262.   Mr. Spedding conjectures that these lines should be transposed.   Steevens, following Farmer, gives the lines thus :
> "*Dem.* And so comes Pyramus.
> *Lys.* And then the moon vanishes."

265. *Gleams.*   The conjecture of K., adopted by St., the Camb. editors,
and others.   The quartos and the 1st folio have "beames ;" the later
folios, "streams."   The latter was sometimes applied to rays of light ;
as in *The Mirror for Magistrates*, ed. 1587 :
> "Which erst so glistned with the golden streames
> That chearfull Phœbus spred downe from his sphere," etc.

But *streams* was probably only the guess of the editor of the 2d folio, and
gleams is to be preferred for the alliteration.   Lettsom thinks that S. has
not used the word *gleam*, as it is not to be found in Mrs. Clarke's *Con-
cordance;* but the verb occurs in *R. of L.* 1378 : "And dying eyes gleam'd
forth their ashy lights."

277. *Thread and thrum.*   "An expression borrowed from weaving :
the *thread* being the substance of the warp ; the *thrum*, the small tuft
beyond, where it is tied" (Nares).   Cf. Herrick, *Poems :*
> "Thou who wilt not love, doe this,
> Learne of me what woman is,
> Something made of thred and thrumme,
> A meere botch of all and some."

We have *thrummed* (=made of coarse ends or tufts) in *M. W.* iv. 2. 75 :
"her thrummed hat."

278. *Quell.* Destroy, kill. Cf. *T. G. of V.* iv. 2. 13 ; *T. of A.* iv. 3. 163, etc. S. has the word once as a noun (=murder) in *Macb.* i. 7. 72 : "our great quell." So *boy-queller*=boy-killer, in *T. and C.* v. 5. 45 ; and *man-queller* and *woman-queller*=murderer, in 2 *Hen. IV.* ii. 1. 58. Steevens quotes the *Coventry Mysteries :* "with stonys her to quell."

279. *This passion, and the death of a dear friend,* etc. The joke would seem to be obvious enough, but the Coll. MS. spoils it by changing *and* to "on." Of course, as W. remarks, the humour of the passage "consists in coupling the ridiculous fustian of the clown's assumed passion with an event which would, in itself, make a man look sad." St. quotes the old proverbial saying : "He that loseth his wife and sixpence hath lost a tester" (the *tester* being=sixpence).

281. *Beshrew.* See on ii. 2. 54.

285. *Cheer.* Countenance. See on iii. 2. 96.

289. *Pap.* Pronounced *pop,* or with "the broad pronunciation, now almost peculiar to the Scotch, but anciently current in England" (Steevens).

295. *Tongue.* Halliwell thinks this "appears too absurd to be humorous," and that it may be a misprint for "Sun."

298. *No die but an ace.* Alluding to dice, and playing on *ace* and *ass.*

303. *How chance.* See on i. 1. 129. Gr. 37.

309. *Mote.* The early eds. have "moth," the old spelling of *mote.* W. changes the name of the fairy *Moth* to "Mote."

Which Pyramus, which Thisbe. Abbott suggests (Gr. 273) that *which* may here be used for the kindred *whether.*

310. *He for a man . . . God bless us.* This passage is in the quartos, but is omitted in the folios ; perhaps, as Coll. suggests, on account of the statute of James I. against using the name of God on the stage.

314. *Moans.* All the early eds. have "means." The emendation is due to Theo.

321. *Lips.* Changed by Theo. to "brows," for the sake of the rhyme. Farmer would read

> "These lips lilly,
> This nose cherry ;"

and the Coll. MS. gives

> "This lily lip,
> This cherry tip."

327. *Sisters three.* The three Fates. Farmer remarked to Malone that this passage was probably intended to ridicule one in Richard Edwards's *Damon and Pythias,* 1582 :

> "Ye furies, all at once
> On me your torments trie :—
> Gripe me, you greedy greefs,
> And present pangues of death ;
> You sisters three, with cruel handes
> With speed come stop my breath."

331. *Shore.* Used instead of *shorn* for the rhyme. We have it as the past tense of *shear* in *Oth.* v. 2. 206 : "Shore his old thread in twain."

343. *A Bergomask dance.* A rustic dance as performed by the peas-

ants of Bergomasco, a Venetian province, whose clownish manners were imitated by all the Italian buffoons (Nares).

356. *Palpable-gross.* Palpably gross, or stupid. For similar compound adjectives, see Gr. 2. We may omit the hyphen, bringing it under Gr. 1.

357. *The heavy gait of night.* Cf. *Hen. V.* iv. prol. 20 : " the cripple tardy-gaited night ;" *Rich. II.* iii. 2. 15 : "heavy-gaited toads."

360. Some editors begin a new scene here. Coleridge says of this speech of Puck's: "Very Anacreon in perfectness, proportion, grace, and spontaneity. So far it is Greek ; but then add, O ! what wealth, what wild ranging, and yet what compression and condensation of English fancy. In truth, there is nothing in Anacreon more perfect than these thirty lines, or half so rich and imaginative. They form a speckless diamond."

361. *Behowls.* All the early eds. have "beholds ;" corrected by Theo. Cf. *A. Y. L.* v. 2. 119 : " 't is like the howling of Irish wolves against the moon."

363. *Fordone.* Exhausted, overcome. Elsewhere it means undone, destroyed. Cf. *Lear*, v. 3. 255 : " She fordid herself ;" *Id.* v. 3. 291 : " Your eldest daughters have fordone themselves ;" *Oth.* v. 1. 129 : " That either makes me or fordoes me quite," etc. See also Spenser, *F. Q.* i. 5. 41 : " A fordonne wight from dore of death mote raise ;" *Id.* iii. 3. 34 : " thy sad people, utterly fordonne ;" *Id.* iv. 9. 28 : " both shamefully fordonne," etc.

365. *Screech-owl.* Cf. *2 Hen. VI.* i. 4. 21, iii. 2. 327 ; *T. and C.* v. 10. 16, etc. *Screech* (verb or noun) is not elsewhere used by S.

368. *Now it is the time*, etc. Cf. *Ham.* iii. 2. 406 : " 'T is now the very witching time of night," etc. See also *Macb.* ii. 1. 51.

369. *That.* When. Cf. iv. 1. 133. Gr. 284.

371. *Church-way.* Used nowhere else by S. Cf. Gray, *Elegy*, 114 : " Slow through the churchway path we saw him borne."

373. *The triple Hecate.* Cf. *A. Y. L.* iii. 2. 2 : " thrice-crowned queen of night ;" also Virgil, *Æn.* iv. 511 : " Tergeminamque Hecaten, tria virginis ora Dianae ;" and Horace, *Od.* iii. 22. 4 : " Diva triformis." *Hecate* is always a dissyllable in S., unless we except 1 *Hen. VI.* iii. 2. 64, the authorship of which is doubtful. See *Macb.* p. 222. Ben Jonson, of course, always makes it a trisyllable ; Marlowe and Middleton make it a dissyllable ; Golding, in his *Ovid*, has used it both ways (Douce).

375. *Following darkness*, etc. See on iv. 1. 93.

376. *Frolic.* Used by S. only as an adjective ; and nowhere else except in *T. of S.* iv. 3. 184.

378. *I am sent*, etc. Cf. *M. W.* v. 5. 48 :

> "Where fires thou find'st unrak'd and hearths unswept,
> There pinch the maids as blue as bilberry :
> Our radiant queen hates sluts and sluttery ;"

and *Id.* v. 5. 59 :

> "About, about,
> Search Windsor Castle, elves, within and out :
>
> .   .   .   .
>
> The several chairs of order look you scour
> With juice of balm and every precious flower ;"

HECATE. FROM THE ANTIQUE.

also *R. and J.* i. 4. 88 :

> "This is that very Mab
> That plats the manes of horses in the night,
> And bakes the elf-locks in foul sluttish hairs ;"

and Drayton, *Nymphidia :*

> "These make our girls their sluttery rue,
> By pinching them both black and blue,
> And put a penny in their shoe,
> The house for cleanly sweeping."

Nash, in his *Terrors of the Night*, 1594, remarks that "the Robin Good-fellowes, elfes, fairies, hobgoblins of our latter age, . . . pincht maids in their sleep that swept not their houses cleane," etc. So in *Robin Goodfellow ; his mad prankes*, etc., 1628 (see p. 15 above), we read : "many mad prankes would they play, as pinching of sluts black and blue, and misplacing things in ill-ordered houses ; but lovingly would they use wenches that cleanly were, giving them silver and other pretty toyes, which they would leave for them, sometimes in their shooes, other times in their pockets, sometimes in bright basons and other cleane vessels."

380. *Glimmering light*, etc. Cf. Milton, *Il Pens.* 79 :

> "Where glowing embers through the room
> Teach light to counterfeit a gloom."

Johnson would read "*in* glimmering light ;" W. changes *Through* to "Though."

385. *Dance it.* See Gr. 226. For *trippingly* see on iv. 1. 93.

390–409. This passage is given to Oberon in the quartos; in the folios it is called *The Song*, and printed in italics. Johnson thinks that two Songs have been lost from the play: one following Oberon's speech, 380–385, and the other after the next speech, by Titania. They were lost, he supposes, "because they were not inserted in the players' parts, from which the drama was printed."

393. *Shall blessed be.* The blessing of the bridal bed was a regular part of the marriage ceremony. Cf. Chaucer, *C. T.* 9693: "And whan the bed was with the preest yblessed." See Douce's *Illustrations of Shakespeare*, vol. i. pp. 199–203; where there is also the copy of an ancient cut (from the French romance of *Melusine*) representing the ceremony.

398. *Never mole,* etc. Cf. *K. John*, iii. 1. 46:

> "Lame, foolish, crooked, swart, prodigious,
>   Patch'd with foul moles and eye-offending marks."

Hare-lip is mentioned only here and in *Lear*, iii. 4. 123, where it is ascribed to "the foul fiend," etc. *Prodigious*=portentous; the only meaning it has in S. See the quotation from *K. John* above; also *J. C.* i. 3, 77, etc.

400. *Nativity.* Birth; especially in its astrological relations. Cf. *R. of L.* 538:

> "For marks descried in men's nativity
>   Are nature's faults, not their own infamy."

402. *Consecrate.* Cf. *Sonn.* 74. 6: "Consecrate to thee." See also *C. of E.* ii. 2. 134; *T. A.* i. 1. 14, and ii. 1. 121. Gr. 342. Douce thinks there may be in this line "a covert satire against holy water."

403. *Take his gait.* Take his way. M. Mason thought that *gait* (or *gate*) meant "the door of each chamber!"

404. *Bless.* Steevens cites Chaucer, *C. T.* 3479:

> "Therwith the night-spel seyde he anon rightes,
>   On the foure halves of the hous aboute,
>   And on the threisshfold of the dore withoute.
>   Lord Jhesu Crist, and seynte Benedight,
>   Blesse this hous from every wikkede wight," etc.

In this case, however, the "night-spel" is pronounced *against* the influence of elves and evil spirits; as in *Cymb.* ii. 2. 9:

> "From fairies and the tempters of the night
>   Guard me, beseech ye!"

406, 407. In the early eds. these lines are transposed. St. arranged them as here, getting the hint from an anonymous correspondent of the *London Illustrated News.* Rowe gives "Ever shall it safely rest;" and Dyce, "Ever shall 't in safety rest," which is very plausible. Halliwell follows Malone in retaining the old reading and arrangement, assuming that the nominative *palace* is understood. Such "ellipsis of the nominative" (Gr. 399–402) is not uncommon in S. We have an example above in v. 1. 98, and possibly another in iv. 1. 64; but in the present passage transposition of the lines seems on the whole the simplest solution of the difficulty.

418. *An honest Puck.* See on ii. 1. 40 above.

419. *If we have,* etc. "That is, if we have better fortune than we have deserved" (Steevens). S. uses *unearned* only here.

420. *To scape,* etc. To escape being hissed. Cf. *L. L. L.* v. 1. 139:

" *Holofernes.* Shall I have audience? he shall present Hercules in minority: his enter and exit shall be strangling a snake; and I will have an apology for that purpose.

Moth. An excellent device! so, if any of the audience hiss, you may cry, 'Well done, Hercules! now thou crushest the snake!' that is the way to make an offence gracious, though few have the grace to do it."

424. *Your hands.* That is, your plaudits. Cf. *Temp.* epil. 10: "With the help of your good hands;" and *A. W.* v. 3. 340: "Your gentle hands lend us, and take our hearts." Douce quotes the epilogue of Stubbes's *Senile Odium:*

"jam vestrae quid valeant manus
Nimis velim experiri: ab illis enim vapulare munus erit."

425. *Restore amends.* A phrase not elsewhere used by S., his ordinary expression being *make amends.* We have *restore*=make amends for, in *Sonn.* 30. 14: "All losses are restored, and sorrows end."

ADDENDA.

THE "TIME-ANALYSIS" OF THE PLAY.—Mr. P. A. Daniel (*Trans. of New Shaks. Soc.* 1877–79, p. 149) sums this up as follows (cf. p. 122 above):

"Day 1. Act I.
" 2. Acts II., III., and part of sc. i. Act IV.
" 3. Part of sc. i. Act IV., sc. ii. Act IV., and Act V."

Flowers (p. 149). In his "Supplementary Notes," prefixed to Vol. I. (the last in order of publication), W. says: "I yielded too readily to the plausibility of the reading found in Mr. Collier's folio of 1632. Read, with the old copies, 'lull'd in these flowers;' *in* having of course the sense of *upon.*"

Knot-grass (p. 168). Mr. H. N. Ellacombe (in the London *Garden,* May 19, 1877) suggests another explanation of *hindering.* He cites Johnstone, who says that in the north of England, the plant "being difficult to cut in the harvest time, or to pull in the process of weeding, it has obtained the soubriquet of *the Deil's-lingels.*"* Shakespeare's "hindering" weed cannot be the *knot-grass* mentioned by Milton, *Comus,* 542:

"the savoury herb
Of knot-grass dew-besprent."

This must be one of the pasture grasses—perhaps *Agrostis stolonifera,* as it is said to be in Aubrey's *Natural History of Wilts.*

---

* A *lingel* (from the Latin *lingula*) is a thong used by shoemakers. Cf. B. and F., *Knight of the Burning Pestle:* "Wrought with lingell and with aul;" Drayton, *Ecl.* v.: "His awl and lingel in a thong," etc.

THESEUS LIFTING THE STONE UNDER WHICH HIS FATHER'S SWORD AND SHOES WERE HIDDEN.

INDEX OF WORDS EXPLAINED.

N

From Prof. F. J. CHILD, *of Harvard University.*

I read your " Merchant of Venice " with my class, and found it in every respect an excellent edition. I do not agree with my friend White in the opinion that Shakespeare requires but few notes—that is, if he is to be thoroughly understood. Doubtless he may be enjoyed, and many a hard place slid over. Your notes give all the help a young student requires, and yet the reader for pleasure will easily get at just what he wants. You have indeed been conscientiously concise.

Under date of July 25, 1879, Prof. CHILD *adds :* Mr. Rolfe's editions of plays of Shakespeare are very valuable and convenient books, whether for a college class or for private study. I have used them with my students, and I welcome every addition that is made to the series. They show care, research, and good judgment, and are fully up to the time in scholarship. I fully agree with the opinion that experienced teachers have expressed of the excellence of these books.

From Rev. A. P. PEABODY, D.D., *Professor in Harvard University.*

I regard your own work as of the highest merit, while you have turned the labors of others to the best possible account. I want to have the higher classes of our schools introduced to Shakespeare chief of all, and then to other standard English authors ; but this cannot be done to advantage unless under a teacher of equally rare gifts and abundant leisure, or through editions specially prepared for such use. I trust that you will have the requisite encouragement to proceed with a work so happily begun.

From the Examiner and Chronicle, *N. Y.*

We repeat what we have often said, that there is no edition of Shakespeare which seems to us preferable to Mr. Rolfe's. As mere specimens of the printer's and binder's art they are unexcelled, and their other merits are equally high. Mr. Rolfe, having learned by the practical experience of the class-room what aid the average student really needs in order to read Shakespeare intelligently, has put just that amount of aid into his notes, and no more. Having said what needs to be said, he stops there. It is a rare virtue in the editor of a classic, and we are proportionately grateful for it.

From the N. Y. Times.

This work has been done so well that it could hardly have been done better. It shows throughout knowledge, taste, discriminating judgment, and, what is rarer and of yet higher value, a sympathetic appreciation of the poet's moods and purposes.

From the Pacific School Journal, San Francisco.

This edition of Shakespeare's plays bids fair to be the most valuable aid to the study of English literature yet published. For educational purposes it is beyond praise. Each of the plays is printed in large clear type and on excellent paper. Every difficulty of the text is clearly explained by copious notes. It is remarkable how many new beauties one may discern in Shakespeare with the aid of the glossaries attached to these books. . . . Teachers can do no higher, better work than to inculcate a love for the best literature, and such books as these will best aid them in cultivating a pure and refined taste.

From the Christian Union, N. Y.

Mr. W. J. Rolfe's capital edition of Shakespeare . . . by far the best edition for school and parlor use. We speak after some practical use of it in a village Shakespeare Club. The notes are brief but useful ; and the necessary expurgations are managed with discriminating skill.

From the Academy, London.

Mr. Rolfe's excellent series of school editions of the Plays of Shakespeare. . . . They differ from some of the English ones in looking on the plays as something more than word-puzzles. They give the student helps and hints on the characters and meanings of the plays, while the word-notes are also full and posted up to the latest date. . . . Mr. Rolfe also adds to each of his books a most useful "Index of Words and Phrases Explained."

PUBLISHED BY HARPER & BROTHERS, New York.

☞ *The above works are for sale by all booksellers, or they will be sent by* Harper *&* Brothers *to any address on receipt of price as quoted. If ordered sent by mail, 10 per cent. should be added to the price to cover cost of postage.*

OLIVER GOLDSMITH.

SELECT POEMS OF OLIVER GOLDSMITH. Edited, with Notes, by WILLIAM J. ROLFE, A.M., formerly Head Master of the High School, Cambridge, Mass. Illustrated. 16mo, Paper, 40 cents; Cloth, 56 cents. (*Uniform with Rolfe's Shakespeare.*)

The carefully arranged editions of "The Merchant of Venice" and other of Shakespeare's plays prepared by Mr. William J. Rolfe for the use of students will be remembered with pleasure by many readers, and they will welcome another volume of a similar character from the same source, in the form of the "Select Poems of Oliver Goldsmith," edited with notes fuller than those of any other known edition, many of them original with the editor.—*Boston Transcript.*

Mr. Rolfe is doing very useful work in the preparation of compact hand-books for study in English literature. His own personal culture and his long experience as a teacher give him good knowledge of what is wanted in this way.—*The Congregationalist*, Boston.

Mr. Rolfe has prefixed to the Poems selections illustrative of Goldsmith's character as a man, and grade as a poet, from sketches by Macaulay, Thackeray, George Colman, Thomas Campbell, John Forster, and Washington Irving. He has also appended at the end of the volume a body of scholarly notes explaining and illustrating the poems, and dealing with the times in which they were written, as well as the incidents and circumstances attending their composition.— *Christian Intelligencer*, N. Y.

The notes are just and discriminating in tone, and supply all that is necessary either for understanding the thought of the several poems, or for a critical study of the language. The use of such books in the school-room cannot but contribute largely towards putting the study of English literature upon a sound basis; and many an adult reader would find in the present volume an excellent opportunity for becoming critically acquainted with one of the greatest of last century's poets.—*Appleton's Journal*, N. Y.

PUBLISHED BY HARPER & BROTHERS, NEW YORK.

☞ *The above works are for sale by all booksellers, or they will be sent by* HARPER & BROTHERS *to any address on receipt of price as quoted. If ordered sent by mail,* 10 *per cent. should be added to the price to cover cost of postage.*

THOMAS GRAY.

SELECT POEMS OF THOMAS GRAY. Edited, with Notes, by WILLIAM J. ROLFE, A.M., formerly Head Master of the High School, Cambridge, Mass. Illustrated. Square 16mo, Paper, 40 cents; Cloth, 56 cents. (*Uniform with Rolfe's Shakespeare.*)

Mr. Rolfe has done his work in a manner that comes as near to perfection as man can approach. He knows his subject so well that he is competent to instruct all in it; and readers will find an immense amount of knowledge in his elegant volume, all set forth in the most admirable order, and breathing the most liberal and enlightened spirit, he being a warm appreciator of the divinity of genius.—*Boston Traveller.*

The great merit of these books lies in their carefully edited text, and in the fulness of their explanatory notes. Mr. Rolfe is not satisfied with simply expounding, but he explores the entire field of English literature, and therefrom gathers a multitude of illustrations that are interesting in themselves and valuable as a commentary on the text. He not only instructs, but stimulates his readers to fresh exertion; and it is this stimulation that makes his labor so productive in the school-room.—*Saturday Evening Gazette*, Boston.

Mr. William J. Rolfe, to whom English literature is largely indebted for annotated and richly illustrated editions of several of Shakespeare's Plays, has treated the "Select Poems of Thomas Gray" in the same way —just as he had previously dealt with the best of Goldsmith's poems.—*Philadelphia Press.*

Mr. Rolfe's edition of Thomas Gray's select poems is marked by the same discriminating taste as his other classics.—*Springfield Republican.*

Mr. Rolfe's rare abilities as a teacher and his fine scholarly tastes enable him to prepare a classic like this in the best manner for school use. There could be no better exercise for the advanced classes in our schools than the critical study of our best authors, and the volumes that Mr. Rolfe has prepared will hasten the time when the study of mere form will give place to the study of the spirit of our literature.—*Louisville Courier-Journal.*

An elegant and scholarly little volume.—*Christian Intelligencer*, N. Y.

PUBLISHED BY HARPER & BROTHERS, NEW YORK.

AFTERNOONS WITH THE POETS.

AFTERNOONS WITH THE POETS. By C. D. DESHLER.
Post 8vo, Cloth, $1 75.

This pleasing work is made up of citations from the poets, accompanied with easy and familiar discussions of their merits and peculiarities. Seven afternoons are thus agreeably occupied, and take the shape of as many interesting chapters. The participants are the "Professor" and his pupil, who are represented as on terms of the utmost intimacy, and express their sentiments to each other with perfect freedom. * * * Mr. Deshler has happily selected the sonnet, and confined his view of the poets to their productions in this single species of verse. * * * The author's extensive research has been accompanied by minute scrutiny, faithful comparison, and judicious discrimination. His critical observations are frank, honest, good-natured, yet just, discreet, comprehensive, and full of instruction. It would be difficult to find a volume that in so small a compass offers equal aid for the cultivation of literary taste, and for reaching an easy acquaintance with all the great poets of the English tongue. The style is pure and transparent, and though colloquial in form, it is exceedingly correct and elegant, embodying every chaste adornment of which language is capable.—*Boston Transcript.*

A very unconventional and pleasant book.—*N. Y. Herald.*

The substance of the book is decidedly meritorious, far better than most of the criticism published in these days. It shows careful study, extensive reading, a nice taste and discrimination, and also a genuine appreciation and insight which are rare.—*N. Y. Evening Express.*

A volume of much literary interest, and is very pleasantly written.* * * Mr. Deshler's discussions of literature are extremely interesting. * * * It will be a source of enjoyment to all who have a taste for poetry, and can appreciate the highest triumphs of poetic art as displayed in the sonnet. —*Hartford Post.*

We have to thank Mr. Deshler for a collection of some of the most exquisite sonnets in the English language, with an animated, appreciative, and suggestive comment which shows a fine poetical taste and is an interesting and instructive guide in a charming field.—*N. Y. Mail.*

PUBLISHED BY HARPER & BROTHERS, NEW YORK.

☞ *The above work is for sale by all booksellers, or will be sent by the publishers, postage prepaid, to any part of the United States, Canada, or Mexico, on receipt of price.*

ROBERT BROWNING.

A BLOT IN THE 'SCUTCHEON AND OTHER DRA-
MAS. By ROBERT BROWNING. Edited, with notes, by
WILLIAM J. ROLFE, A.M., and HELOISE E. HERSEY.
With Portrait. 16mo, Paper, 40 cents ; Cloth, 56 cents.
(Uniform with Rolfe's Shakespeare.)

Prepared in the same thorough manner as the previous volume upon
the Select Poems of the same author and the numerous manuals of Mr.
Rolfe. No poet needs, for the average reader, such an interpretation
as is here given more than Browning. Read carefully, with reference to
the notes of the editors, the richness of the great poet's thoughts and
fancies will be the better apprehended.—*Zion's Herald*, Boston.

Out of the eight dramas which the poet wrote between 1837 and 1845
the three most characteristic ones have been selected, and a full idea of
his dramatic power may be gained from them. A synopsis of critical
opinions of Mr. Browning's works is included in the volume. The same
careful scholarship that marked Professor Rolfe's editions of Shakespeare
is shown in this edition of Browning. The lovers of the poet will be
pleased to have old favorites in this attractive form, while many new
readers will be attracted to the author by it. Robert Browning will fill
a larger space in the world's eye in the future than he has done already.
—*Brooklyn Union.*

The introduction and notes are all that could be desired.—*N. Y. Sun.*

The book itself is not only a compact compilation of the three plays,
but it is valuable for the commentatory notes. The editing work has
been done in an able manner by Professor Rolfe and Miss Hersey, who
has gained a high place among the modern Browning students.—*Philadelphia Bulletin.*

This dainty volume, with flexible covers and red edges, contains not
merely Browning's dramas, with the author's latest emendations and corrections, but notes and estimates, critical and explanatory, in such volume, and from sources so exalted, that we have not the temerity to add
one jot of tittle to the aggregate.—*N. Y. Commercial Advertiser.*

PUBLISHED BY HARPER & BROTHERS, NEW YORK.

☞ *The above works are for sale by all booksellers, or they will be sent by* HARPER
& BROTHERS *to any address on receipt of price as quoted. If ordered sent by
mail, 10 per cent. should be added to the price to cover cost of postage.*

ROBERT BROWNING.

SELECT POEMS OF ROBERT BROWNING. Edited, with Notes, by WILLIAM J. ROLFE, A.M., formerly Head Master of the High School, Cambridge, Mass., and HELOISE E. HERSEY. Illustrated. 16mo, Paper, 40 cents; Cloth, 56 cents. (*Uniform with Rolfe's Shakespeare.*)

Probably no critic yet has gone to the heart of Browning's true significance as does Miss Hersey. There is something in the fineness of her insight and her subtle, spiritual sympathy that truly interprets him, while others write in a more or less scholarly manner about him. Miss Hersey's work indicates the blending of two exceptional qualities—the poetic sympathy and the critical judgments. She feels intuitively all the poet's subtle meanings; she is responsible to them by virtue of temperament; yet added to this is the critical faculty, keen, logical, and constructive.—*Boston Traveller.*

To say that the selections have been made by Mr. Rolfe is to say that they have not only been made by a careful and accurate scholar, but by a man of pure and beautiful taste. . . . The Notes, which fill some thirty pages, are admirable in their scope and brevity.—*N. Y. Mail and Express.*

We can conscientiously say that both the arrangement of the selections and the fulness, as well as the illuminating character, of the annotations are all that the most exacting taste could require; and the whole work is well fitted to charm the poet's established admirers, and to awaken in others who have not been among these a new sense of Browning's strength and beauty as a writer.—*Hartford Times.*

The "Select Poems of Robert Browning" is a marvel of industrious editing, wise, choice, and excellent judgment in comment. . . . An introduction, a brief account of Browning's life and works, a chronological table of his works, and a series of extracted critical comments on the poet, precede the series of selections. Besides these there are at the end of the book very extensive, valuable, and minutely illustrative notes, together with addenda supplied by Browning himself on points which the editors were unable fully to clear up.—*N. Y. Star.*

PUBLISHED BY HARPER & BROTHERS, NEW YORK.

☞ *The above works are for sale by all booksellers, or they will be sent by* HARPER & BROTHERS *to any address on receipt of price as quoted. If ordered sent by mail,* 10 *per cent. should be added to the price to cover cost of postage.*

ENGLISH MEN OF LETTERS.

EDITED BY JOHN MORLEY.

The following volumes are now ready:

12mo, Cloth, 75 cents per volume.

PUBLISHED BY HARPER & BROTHERS, NEW YORK.

☞ *The above work is for sale by all booksellers, or will be sent by the publishers, postage prepaid, to any part of the United States, Canada, or Mexico, on receipt of price.*